EFFECTIVE DIRECTORS

Being a good board member is not about knowing everything; it is about asking the right questions and challenging appropriately. *Effective Directors: The Right Questions to Ask (QTA)* is a reference book for board members and executives globally to support them in their work.

With chapters written by senior company board members and respected figures in corporate governance, the questions have been drawn together to offer food for thought and useful prompts that take boards beyond operational discussions. The book clearly presents key areas to be considered by the board (there are over 50 in total) and range from board composition, to data security, diversity and inclusion, and succession planning. The questions are ones that boards, in any organisation, should be asking themselves, their fellow board members, service providers, executives, and other stakeholders to ensure that the right issues are raised, transparency and effective oversight are achieved, and the board is fulfilling its role in governing the organisation.

In addition to being invaluable for board members, the book is also a very useful tool for executives in understanding the kind of questions their board members are likely to ask, and the kind of questions that should be asked and discussed in the boardroom.

Charlotte Valeur and Claire Fargeot have over 60 years combined experience of working in and around boards in all types of organisations, all over the world. They deliver training, conduct board reviews, and advise and support boards on governance and sustainability issues through their company, Global Governance Group.

QUESTIONS TO ASK (QTA)

Series Editors: Charlotte Valeur and Claire Fargeot

The book series **Questions to Ask (QTA)** explores the key questions to ask in organisational governance and leadership. The questions are ones that boards and leaders globally, in any organisation, should be asking themselves, their fellow board members, service providers, executives, and other stakeholders to ensure that the right issues are raised, transparency and effective oversight are achieved, and the board is fulfilling its role in governing the organisation. It includes books that focus on questions to ask for boards within specific industries and sectors, for example, the construction industry, renewable energy, the fashion industry, the oil industry, universities, charities, and NGOs. It also includes books that cover specific scenarios, such as merger & acquisition situations, hostile takeovers, and activism.

Effective Directors: The Right Questions to Ask (QTA)
Edited by Charlotte Valeur and Claire Fargeot

EFFECTIVE DIRECTORS

The Right Questions to Ask (QTA)

*Edited by Charlotte Valeur and
Claire Fargeot*

LONDON AND NEW YORK

First published 2022
by Routledge
2 Park Square, Milton Park, Abingdon, Oxon OX14 4RN

and by Routledge
605 Third Avenue, New York, NY 10158

Routledge is an imprint of the Taylor & Francis Group, an informa business

© 2022 selection and editorial matter, Charlotte Valeur and Claire Fargeot; individual chapters, the contributors

The right of Charlotte Valeur and Claire Fargeot to be identified as the authors of the editorial material, and of the authors for their individual chapters, has been asserted in accordance with sections 77 and 78 of the Copyright, Designs and Patents Act 1988.

The Open Access version of this book, available at www.taylorfrancis.com, has been made available under a Creative Commons Attribution-Non Commercial-No Derivatives 4.0 license.

Trademark notice: Product or corporate names may be trademarks or registered trademarks, and are used only for identification and explanation without intent to infringe.

British Library Cataloguing-in-Publication Data
A catalogue record for this book is available from the British Library

Library of Congress Cataloging-in-Publication Data
Names: Valeur, Charlotte, 1964– editor. | Fargeot, Claire, 1967– editor.
Title: Effective directors: the right questions to ask (QTA) / edited by Charlotte Valeur and Claire Fargeot.
Description: Milton Park, Abingdon, Oxon; New York, NY: Routledge, 2022. | Series: Questions to ask (QTA) | Includes bibliographical references and index.
Identifiers: LCCN 2021014796
Subjects: LCSH: Boards of directors. | Corporate governance–Evaluation. | Industrial management–Evaluation.
Classification: LCC HD2745.E34 2022 | DDC 658.4/22–dc23
LC record available at https://lccn.loc.gov/2021014796

ISBN: 978-1-032-06202-0 (hbk)
ISBN: 978-1-032-06204-4 (pbk)
ISBN: 978-1-003-20118-2 (ebk)

DOI: 10.4324/9781003201182

Typeset in Joanna
by Newgen Publishing UK

Charlotte: For my three amazing children, Giles, Oscar, and Isabella, who provide me with no end of love, inspiration, and passion to make the world a better place for them to prosper in.

Claire: For my daughter, Annabella, and husband, Roger — forever grateful for showing me how to be a better human.

CONTENTS

List of figures — xiii
List of tables — xiv
List of contributors — xv
Foreword: effective directors and professional boards — xxvi
Preface — xxix
Acknowledgements — xxxi
Editor biographies — xxxiii

Part I The board — 1

1 **Board composition** — 3
   Chris Hodge

2 **Board appointment** — 9
   Carol Rosati OBE

3 **Director self-assessment** — 15
   Alison Gill OLY

4 **Assessing the chair's performance** — 22
   Charlotte Valeur

5 Due diligence for new appointments and new directors — 25
Charlotte Valeur

6 Succession planning for the board — 31
Ray Crofts

7 Board evaluation — 36
Dr Tracy Long CBE

Part II Officers of the company — 43

8 Chief executive succession planning — 45
Kit Bingham

9 Chief executive review — 51
Charlotte Valeur

10 Equality, diversity, and inclusion — 57
Marianne Egelund Siig

11 Health and well-being — 63
Alison Charles

12 Human resources — 68
Reena Dayal

13 Remuneration for executives and management — 74
Brian Kearney

14 Succession planning for executives — 79
Tim Drake

Part III Leadership — 85

15 Leadership in the boardroom — 87
Dr Randall S. Peterson

16 Tone from the top — 92
Sir John Parker

17	Culture Charlotte Valeur	97
18	Ethics and why they matter Knut N. Kjaer	101

Part IV Strategy — 107

19	Purpose R. "Bob" Garratt	109
20	Strategy Jean Pousson	115
21	Valueism Paul Barnett	120
22	Intellectual property Dr Janice Denoncourt	126
23	Data ethics Tony Fish	131

Part V Sustainability — 139

24	Environmental, social, and governance Sir Mark Moody-Stuart	141
25	Climate change Dr Geoff Kendall and Martin Rich	145
26	Sustainability Sara Lovisolo	152
27	Social impact Oonagh Harpur	156

Part VI Board meetings — 165

28	Role and responsibilities of the board Natalie Sykes	167

29	**Board meetings and the agenda** Dineshi Ramesh	172
30	**Board support** Siobhan Lavery	178
31	**Third-party providers** Charlotte Valeur	183
32	**Board committees: purpose, tasks, and value** Jenny Simnett, Filipe Morais, and Andrew Kakabadse	188
33	**Matters reserved for the board** David Doughty	196
34	**Soft governance** Dr Meena Thuraisingham	201

Part VII   Accounts   209

35	**Accounts** Ian Wright	211
36	**External auditors** Helen Gale	218
37	**Solvency and going concern** Heather MacCallum	223
38	**Insolvency** Amaechi Nsofor	230
39	**Viability** Steve Maslin	236
40	**Finance** Jean Pousson	243

Part VIII	Compliance and risk management	251

41 Compliance 253
Charlotte Valeur

42 Cybersecurity 257
Anjola Adeniyi

43 IT governance 265
Tony Fish

44 Financial performance management 270
Virginia Bombín Moreno

45 Risk oversight, management, and controls 278
Rajiv Jaitly

Part IX	Communications	285

46 Reputation 287
Alice Hunt

47 Corporate brand 292
Elliot S. Schreiber

48 Social media 297
Marshall Manson and Craig Mullaney

49 Shareholder relations and communication 303
Claire Fargeot

50 Stakeholder engagement and management 308
Alice Hunt

Part X	External pressure and disruption	313

51 Crisis management 315
Charlotte Valeur

52	**Digitalisation** *Claudia Heimer*	321
53	**Disruption** *Simon Devonshire*	328
54	**Artificial intelligence** *Lord Clement-Jones*	336

FIGURES

23.1 Interface to ecosystem 134
34.1 High-performing board 206

TABLES

23.1	Ethics and philosophy	136
33.1	Board responsibilities for the unitary board	198
33.2	Board responsibilities for the two-tier board	198

CONTRIBUTORS

Anjola Adeniyi, Dip IoD, EMEA Account Management, Securonix
Anjola is a board-level information security leader in the financial services, public services, FCMG, retail, and manufacturing industries. He is past master of the Guild of Freemen and board member of the Royal Over-Seas League, Getting on Board, Cyber Rescue Alliance, as well as being cyber security ambassador for the IoD (UK).

Paul Barnett, CEO, Enlightened Enterprise Academy
Paul is founder and CEO of the founder and CEO of the Enlightened Enterprise Academy, part of the Enlightened Enterprise Academy.[1] The academy is to be a platform for progressive thinking for enterprise in business, and he aims to create a global multidisciplinary faculty that will ensure sustainable shared prosperity measured in terms of human flourishing and well-being.

Kit Bingham, Partner and Head of Practice, Chair and Board, Odgers Berndtson
Kit is a partner in the Board Practice at Odgers Berndtson, following a career in financial journalism and financial public relations. He developed

1 www.enlightenedenterprise.ac

and tutored an MBA in board effectiveness at Henley Management College and is a member of the Development Board of the Bingham Centre for the Rule of Law, an independent research organisation.

Virginia Bombín Moreno, Adjunct Professor, IE University
Virginia is an instructional designer and pioneer in online and blended learning. She has primarily focused her career on corporate finance executive education. She is an adjunct professor at IE University and an active educator of Headspring, a joint venture created by IE and the Financial Times for international executive custom programmes.

Alison Charles, Founder, Alison Charles Ltd
From the Army Intelligence Corps to the battlegrounds of boardrooms and corporate strategies, Alison has delivered results in many highly stressful environments. Now she helps corporates deliver results through well-being programmes that support your people, minimising their stress levels and maximising their productive engagement.

Lord Clement-Jones
Lord Clement-Jones was made CBE for political services in 1988, life peer in 1998. He is Liberal Democrat House of Lords spokesperson for Digital; former chair of the House of Lords Select Committee on AI; co-chair, All-Party Parliamentary Group on AI; founding member of The OECD Parliamentary Group on AI; consultant to Council of Europe's Ad-hoc Committee on AI; consultant of global law firm DLA Piper; chair of Ombudsman Services Limited, and chair of the Council of Queen Mary University London.

Ray Crofts, Norman Broadbent
Ray is an associate at Norman Broadbent Executive Search and works mostly within the board practice, with a wide range of experience across multiple industries. Extremely passionate about diversity and governance, she holds a Master's degree in English and writing from the University of Warwick.

Reena Dayal, Founder, The Collaborators (UK) Ltd
Reena is an author, leadership coach, and mentor, with a global HR transformation track record of 22+ years across multiple sectors and countries, facilitating business expansion, integration, JV launch, global restructuring, talent/leadership alignment, and cultural change. She works with C-suite, SME entrepreneurs, and young leaders via The Collaborators UK Ltd.

LIST OF CONTRIBUTORS   xvii

Dr Janice Denoncourt, BA McGill, LLB Western Australia, PhD Nottingham, SFHEA, GAICD
Janice Denoncourt is a senior lecturer in law at Nottingham Law School in the UK where she teaches and researches in the field of intellectual property (IP) law, and company and business law. She was formerly in-house general counsel for a publicly listed technology company in Western Australia where she acted as an alternate director and IP manager for a large private UK company.

Simon Devonshire, OBE
Simon is currently chair of Ploughshare Innovations and non-executive director at Student Loans Company and Mercia PLC as well as being entrepreneur-in-residence at the National Physical Laboratory. Previously he was director of Wayra Europe and the entrepreneur-in-residence of Scale-up, the UK Government Department of Business, Innovation and Skills. Simon is an agent for the mass adoption of new technologies and is a passionate advocate for thriving businesses and people at work.

David Doughty, Chief Executive, Excellencia Ltd
As an experienced chartered director, chief executive, chair, and non-executive director who specialises in corporate governance, David works with executives and other board members to help them be more effective. He helps directors, trustees, and governors understand their board roles and what is required in order to succeed at board level.

Tim Drake, Norman Broadbent
Following senior roles with a number of consulting firms, Tim joined Norman Broadbent in early 2020. There, he works with clients to help them develop and implement solutions to meet the challenges created by the new world of work. Tim is also an experienced coach, working at both individual and team levels to build effectiveness and drive success.

Marianne Egelund Siig, CEO, Mannaz
Marianne is CEO of Mannaz and a recognised strategic leader, dedicated to creating value and purpose for people, businesses, and society as a whole. She has occupied various leading positions in the largest bank in the Nordics as well as being head of D&I. A renowned speaker and thought leader within the fields of gender equality and D&I, Marianne has led successful business

transformations in the fields of leadership, talent and organisational strategies, and development.

Tony Fish, Managing Director, Digital20
Tony has founded, invested in, and exited many digital businesses. He focuses on how data affects the future of corporate governance in times of complexity, decision-making to be better ancestors, and the unintended consequences of board judgement. He remains deeply passionate about new ways of creating value and inspiring the next generation of thinkers and doers.

Helen Gale, Project Director, Financial Reporting Council
Helen Gale is currently undertaking a project to assess and monitor the culture of audit firms and shape the development of a new approach to the regulation of the audit profession. She started her career with Arthur Andersen and was an audit partner at Deloitte, specialising in the private equity and investment management sectors.

R. "Bob" Garratt, Founder, Good Governance Development
Bob is a director and international board consultant. He is an honorary visiting professor at Bayes Business School, University of London and Professor Extraordinaire at the University of Stellenbosch Business School. He is the external examiner of the Gulf Co-operation Council's Board Development Institute's Director Development Programme. This material is a development from his book, *Stop the Rot: Reframing Governance for Directors and Politicians* (2017).

Alison Gill, OLY, CEO, Bvalco
Alison is a founding director and CEO of Bvalco. She helps boards and leadership teams by designing and delivering external board reviews, with a particular emphasis on the human behaviour and dynamics elements that can contribute to, or undermine, board effectiveness. By background Alison is a behavioural psychologist.

Oonagh Harpur, INED and member, Public Interest Committee, KPMG U.K. LLP
Oonagh sits on KPMG's Public Interest Committee as an independent non-executive and has considerable experience as a serial CEO, chair, non-executive director, and trustee in energy, health, financial, and professional services in the private and public sectors both in the UK and USA.

LIST OF CONTRIBUTORS xix

Claudia Heimer, Founding Director, Boardroom of the Future
Claudia Heimer is a director and internationally active coach for talents and teams working with global tech players for the past 30 years. She helps directors develop strategy, transform their organisations, and navigate the boardroom. A clinical and organisational psychologist, she understands how best to engage, resolve conflict, innovate, and align around a new strategy.

Chris Hodge, Director, Governance Perspectives
Chris is an independent adviser on corporate governance and regulation. He was formerly director of corporate governance at the UK's Financial Reporting Council in which capacity he was responsible for the UK Corporate Governance Code and for the first national stewardship code for investors.

Alice Hunt
Alice Hunt is a FTSE 100 group corporate affairs director with experience in purpose development and reputation management, for PLCs, charities, and in politics. She has overseen the full suite of communications disciplines and is a passionate advocate of civil society, being the CEO of the 2012 Olympic Legacy Volunteering initiative as well as campaigning for TheirWorld and Girl Effect.

Rajiv Jaitly, Managing Partner, Jaitly LLP
Rajiv Jaitly is a risk management specialist, chartered accountant, licensed insolvency practitioner and a CISI diploma holder. He is a widely experienced board member and committee chair as well as having held roles as chief risk officer for major international organisations. Rajiv is currently a NED on a number of boards.

Andrew P. Kakabadse, Professor of Governance and Leadership, Henley Business School
Andrew Kakabadse is Professor of Governance and Leadership at Henley Business School and Emeritus Professor at Cranfield School of Management. Andrew's research covers boards, top teams, and the governance of governments. He has published over 47 books, 88 book chapters, over 240 articles, and 18 monographs. He is adviser to the UK Parliament and numerous corporations, NGOs, and other governments.

Brian Kearney, FCA, Non-Executive Director

Brian Kearney has extensive board experience occupying senior NED as well as chair roles. He has run his own consultancy firm for more than 30 years and served on the Professional Standards Committee of the Chartered Accountants Regulatory Board. Brian is a fellow of Chartered Accountants Ireland and has been a member of its Strategy Review Board.

Dr Geoff Kendall, Co-founder & CEO, Future-Fit Foundation

Geoff Kendall is an entrepreneur whose experience spans sustainability consulting, high-tech start-ups, corporate communications, and academic research. Geoff holds a PhD in artificial intelligence and co-founded two software businesses. He has advised some of the world's biggest corporations on sustainable business models and co-founded Future-Fit Foundation[2] to help companies measure their sustainability

Knut N. Kjaer, Chairman FSN Capital

Knut N. Kjær is chairperson and partner of FSN Capital, a Northern European PE firm. He is member of the cupervisory board of the Dutch pension fund manager APG and adviser to the Monetary Authority of Singapore and Central Bank of Thailand. Previously, Knut was the founding CEO of Norges Bank Investment Management, responsible for the Norwegian Oil Fund, and president of RiskMetrics Group. He has been board member of the Irish National Pensions Reserve Fund and adviser the Singaporean and Chinese sovereign wealth funds.

Siobhan Lavery, FCG

Siobhan is a fully qualified company secretary with over 15 years' experience providing company secretarial services to a wide variety of LSE-listed and private companies. She was the winner of the Jersey ICSA Company Secretarial Officer of the Year Award in 2015.

Dr Tracy Long, CBE, Founder, Boardroom Review

Tracy Long is a leader in the field of board effectiveness, and an experienced board member. Tracy founded Boardroom Review Limited in 2004, working with chairs and board members to optimise the contribution of the board

---

[2] https://futurefitbusiness.org/

and prepare for the future. As a trusted adviser to the most senior decision makers, she has conducted over 300 international reviews across all sectors.

Sara Lovisolo, Group Sustainability Manager, London Stock Exchange Group

Sara has been working in sustainability in finance for the past ten years. She has been involved in a technical expert capacity with advisory groups set up by the UN and the European Union to provide input into sustainability regulation and the transformation of the financial sector.

Heather MacCallum, CA

Heather is a chartered accountant and was a partner with KPMG Channel Islands for 15 years before retiring in 2016. She now holds a portfolio of non-executive directorships including Aberdeen Latin American Income Fund Limited, City Merchants High Yield Trust Limited, and Blackstone Loan Financing Limited, all of which are listed on the London Stock Exchange. She is also the non-executive chair of Jersey Water, co-chair of The Jersey Community Foundation Limited, and a trustee of The Lloyds Bank Foundation for the Channel Islands.

Marshall Manson

Marshall leads Brunswick's Digital specialty across Europe, the Middle East and Africa, and India. He develops digital strategies to help clients solve complex communications challenges. Marshall also leads Brunswick's global strategic communications planning discipline.

Steve Maslin

Steve is a chartered accountant and a serial non-executive director. He spent his executive career at Grant Thornton where his leadership roles included: chair, Partnership Oversight Board; head of audit, and managing partner of London satellite offices as well as chairing the public policy committee jointly established by the CEOs of the six largest global accounting networks.

Sir Mark Moody-Stuart

Mark Moody-Stuart has lived and worked in ten different countries and led as CEO or chairman two major global resource companies. He has been a

NED of several major companies and a member of the board of the UN Global Compact, the Global Reporting Initiative, the International Institute for Sustainable Development, and other not-for-profits. He has written papers on sustainability and ethics, and a book.[3]

Filipe Morais, Lecturer in Governance, Henley Business School

Dr Filipe Morais is a lecturer in governance and programme director of the MSc in Management for Future Leaders at Henley Business School. He is an independent member of the Ratings Ratification Committee at Risk Insights (Pty) Ltd.

Craig Mullaney

Craig leads Brunswick's team supporting executive communications in digital and social media. Craig previously founded Facebook's Global Executive Program. Craig is the author of the 2009 *New York Times* bestseller *The Unforgiving Minute: A Soldier's Education*.

Amaechi Nsofor, Partner Grant Thornton

Amaechi is a partner in Grant Thornton UK LLP's insolvency and asset recovery team, which has recovered over $3 billion for creditors in the last eight years. He is at the forefront of the drive to develop insolvency frameworks in Africa. Amaechi also serves as a non-executive director of the UK's Institute of Directors, the influential body empowered under Royal Charter to protect and promote companies' interests.

Sir John Parker, Chairman Laing O'Rourke Group

Sir John Parker is currently chair of the construction group Laing O'Rourke, NED of Carnival Corporation, and chair of the Government-commissioned review on Ethnic Diversity in the Boardroom. Trained as a naval architect and engineer and a former president of the Royal Academy of Engineering, he has chaired 6 FTSE 100 Companies, including National Grid plc and the international Mining group Anglo American plc.

---

3 *Responsible Leadership: Lessons from the Front Line of Sustainability and Ethics*, Greenleaf Publishing, 2014

Dr Randall S. Peterson

Randall Peterson is professor of organisational behaviour and founding director of the Leadership Institute at London Business School. His research on boards and team dynamics has been published in the top scholarly and practitioner journals. He is also an experienced director who is passionate about developing evidence-based advice to boards on how to improve their practice.

Jean Pousson, Founder, Board Evaluation Limited

Jean Pousson is an experienced management consultant with over 30 years' experience. He is a senior consultant of the UK Institute of Directors (IoD) and has conducted numerous consultancy assignments, board reviews, and strategic assignments in more than 30 countries in that time. In a typical year, he will interface with approximately 600 directors and work with 8–10 boards. He was voted 2018 Lecturer of the Year for UK Finance, and has also written many articles.

Dineshi Ramesh, Executive Director, Specialist Delivery

Dineshi is a director at Board Intelligence specialising in board information and effective meetings. Dineshi leads Board Intelligence's consulting arm and Academy, an online learning platform for board members and executives. Prior to BI, she worked as strategy consultant for 20 years and holds an MEng from Imperial College.

Martin Rich, Co-founder & Executive Director, Future-Fit Foundation

Martin Rich is a sustainable investment specialist, with over 20 years' experience in mainstream and impact finance. He co-founded Future Fit Foundation3 to find a solution for investors wanting to understand the impact of their portfolios. Martin is chair of the Endowment Investment Committee for Access Foundation, and a member of assorted investment/advisory committees.

Carol Rosati, OBE, CEO, V2 Coaching

Carol, a talent management specialist, is a passionate advocate for improved gender diversity and inclusion since founding her women's board network, Inspire. She was awarded an OBE for Services to Women in Business in 2015. She is vice chair of UN Women UK, senior independent director at Southern Housing, where she also chairs Spruce Homes, and chair of the Remuneration and Nominations Committee at Alliance Group.

Elliot S. Schreiber, PhD, Adjunct Professor, Florida Atlantic University
Elliot Schreiber, PhD, is a former chief marketing officer of three global companies and currently is an independent consultant to companies and boards in brand and reputation and governance. He holds a PhD from the Pennsylvania State University. He a citizen of both the US and Canada.

Jenny Simnett, Doctoral Researcher, Henley Business School
Jenny is a non-executive director and chair of nomination and remuneration committee at Tower Hamlets Community Housing. She is also a doctoral researcher in corporate governance at Henley Business School.

Natalie Sykes, Head of English Branches, Executive Management Team, IoD
Natalie is a chartered director, NED, chair, and trustee with experience across an array of industry sectors and with a passion for enterprise. She has won industry awards for her work with national and international luxury hospitality groups and is the youngest chair ever appointed to a regeneration charity, the Groundwork Federation, where she served for eight years. Natalie is also a director for the Royal Armouries.

Dr Meena Thuraisingham, Founder, Principal BoardQ
Meena Thuraisingham is an organisational psychologist and founder of BoardQ, an advisory practice working with boards and top teams on culture. She is the author of *Identity, Power and Influence in the Boardroom* (Routledge, 2019), offering strategies for developing high-impact directors and boards. She is a non-executive director of The George Institute for Global Health, a member of the International Women's Forum, and alum of Manchester University and London Business School.

Ian Wright, Former Deputy Chairman, Jersey Financial Services Commission
Ian Wright is a chartered accountant and is the former deputy chairman of the Jersey Financial Services Commission. He trained with PwC, becoming

Global IFRS leader and committee member of the International Financial Reporting Interpretations Committee. After retiring from PwC, Ian was appointed director of corporate reporting at the FRC and deputy chairman of the Financial Reporting Review Panel.

FOREWORD: EFFECTIVE DIRECTORS AND PROFESSIONAL BOARDS

For millennia, humans have known that it is better to apply more than one brain to an issue to ensure more effective problem-solving. This is especially so if the owners of those brains have responsibility for the oversight of the complexity of a company and its impact on the financial, social, and physical environments – the ecological system within which it exists. These diverse directorial brains are essential for the continual resolution of the directors' dilemma. Such brains, thoughtfully chosen and regularly assessed, help ensure sufficient diversity of thinking and experience to generate wise and subtle solutions. To survive and develop, the board of directors needs to become the business brain – the central processor – of a continually learning organisation. To be effective, both the board and the operational side of the company need to generate a sufficient rate of learning to be equal to, or greater than, the rate of change in their external environment. Few boards achieve this; even fewer sustain it.

In the twentieth century, most people became "directors" by default; they signed the forms, were given a short talk by the chair and company secretary, then given a pile of legal papers that spelled out their onerous and legally binding directorial duties. These tended to then be put aside as the director became overwhelmed by the day-to-day demands of their "real" job. Directors rarely appreciated that they have a second and more onerous real job: directing the company. This is very different from managing, but they rarely allow the time to generate the intellectual energy and skills to learn how. It is only when a crisis happens that the wider world questions their lack of diligence in their directorial duties. Then the full extent of their legal responsibilities and liabilities become clear. By then it is too late because ignorance is no defence under the law.

When I use the phrase "professional board," I mean one that fully understands its legal and governance duties, delivers them effectively, assesses them regularly, and learns continuously. So as we develop the companies of the future, how do we develop these professional boards? One thing we know is that they will be very different from the narrowly defined and relatively undemanding boards of the twentieth century. For example, the new demands of diverse stakeholders coupled with the loss of "shareholder supremacy," the rapid growth of national and international legislation, and new audits about the social, environmental, governance, and financial decisions of boards, all pose new challenges. These intellectual, behavioural, and emotional challenges are rarely ever considered to be relevant to board competence. The old, simplistic issues of shareholder value priorities, the irritation at the rise of stakeholders, the nagging doubts as to the validity of assessing social and environmental impact, even the background debate on capitalism versus socialism, all now look increasingly minor when faced with the new global challenges. Boards will have to learn how to cope, yet few feel capable or even motivated to do so.

Directors' duties require an intellectual and ethical stance way above what is required from day-to-day management. In this foreword it is not possible to go into great detail. But, as examples, here are just four challenges. First, in exercising independent judgement, a director must rise above their often single, professional discipline to consider the future health of the company as a whole. Second, it is unlawful for a director to act on behalf of a third party; any director acting merely as an agent of another is not fulfilling their duty of independent thought. Third, sufficient time needs be set aside to ensure that board decisions are taken jointly to demonstrate carefulness, skilfulness, and diligence. Decisions taken beyond the existing competences of the board need to show that appropriate professional advice was sought.

Fourth, boards and directors need be provided with suitable professional support to deliver their duties and so ensure their effectiveness.

And finally, the written declaration of conflicts of interests, offered or accepted benefits from third parties, or involvement in third-party transactions must be produced well before any board vote on a proposal. While it is for the board to decide and record whether the director involved attends, has a say in the meeting, and is able to vote, they should not be in the room when the vote is taken. These issues need careful handling in specific circumstances, for example, when decisions are taken by the board of family companies where conflicts of interest can be complex.

Given these complex demands and ever-growing stakeholder expectations, who would want to be a director now? I am however reassured by those who see the chance of becoming professional in reframing their company within a more integrated and publicly agreed compact for their social community and its ecology. Most are willing to learn how to handle environmental, social and governance, and triple bottom line reporting. They want to become professional directors.

Recent events have meant that we have the opportunity of creating a new workable model of the purpose of a company with governance arrangements fit for the twenty-first century. Directors need to play their part and continue to professionalise, being the business brains of a continually learning organisation. It is only then that a board can deliver effectively their roles related to their duties as a director, and the purpose of their company.

It has been a pleasure to work with Charlotte and Claire on this book that has as its aim to provide directors, and those seeking directorship, the key questions to ask in the boardroom in order to be an effective and professional director.

Professor R. "Bob" Garratt

PREFACE

Putting together a book about what questions to ask in the boardroom was an idea I first had almost three years ago when I decided to do something about all the requests I was getting for help with the right sorts of questions to ask at board. People wanted to make sure that the right outcomes are generated, and that decision-making was effective through asking the right questions.

Over the years I have come across so many expert people with so much accumulated wisdom within governance and boardrooms, and I felt that one way of delivering key knowledge transfer would be for them to contribute to this book. Drawing out the key 20 questions to ask in the boardroom from the contributors' expert fields of knowledge, would in this way benefit the world at large.

Board members everywhere can use this as a reference book for inspiration as to what questions to ask in discussions for the boards they serve on. Executives can draw on the book to ensure they cover questions that could or should be asked in the boardroom and ensure the right discussions occur. Their boards would be so lucky to have executives able to envisage which kind of questions their board might ask them in different areas and maybe answer the questions before they are even asked.

The sorts of questions that directors of any type of organisation should be asking or considering (and ensuring that they are noted in the minutes), would be:

- What is the business rationale behind this ...?
- Is there anything in this document that the lawyers and/or management want to specifically bring to the directors' attention?
- Are you aware of any reason the board should not approve this ...?

And as a point of care, always ask for back-up letters for any representation the board is asked to give where the board members themselves haven't actually completed the work or have the information directly.

In addition, I would love to see the book being used as a learning tool for aspiring directors and executives as a way to better understand the level boards operate at and how asking the right questions can draw out deeper thinking. In general, it is clear that directors need to evolve from the last century to this century if they want to be able to thrive in this increasingly complex world – a world where we all face existential issues – and one that we want to reverse for our children and grandchildren or for the people who come after us.

Of course, in writing the book I also had a close eye on achieving appropriate diversity within the group of contributors and ensured getting a broad variety of people involved, which all together illustrates the full power that diversity brings. It has been such a thrilling experience seeing how beautifully it all came together at the end, and I hope our readers will enjoy the book as much as I have enjoyed putting it together.

ACKNOWLEDGEMENTS

I am delighted to have been able to put this book together with the help of so many people who are passionate about what goes on in the boardroom and about improving governance around the world.

Trying to limit yourself to the most important topics and the top 20 or so questions for each topic has seen this book's remit grow. Already therefore we have agreed that this will be the first in a series of books to explore all the topics and issues of boardroom discussions within different industries and different types of organisations – a plethora of books to write for many years to come.

My first thanks go to Claire Fargeot, my co-editor, who without hesitation gave up her time and energy to support me in completing this book. Her willingness to help with her network, her efficiency, and ability to hold me to account have been invaluable as we started the journey of first completing and then publishing my first book.

The chapter authors deserve real acknowledgement too as all of them are busy working senior practitioners or academics who have either found the time, or found the patience, to put up with our demands. Often at incredibly short notice chapters have been drafted, reviewed, and completed. Other authors have seen their initial drafts from over two years back suddenly be reinvigorated. Without their help this book would never have been started and I wouldn't be looking forward with excitement to seeing this book available for everyone to read.

Thank you also to Routledge's commissioning editor, Rebecca Marsh, and the editing team for working with me in this endeavour.

EDITOR BIOGRAPHIES

Charlotte Valeur

Charlotte has over 35 years of experience in finance, primarily as an investment banker in Denmark and the UK. She is an experienced FTSE chair, non-executive director, and corporate governance expert, serving on a variety of boards, as well as delivering training, conducting board reviews, and advising boards on corporate governance through her company, Global Governance Group.

She is a visiting professor in governance at the University of Strathclyde and on the advisory board of the Moller Institute at Churchill College, Cambridge University.

Charlotte has been a director of seven public companies, including three appointments as the chair. She has taken part in a complete restructuring of NTR Plc, the sale of REG Plc to BlackRock and, as chair, overseen a $8bln Merger of FTSE250 Kennedy Wilson Europe Real Estate Plc with its US NYSE-listed parent company. She currently chairs Blackstone Loan Financing Plc. Charlotte also has board experience with a range of unlisted companies including international engineering firm Laing O'Rourke, BT Pension Fund, chair of Institute of Directors U.K., and is the founder and chair of Board Apprentice.

Claire Fargeot

Claire is a non-executive director and corporate governance scholar working as a consulting adviser with listed, as well as entrepreneurial or private companies, to improve their governance, sustainability, and reporting practices. As well as delivering impactful governance training around the world on behalf of the London Stock Exchange and Euronext, she regularly conducts board evaluations and governance due diligence on behalf of investors.

She is also an expert witness in capital markets and an associate lecturer at Nottingham Business School.

Claire has board experience in the listed, private, entrepreneurial, youth and health charity, government, and education sectors, and provides mentoring support to leadership teams to find solutions to particular governance, growth, and sustainability challenges.

Part I

THE BOARD

1

BOARD COMPOSITION

Chris Hodge

Board composition is one of the keys to good governance. Getting the right people around the board table does not guarantee the company will be effectively governed, but not doing so guarantees that it won't be, no matter how good the policies and processes you put in place.

Unfortunately, there is no standard template to help you. Just as the needs and challenges of every company are unique, so they are for boards. However, while boards must be bespoke, there are certain factors that all companies should consider when deciding on their board structure and balance.

The starting point must be the company's strategy, business model, and operations. The board clearly needs to be capable of understanding them if it is to provide effective oversight, but if it is to provide leadership, not just oversight, then it needs to have the ability to guide their development as well. Ideally, the board will have skills, experience, and perspectives that will enhance those of management.

Even companies with a relatively simple business model may struggle to find room for all the attributes they would ideally want the board to have. Prioritisation and trade-offs will be required. The rest of this chapter highlights some of the choices that boards will need to make.

Board size

The size of a company's board tends to be determined by its size, sector and the complexity of its operations, and the issues with which the board needs to deal. In large, listed companies, boards will typically have between nine and eleven members – or even more in regulated sectors like financial services – while the boards of private and smaller listed companies will typically have fewer.

Conventional wisdom is that big boards are bad. They are harder to chair, making discussion and decision-making more difficult; cliques can form, splintering the unity of the board; and there is a greater risk of some directors losing interest and becoming passengers, not participants.

While these problems are less prominent on smaller boards, they bring challenges of their own. The most obvious is finding a small number of individuals who can collectively provide all the skills and experience the board and company require, although this difficulty can be mitigated, for example, by bringing in advisers to assist with specific issues.

Each company needs to make a judgement as to how many board members it needs. Ideally, that number should be the minimum required to ensure the board has the capacity to carry out its responsibilities fully and the range of attributes needed for it be effective.

In some cases, that may require a bigger board. Regulatory requirements and public expectations have seen the list of the board's responsibilities lengthen considerably; and while the use of board committees can alleviate pressure on the board's time, the more committees there are, the more board members are needed to run them.

Expertise and independence

Many boards benefit from the greater objectivity that directors who are independent of the company's management and owners can bring. Their presence can also provide a degree of reassurance to external shareholders, stakeholders, and regulators that the interests of the company will take priority over the interests of management where the two diverge.

It is sometimes argued that too much emphasis has been placed on independence at the expense of relevant expertise, particularly in the listed sector. I do not personally believe that the two are incompatible. Depending on their size and sector, most companies should be able to find board candidates who are both independent and expert. This may mean looking a bit harder than is sometimes the case, and not limiting your search to the "usual suspects."

What is often more difficult is prioritising one type of expertise over the other. Some boards consider it important to have non-executive directors (NEDs) with direct sectoral experience. This can be invaluable if, for example, the company has a relatively inexperienced management team; but it is arguably less useful if it just replicates the expertise that the company already has, leaving other gaps unplugged.

Many companies use a skills matrix when developing or refreshing the board. These can be a useful starting point as they prompt you to think about the expertise required by the board as a whole or for specific positions (for example, committee chairs) and compare it with what the current board has to offer – informed by the results of the board's evaluation of its own effectiveness, where one has been undertaken.

Looking ahead at the risks, opportunities, and changes in the operating environment facing the organisation in the next few years, and building these into the matrix can help identify what the board needs if it is to shape these developments rather than simply respond to them.

Executive directors

There are different views on the merits of having executive directors (that is, senior management) on the board.

In some countries, companies will typically have a "two-tier" board structure which formally separates the oversight and management functions, with a top-tier supervisory board that is completely non-executive. In countries where the single or "unitary" board is common, companies will usually have the CEO and perhaps the chief finance officer on the board, but rarely more than two or three executives in total.

One view is that having more executive directors at the board table leads to more effective oversight of senior management, enhances the quality of board discussion by ensuring it is informed by a good understanding of the operational considerations, and creates a shared sense of purpose.

Opposing that, others argue that executives reporting to the CEO are unlikely to be willing to demonstrate the independent judgement expected of directors when he or she is in the room; and that the larger the executive contingent on the board, the more likely that the atmosphere will become too cosy and the non-executives will be reluctant to challenge them.

There is no right answer, but there may be certain circumstances in which the arguments for having more executive directors are stronger; for example, if the company is operating in multiple sectors or geographical markets, or where the board feels it needs more direct line of sight of functions critical to the organisation's success.

Bringing in outsiders

For some companies, particularly those run by entrepreneurs and families, deciding whether to bring an outsider onto the board can be agonising. Some see it as a threat to their control, others as a betrayal of the company's values.

Smaller companies with no ambition to grow may not need to look outside the family or employees to find the skills and experience that the board requires. For most others, though, there comes a point when the benefit of drawing on a broader pool of talent outweighs their concerns.

Opening the board up need not be, and should not be, at the expense of developing in-house talent, of course. All companies can benefit from investing in senior managers to enable them to be "board ready" when required, for example, by encouraging them to take on non-executive positions elsewhere.

"Fit" versus diversity

When asked what they look for in new board members, you will often hear chairs talk about the importance of being a "good fit." This phrase has different meanings. It can mean "someone who shares our values and will embody the culture we are trying to create," which is clearly highly desirable. But it can also mean "someone who looks and thinks just like the rest of us" or "someone who won't rock the boat."

It is understandable that boards tend to choose members who they believe will be able to work constructively with their colleagues. A board that is constantly at war with itself cannot be an effective one. An "identikit" board, however, is unlikely to be effective either. There is a huge danger of "groupthink," of risks and opportunities being missed because everyone comes at an issue from the same direction, with the same assumptions and perspective.

Boards benefit from having a diversity of views and being able to draw on a wide variety of experience. This is more likely to be achieved if the members of the board are diverse as well. In recent years there has rightly been a lot of focus on gender diversity. This is important, but there are other aspects of diversity that boards ought to think about, such as age, ethnicity, and the range of different experiences and expertise already mentioned.

Refreshing the board

The challenges organisations face change over time, and the board will need to change as well. The board that stands still when everything beneath and around it is moving is a board that becomes out of touch. That said, a degree of stability is important to provide clear leadership and to ensure that the corporate memory is not lost. Continual churn can be unsettling not just for the board itself but for those who look to it for direction and support.

All boards can benefit from being refreshed from time to time; the challenge is in judging the appropriate pace. The boards of companies that are growing or entering new markets may benefit from regular turnover, as the skills and experience required change, while those whose business models are at risk of being made obsolete by disruptive competitors may require a radical restructuring. For other, more established, companies it may be that occasional fine-tuning is all that is required.

Making this judgement comes back again to an understanding of the organisation's current and future opportunities and risks, and the strategy that is needed if the company is to survive and grow. It also requires directors to be humble enough to recognise that the board that develops that strategy is not necessarily the board that is best able to deliver it, and that there will almost inevitably come a time when it is in the best interests of the company for them to step aside.

Questions

- Does the board have the capacity to carry out all its responsibilities? If not, do you need more people or more delegation?
- How satisfactory are board discussions? Do all board members participate fully?
- Does the board collectively have sufficient expertise to understand the company's business model and performance data?
- Does the board collectively understand the views of its key stakeholders, and the likely impact on them of the board's decisions?
- What are the main challenges facing the company in the next five years? What skills and knowledge will the board need to overcome them?
- What are the culture and values the board seeks to promote, and how do you assess whether board members and candidates share them?
- Is there a skills matrix for the board? Does it include the desired personal attributes and mix (for example, diversity) as well as relevant experience?
- Is the board evaluation used to identify skills gaps?
- What knowledge and experience does senior management have, and where are the gaps? Do these need to be filled by the board or by some other means?
- Which members of the senior management team sit on the board? How open are they with the NEDs?
- When was the last time the board was refreshed? What is the average length of tenure of the current board members?
- Does the company have a formal succession plan for board member and senior management? How far ahead does it look?
- How does the board identify and select new NEDs? Is there a formal process, and how widely does it search?
- What is being done to develop potential internal board candidates?

2

BOARD APPOINTMENT

Carol Rosati OBE

Boards today are expected to be more engaged, more knowledgeable, and more effective than ever, so getting the right composition is critical. There has to be a broad range of skills, knowledge, backgrounds, and business acumen to avoid groupthink, promote diversity of thought, and reflect the needs of stakeholders and customers.

It is important to ensure the board has a broad perspective, is able to offer constructive challenge, and has a robust debate. To do that, there has to be a rigorous ongoing process in place that will identify individuals who will challenge the status quo, bring new perspectives, and enhance collective knowledge.

A nomination committee often sits alongside, or is even combined with, the remuneration committee and is there to evaluate a firm's board of directors and evaluate the skills and characteristics required of board candidates and ensure all the necessary skills are present on the board. It is essential that it has formal and transparent procedures for making recommendations on appointments and re-appointments to the board.

Questions for the nominations committee

- How balanced is the current board? Is there true diversity of thought?
- Is there fair representation of gender, ethnicity, age, and sexual orientation on the board?
- Is the board too comfortable, and do we have groupthink?
- Are we able to provide enough challenge from a broad knowledge perspective?
- In terms of succession planning which board members are due to finish their rotation, and what skills do new appointees need to have?
- Are the skill sets clearly defined?
- Are there any knowledge gaps or skills that need to be filled or areas that need to be improved?
- What are the likely business challenges facing the organisation and does the board have the collective skills to engage effectively with the executive team? For example, digitalisation, the impact of artificial intelligence on talent management, client engagement through social media.
- What areas for improvement did the last board review highlight and what skills could enhance the board's performance?

The board review process also plays a role as well as the board appraisals conducted by the senior independent director (SID) and chair. Both should identify any skills gaps and also strengths of the board. The chair should also be mindful of future challenges the board may face and ensure the individuals will be able to contribute fully and add value.

Once the need for a particular skill set has been identified, a specific job specification/candidate profile should be created to outline the criteria. Applicants, whether from a direct advertisement or search firm, should be asked to fill out an application form against each criterion to demonstrate their suitability, or at the very least provide a covering letter and CV. The latter however may well lead to greater subjectivity in the process, influenced by personal bias and feelings.

It is essential that a fair and transparent interview process is created so that each candidate can demonstrate their suitability for the role. Prior to the interview, check if any reasonable adjustments are necessary. It is preferable to have a balanced interview panel to eradicate any potential bias and avoid the human trait of opting for the individuals most like us or those individuals we feel comfortable with, as this is often the least beneficial person to appoint and will not improve diversity of thought. The panel should consist of the chair, SID, or chair of the remuneration/nominations committee and chair/member of the relevant committee such as audit and risk/finance depending on the skills requirement. Wherever possible, there should be a range of gender and ethnicity, and reflect both actual diversity of personality, ethnicity, and so on, as well as diversity of thinking.

Prior to the interviews, there should be a pre-interview briefing session to make the interviewers more aware of their own and others' biases, and pre-prepared questions should be assigned so that each candidate is interviewed in the same way. It is also important to remember to give candidates plenty of time to answer, with enough allocated time for their questions at the end. Try to avoid a common pitfall, namely too much input from the panellists and not enough from the interviewee.

A scoring system (where 5 is optimal and 1 is meets criteria) should be used so that results can be compared at the end of the session.

Notes should be collected at the end of each interview so that the company secretary can give constructive feedback to the candidates.

Interview questions for the potential NED individual

- If this is a first-time NED appointment, does the potential board member understand the boundaries and clear responsibility of a NED versus an executive?
- How do you handle conflict?
- What are the three key skills you feel would add value to our board?
- How would you ensure you have enough information to provide effective executive oversight without overstepping the mark with the management team?
- How would your colleagues describe your communication style?
- How strong is your network and how could you use your connectivity as a resource benefit for the board and the organisation?
- What do you think is the best way a NED can contribute to an organisation?
- Give an example of strategic input that has fundamentally added value to a project or organisation.

- Describe the main characteristics of effective governance present in well-performing boards.
- The time commitment is X. Are you able to commit to it?
- What do you think are the characteristics and traits of a great board member?

Following the update of the UK Corporate Governance Code in 2018, it is also the responsibility of a board to ensure the corporate culture is aligned to the business strategy and promotes diversity. In this regard board members have a role to play in the board appointment process.

Questions a board member should ask about potential board members and the board

- Are we independent, or is there an element of groupthink in our decision-making process?
- What skills are we missing?
- How would this appointment challenge us and add value?
- Is our board truly diverse?
- How can I help this individual settle in and contribute as quickly as possible?
- Is the process fair, transparent, and reflective of our values?

Questions a board member should ask themselves during a board appointment process

- What are my biases and how can I challenge them?
- What can I learn from this individual that will make me a better board member?
- How can I work more effectively with a colleague who may well be different to me?
- When did I last attend a subcommittee meeting to learn more about it?

Finding your first NED role

Once you have decided that you would like to become an NED, it is the start of what can be a fairly long journey as, although progress has been made, there is still a long way to go before boards really reflect the customer base and society they represent. It is also not for the faint-hearted, and you must ensure you understand and accept the legal duties and liabilities and the due diligence you should carry out before accepting a position on a board, as the Companies Act 2006 does not differentiate between executive and non-executive directors.

Your NED/board profile is different to your executive CV and should reflect your commercial and business acumen, and how you would add value to a board rather than be a chronological list of your experience. It should illustrate your strengths and outline your experience of interaction at a senior level.

You need to reflect on the kind of boards you would be most suitable for and be realistic in your expectations. Sector expertise and connectivity are often key, as is the size of an organisation. You also need to think of your time commitments as this can vary enormously from board to board and also where the organisation is in its life cycle. You may also be called in when unexpected challenges arise.

There are many places to look for a NED role, and rightly or wrongly, it is still often your network which will provide the opportunity, so make sure you do invest time in it.

Competition is fierce and you will need to demonstrate how you are different and why the panel should choose you over the other candidates. Preparation is key. Learning your sales pitch will make you more comfortable and appear self-assured, which in turn will inspire confidence in the interview panel. Think about your communication style and interpersonal skills. Believe it or not, 55% of the interview is conducted without a word being said. Thirty-eight per cent is your tone and only 7% is what you actually say.

Questions to ask yourself

- What are my five keys skills I can offer to a board?
- How do I evaluate risk?
- What sectors are relevant? Where I can use my experience?
- How much time can I commit? Do I have time to read the papers and prepare for every meeting?
- What locations are best for me?

- Do I understand my legal duties and liabilities?
- Do I understand the difference between an executive and non-executive and where is the line?
- Can I add value to this board?

3

DIRECTOR SELF-ASSESSMENT

Alison Gill OLY

The work of the board is both challenging and rewarding. Brain health, emotional and moral intelligence, and boardroom behaviour are four areas for board directors to develop self-awareness in and to continually self-assess and self-develop. Overconfidence and complacency undermine judgement and ultimately performance, so it is important to feel that we have never really cracked learning about ourselves and remain open-minded to learning experiences, feedback from colleagues, and to insights gained from success and failure.

Gaining an accurate impression of oneself is an intrinsically difficult task, one for which people often do not have crucial information, and when they do, they find it easy to ignore. That said, directors can take steps to reach more objective conclusions about themselves by setting clear and objective criteria, seeking regular, situational and specific feedback from others, and asking more profound open-ended questions that stimulate us to think as much about the things we don't want to face up to, as much as the ones we do.

How can you improve your self-awareness and self-assess?

The most important thing to do before beginning any self-assessment is to anchor the assessment to specific criteria. Judging performance is difficult if the criteria are ambiguous, open to disagreement, or are just unknowable. Research shows that the more ambiguous the performance criteria, the more likely people are to self-enhance and misjudge ability.

Brain health: A board director's job is a thinking job. In the last few years, neuroscience has made significant advances that show that insufficient sleep and cognitive overload have a direct bearing on the brain's capacity to think. If you are not getting enough sleep (latest research from the Centre for Human Sleep Science indicates seven to nine hours) or are working more than 40 hours a week, you don't just get tired, you make mistakes.

When fatigued or sleep deprived, we literally become less able to think effectively and to make judgements. The parietal and occipital lobes and the prefrontal cortex literally become less active. These are the areas of the brain we need for social perception, to be able to differentiate between good and bad and for thinking and processing information. Reports from serious corporate failures like the BP oil refinery explosion and "EA: The Human Story" make clear the role of fatigued and sleep-deprived people in corporate disaster. The board is the last stop for organisational oversight and challenge, and never before has it been so evident why board directors need to take the health of their brain and the health of their workers brains' so seriously.

Moral compass: Board work involves navigating dilemmas; situations in which a difficult choice has to be made between two or more alternatives, often choices that are equally undesirable. When faced with dilemmas, we make decisions that not only impact us but those around us. The consequences of the decisions we make at board level ripple far and wide, and the actions we take really matter to colleagues and their families, customers, and the economy. Doing the right thing isn't always easy. Understanding how we make up our minds when faced with a dilemma, means that we are more likely to do the right thing, in the right way, more of the time.

Emotional intelligence: Emotional intelligence is the capacity to blend thinking and feeling to make optimal decisions about ourselves, and how we relate to and work with others. It is not traditional to think of boards and board decision-making as involving feelings and emotion; instead, we prefer to think of the board centred around logic and reason. However, this traditional view defies both experience and research. Emotional intelligence is central to effective boards because emotions transmit much faster than ideas and they are a significant driver of behaviour.

From research studies of brain-damaged patients whose amygdala (the emotion centre of the brain) is damaged, we find that they literally cannot make decisions. Emotions and feelings are a source of information, and emotional intelligence is the ability to explore this information to gain insight. For example, feeling anxious typically means that you perceive something or someone you care about to be under threat. Noticing the feeling of anxiety and considering what is making you feel like this puts you in a better place to consider your options: Are you really under threat? How big is the threat? What might you do to neutralise the threat?

There are four fundamental domains of emotional intelligence that directors can self-assess against.

- Self-awareness – can I name how I feel, and what insight is the feeling offering me?
- Self-management – do I consciously choose how I respond to my feelings, or conversely just react without exploring or reframing?
- Social awareness – how well do I empathise with the feelings of others?
- Relationship management – how effectively do I relate to others, navigating different relationship states?

Leadership Behaviour: Behaviour is important because how we behave directly impacts outcomes. There are four specific behavioural clusters directly related to the work of the board.[1] Each behaviour is definable, observable, and learnable, therefore making it possible for directors to self-assess against, to gain feedback on, and to learn to affect the desired outcomes.

  i. **Purpose, objectives, and strategy formation** (thinking behaviours: seeking information, forming concepts, conceptual agility). The board

---

1 Specified by the UK Corporate Governance Code Principles of Board Leadership and Company Purpose.

is responsible for establishing the company's purpose and strategy. The act of strategy formation requires the director to *seek information* about the competitive landscape and markets; to be able to *form concepts* about the objectives the organisation wishes to pursue; and to demonstrate *conceptual agility*, comparing the pros and cons of different strategies. The quality of the strategic thinking by the board literally determines the quality of strategy.

ii. **The board as a leadership team** (involving behaviours: enabling openness, facilitating and developing capability). The board is comprised of independent directors and executive directors who have shared accountability for the long-term success of the company and to deliver value for shareholders and contribute to the wider society. The board is *facilitated* by the chair, who is responsible for the effectiveness of the board. The capacity to *enable openness* in each other is vital in order for each director to be listened to and feel a sense of shared ownership for the outcomes. As with any team, each board member is responsible for *developing the capability* of themselves and the board as a whole. Feedback exchange and supporting peers to develop is a crucial precursor to optimising group effectiveness.

iii. **Stakeholder engagement** (inspirational behaviours: inspiring communication, influence and building confidence). In order for the company to meet its responsibilities to shareholders and stakeholders, the board should ensure effective engagement with, and encourage participation from, these parties. This requires directors to be *inspiring communicators*, work with *influence*, and *build confidence*.

iv. **Performance oversight** (performance behaviours: enabling action and measuring and monitoring performance). The board should ensure that the necessary resources are in place for the company to meet its objectives and measure performance against them. To do this, directors need to *empower action* to ensure what's agreed is delivered and to *measure and monitor performance* by seeking to understand a breadth of metrics from culture assessment to customer engagement to financial measures.

Effective self-assessment requires directors to seek and collate evidence of effectiveness against criteria from yourself and from others. This is best done by seeking feedback regularly and in relation to specific situations.

Fellow board members are much more likely to provide sincere and accurate feedback if, for example, after a particular meeting, you pose a series of questions relevant to the situation and related to a particular behaviour. For example, to understand how well you listened, you might ask: "How would you describe the quality of my listening in the meeting we've just finished?"; "Which issues could I have explored at a deeper level?"; "In my summary of the conversation, was there anything you might have added or concluded differently?"; "What might help me develop better rapport with X?". Exploration of issues, summarising, and rapport building are all components of effective listening.

For those of you who have tried to fill out a feedback questionnaire, at the end of the year, about a colleague, hopefully you will instantly recognise this as a more beneficial way to gain and give accurate and specific feedback. Research shows that when feedback is given often, immediately, and with objectivity, it improves a person's ability to self-assess. Seeking regular, immediate, and specific feedback can improve your ability to self-assess by 50% – priceless!

Twenty questions to generate self-awareness and monitor progression

There are two types of questions here. The first are those that you can use to monitor yourself. Regularly assessing your brain health, moral compass, emotional intelligence, and boardroom behaviour will help with maintenance and continuous improvement. The second type of question is designed to help you think at a deeper and more profound level about your contribution and the impact that you are having as a director on a board.

Brain health

1. How would I rate my sleep quality and sufficiency over the last week?
2. How many hours have I worked this week and on average over the last month?
3. Honestly, looking back over my preparation for board meetings, my attendance at board meetings, and other board work, how optimal has my brain functioning been?

4. In the last year, to what extent have I identified, explored, and challenged evidence of fatigue and cognitive overload in other directors or the workforce?

Moral compass

5. If I had the opportunity to talk to anyone that you have worked with over the years, what would be the most embarrassing thing I'd find out?
6. When faced with a difficult moral dilemma, what is your method for deciding what is the right thing to do and the right way to do it?

Emotional intelligence

7. Emotional intelligence has four fundamental elements. Which do you need to work on and what will the benefits be?
8. Can you name the 22 primary emotions and what each emotion is a signal of?
9. If your emotions were a friend who'd popped round for coffee, what would they tell you about yourself and how you feel about your role as a board director right now?

Behaviour thinking

10. All groups work with unconscious social dynamics and biases, for example, "groupthink" and "confirmation bias," which affect their ability to think strategically. Which dynamics and biases are you and your board particularly susceptible to and why? What is your evidence for this?
11. Last time you made a strategic decision, how many options did you thoroughly consider the pros and cons of before settling on your choice?
12. What strategic issues is your board ignoring and why? What might you do about this?

Involving

13. How do you rate your ability to get others to say what really think and feel?
14. Conformity means to behave in ways which are socially acceptable in a group. Which socially acceptable norms are rewarded in your board?
15. When did you last give another director feedback? Be honest. How accurate versus sugar-coated was it? How well timed was it? And how was it received?

Inspiring

16. How could you measure your level of influence?
17. Right now, what do you feel most ambiguous about with regard to the work of your board and your fellow board directors? What is this telling you?
18. Who or what is inspiring you, and what does that tell you about your values?

Performing

19. How effective have you been at raising performance standards of directors?
20. What stretching performance measures have set for yourself?

4

ASSESSING THE CHAIR'S PERFORMANCE

Charlotte Valeur

The chair of an organisation has an important role to play for both the wider board and the executives. The chair's role is to lead the board in discharging their duties and to support the executives as well as be the main contact to the board for the executives.

There are a number of attributes which make for a great chair. Leadership styles in the twenty-first century have moved towards a greater emphasis on emotional intelligence, coaching skills and an ability to influence others without dominating. A good chair gives support to others and, like any good leader, creates an environment where others succeed. They lead the board without ruling the board. They should demonstrate the highest personal standards with regard to integrity, reliability, credibility and honesty, always leading by example.

It is generally expected, especially by large institutional investors, that a chair should not also be the CEO, as the role of a chair is to lead the board, not the organisation. The chair's focus is to ensure that the board is fully enabled to function as the highest decision-making and oversight(?) body of the organisation. A chair should be clear about the vision for the organisation and ensure that the board and executives share the same vision. A great

DOI: 10.4324/9781003201182-5

chair leads the board in setting the vision and values for the organisation and ensures these are clearly communicated to executives, employees and other stakeholders.

A board, consisting of a majority of non-executive directors, is not your standard team. As such, they don't need to like each other, but they do need to be able to collaborate and have trust in each other. The chair is responsible for ensuring all board members have the opportunity to be heard and that the members are using all of their skills for the best organisational outcomes. The chair ensures that the directors are working together collaboratively, and as such, emotional intelligence has become possibly the most important attribute of leaders of the twenty-first century.

Good chairs are passionate about their role and take the time to develop a strong relationship with the CEO. They generally work as a supportive sounding board to the CEO and develop the board meeting agendas in close collaboration with them.

On an annual basis the board should conduct a review of the performance of the chair where a number of questions should be asked. The list of questions below covers the main body of what should be asked both in the review and on an ongoing basis.

Key questions to ask of the chair:

- Does the chair act with integrity and demonstrate ethical leadership at all times?
- Is the chair effective in planning, coordinating and managing board meetings?
- Does the chair consistently display a sense of purpose?
- Does the chair encourage healthy board dynamics and interactions?
- Does the chair welcome different perspectives and robust exchanges of views?
- Is the chair open to being challenged themselves?
- Does the chair enable all board members to raise issues and concerns?
- Does the chair demonstrate fairness and objectivity in managing board discussions?
- Does the chair have a role in creating trust between board members?
- Does the chair lead the setting of the agenda and board calendar to ensure all relevant subjects are being discussed in a balanced way throughout the year?

- Is the chair ensuring that adequate time is available for discussion of all agenda items?
- Is the chair ensuring time is spent on discussing strategic issues on a regular basis?
- Is the chair coordinating the work of the committees, ensuring that they interact with the board in an appropriate manner?
- Is the chair accessible to board members and executive management both in and outside of board meetings?
- Is the relationship between the chair and the CEO constructive?
- Does the chair engage effectively with shareholders, employees and other significant stakeholders?
- Does the chair ensure that directors are made aware of the views of stakeholders?
- Is the chair regularly in individual contact with each director?
- Does the chair seek ways to enhance directors' contributions and effectiveness?
- Does the chair understand the strengths and weaknesses of the board?
- Is the chair committed to developing the overall effectiveness of the board?
- Does the chair live and breathe the organisational values?

5

DUE DILIGENCE FOR NEW APPOINTMENTS AND NEW DIRECTORS

Charlotte Valeur

Conducting due diligence for board members should be seen from two different angles. A new board member should conduct due diligence on the organisation, its executive and the board members before taking on a new appointment. The board/organisation should conduct due diligence on any new board member before appointing them.

New appointment

The potential risks of joining a board are ever increasing, and any candidate should conduct appropriate due diligence before accepting a new position. The process of conducting due diligence will enable the candidate to determine whether or not they will add value to the board, assess the level of risk within the appointment and identify potential conflicts of interest.

The first level of due diligence is to research any public information, annual accounts and news articles, recent and historical, about the organisation, its leadership and reputation. The candidate should also ask about the financial plans and budgets, and information about any litigation filed. Ideally, minutes should be reviewed together with the agendas and board packs from the last one to two years. This can usually be carried out under a non-disclosure agreement to protect any confidentialities.

Any board candidate should also look into the board composition and background of the current directors. It is worth also looking into: How were they identified and appointed? What is their reputation? Do they have any conflicts of interest? Do they have any personal relationships with other board members or the executives?

Most information will be available publicly, and the rest should be obtained directly from the organisation through the interview process and the relevant papers. This due diligence makes it possible for the prospective director to assess the potential risks associated with being a director of the organisation. It can also reveal which main areas will require extra time and input from the board members.

Questions to ask about the organisation

Financial

- What do the public documents reveal about the current and historical state of the finances?
- What is the future expected to bring?

Insurance

- What is the D&O insurance coverage and is it adequate?
- Does the organisation have adequate insurances in place covering all aspects of the business?
- Have there been any claims or notifications during the last ten years?

Legal and regulatory

- What is the legal entity of the organisation?

- Is the organisation carrying out any regulated activity? If so, what activity and what regulator is regulating it?
- Have there been any legal or regulatory breaches during the last ten years?

Reputationally

- What is the reputation of the organisation?
- How has reputation been managed historically?
- How is reputation being managed now?

Culture

- What is the culture of the organisation and the board?
- Can you support the culture and values of the organisation and its board?
- Can you stand behind the behaviours of the board and executives?
- What do the public comments/posts on social media tell you about the culture of the organisation?

Governance

- Does the organisation adhere to a specific code of corporate governance?
- If yes, which one?
- If no, why not?
- What do the historical books and records (minutes/agendas) reveal about governance and board dynamics?
- How frequently are board meetings being held, where and how (in person/on phone/online)?
- Is attendance by directors at meetings appropriate?

Risk management

- Does the organisation perform adequate risk management, so the board is able to discharge its duties with regards to risk oversight?
- How often is the risk register tabled to be discussed in board meetings?
- Does a risk-taking culture exist among executives?

Stakeholder engagement

- Does the organisation have a stakeholder engagement and management plan in place?
- Are stakeholder communications appropriate and relevant?
- How engaged is the board in stakeholder management?

Public statements/Press

- What historical press has been published about the organisation?
- How is the organisation regarded by the press?
- How is the organisation spoken about on social media/online?

Questions to ask about the board and board members

- How were the current directors identified?
- What is the board composition in terms of experience, skills, gender, age, ethnicity, background, tenure?
- What are the areas of expertise and professional qualifications of existing board members?
- Do any of the directors serve on several boards together?
- Do any of the directors have any other business connections between them?
- Are the board members unified and aligned generally?
- Are there any current or historical relationships among board members?
- What is the board's relationship with stakeholders?
- Is there any historical press about individual board members?
- Are the director fees paid (if any) appropriate for the risk profile, liability and time commitment required of the role?
- Are the fees in line with fees of similar organisations?

Questions to ask yourself

- Do I have the necessary capacity to take on the appointment?
- Do I fully understand the time commitment involved with the engagement?

- Do I understand the vision, mission, strategy and purpose of the organisation?
- Am I aligned with the purpose, values and culture of the organisation?
- Do I believe in the capabilities of the executives to execute the strategy?
- Do my specific skills and experience add value to the organisation and its board?
- Is the appointment letter clear about time commitment, D&O insurance, termination and so on?
- Do I have any conflict of interests?

New director

Any board taking on a new director should conduct due diligence on the candidate to ensure they are fit and proper for the position. Individuals appointed as board members are often chosen for their breadth of experience in certain areas. They are expected to play a key role in providing an objective, independent and constructive view of how the executive team is performing. They also perform a valuable role in determining appropriate levels of executive remuneration and advice on succession planning. For these reasons, they need to be able to act independently and have an independent state of mind. They should be able to challenge and support executives freely and have an objective view on matters.

Questions to ask of a prospective new director

- Are they regulated as directors? If yes, under which regulations?
- What other commitments do they have?
- What other board appointments do they have?
- Are they financially dependent on the income from the appointment(s)?
- Do any of the appointments or commitments represent a conflict of interest with the organisation?
- Do they have any business, interests or personal connections material to the position?
- Do they have any conflict of interest with the business of the organisation?
- Do they have any interest in, or connections with, stakeholders of the organisation?

- Can they give enough time to this appointment?
- What particular contribution do they bring to the board?
- Are they politically engaged? If so, how?
- Do they hold membership of any relevant professional body?
- Have they been convicted of any offence involving fraud or other dishonesty?
- Have they been convicted of any offence under any enactment relating to banking or other financial services, building societies, collective investment funds, companies (including insider dealing), consumer credit, consumer protection, credit unions, friendly societies, industrial and provident societies, insurance, insolvency or money laundering?
- Have they been convicted of an offence of perjury or conspiracy to pervert the course of justice?
- Have they been convicted of an offence in connection with, or in relation to taxation, for which a person aged 21 or over may have been sentenced to a term of two years or more?
- Have they been censured, disciplined, or criticised by any professional body to which they belong or have belonged?
- Are they the holder of a practicing certificate and have they surrendered it, had it revoked, withdrawn, or had conditions attached to it?
- Have they been censured, disciplined, or publicly criticised by, or made the subject of, a court order at the instigation of any regulatory authority?
- Have they been dismissed from any office, employment, fiduciary office, or position of trust, or barred from entry to any profession or occupation, whether or not remunerated, at any time in the last ten years?
- Have they ever been the subject of internal enquiry or suspended from office or asked to resign?
- Are they currently, or have they ever been, involved in any litigation or are they aware of any pending involvement in litigation?

6

SUCCESSION PLANNING FOR THE BOARD

Ray Crofts

For many boards, succession planning is a reactive activity, triggered by the imminent departure of an existing member, usually through retirement or exhaustion of tenure. For developed organisations it is the role of the nominations committee to forecast upcoming departures, anticipate what may be required in a replacement – and source the individual who would be that replacement.

However, as many businesses seek to become more agile and find that the pace of change is accelerating, waiting for a board member to retire or exhaust their tenure can result in stale boards which lack diversity of thought. The most efficient boards engage in a continual process of assessment and review to ensure their make-up is best suited to meet the upcoming strategic challenges of the business. There are a number of questions a board should be asking itself regularly:

- What is our purpose as a board? What do we need to fulfil that purpose?
- What are the reasons behind our current size and formulation?
- When was the last time we brought a new member to the board?

DOI: 10.4324/9781003201182-7

- How do we classify the skills and attributes we need, and how often do we assess how well we fulfil those categories?

Diversity of thought

The most effective boards embrace diversity of thought by ensuring they contain a blend of skills, experience, and attributes. It is vital to ensure industry expertise, but also boards can benefit from external perspectives. Boards should continually challenge their assumptions, and a board which has been static for some time will often fall prey to groupthink. External assessment can play a crucial role in ensuring the board has the right blend of personalities and culture, as well as the requisite experience and knowledge to lead a business forward.

- Do we regularly challenge our decisions and assumptions?
- How do we demonstrate diversity of thought?
- What are our backgrounds? How are they similar/different?
- What unique skill/attribute do we each bring to the table?
- Do we actively seek opinions/advice from outside of our industry?
- What are the skills and knowledge that the organisation will need in the future that are currently under-represented on the board?
- Are we over-represented in certain areas/too dependent on certain skill sets?
- How well do we fulfil our obligations regarding length of tenure on boards? Why is this?

For board succession planning to be effective, it must be acknowledged as a priority by the whole board, which should be able to have regular, if difficult, conversations about how the board make-up aligns with the business strategy. However, it is also vital that overall ownership remain with the majority independent nominations committee, as it is their role to remain objective. Although stakeholders like the CEO are included in the process, no one individual is given the power of veto, as this can result in boards of like-minded individuals rather than a more diverse board. Well-managed succession planning should include as wide a range of stakeholders as possible. For example, offering shareholders visibility of a structured and planned process has been known to diffuse tensions between board and shareholders, heading off the threat of activism on the part of frustrated shareholders, who often cite "ineffective boards" or "poor board composition" when raising challenges or seeking better representation.

- How do we demonstrate transparency in our process of recruitment to the board?
- Who has ownership of the succession planning process? How does this manifest?
- How do we communicate our plans for future recruitment on the board to other stakeholders?

Effectiveness reviews

Board effectiveness reviews can be carried out internally or via an external consultant. These regular assessments give a board a framework to think about its own make-up and consider making changes. If changes are required, they also offer a basis to consider where the gaps in knowledge and skills lie, enabling the board to construct a candidate profile which covers not just experience and skills but also style and the all-important cultural fit.

- How frequently do we review our effectiveness as a team?
- What improvements have we made as a result of an effectiveness review?
- How do we collectively demonstrate our commitment to the review process?
- What key elements define our culture? How are these demonstrated?

Role specifications

When building a specification, it is important to be pragmatic, and understand which elements are essential and which are not. It is also an opportunity to take a fresh look at previous restrictions on specifications and challenge these. Some boards for example prefer not to take on first-time non-executive directors, but these individuals are often younger, with a valuable, forward-looking skill set. Or you may consider looking outside of your own industry. Increasingly, boards are looking to "future proof" with a broader range of skills and experiences, and seeking directors with experience in sectors like tech, marketing, human resources, and even sustainability. Some businesses even seek to have a representative of employees on the board, to offer a different perspective. Diversity amongst the board – be it in skill set, experience, gender, age or race – should be actively encouraged.

- In what way will the business develop over the next five years, and what skills and attributes will the board need to support that development?
- What assumptions are we making about suitable/unsuitable candidates? Where do these come from?
- Have we considered a workers' representative on the board?
- What associated industries could provide alternative candidates with a fresh perspective?

Recruitment process

An objective and transparent recruitment process serves to reassure stakeholders and governing bodies. Many boards choose to use an external supplier when recruiting new directors for this reason. It is vital that any internal candidates proposed for a role be included in the same process, to be benchmarked against the same criteria to ensure transparency and objectivity.

- How can we demonstrate that our process is objective?
- Whom do we allow visibility of the recruitment process? Why?
- When we recruit, what kind of restrictions do we place on the recruitment process? Are these necessary?
- Do we ensure that our criteria are balanced and accurately reflect our needs? How do we benchmark against these?

To close the circle, the process must be subject to constant review and evaluation. Only by considering the success of the appointment, the current strength of the board, and its fitness to lead the future strategy of the business will you ensure the board remains ready to tackle the challenges of tomorrow.

- Looking back, how well do we anticipate individual departures from the board?
- How successful is our appointment process?
- Why have previous appointments been successful/unsuccessful?

7

BOARD EVALUATION

Dr Tracy Long CBE

A board effectiveness review, or evaluation, should provide an important catalyst for discussion and change, encouraging directors to step back from the day-to-day business in order to question the board's contribution to the long-term health and success of the company, and its preparation for future challenges.

Clearly this is not a compliance function. Conducting or commissioning a review is a critical decision; the process demands a combination of skills, maturity, and courage from the board; wisdom and perspective from the reviewer; and integrity and legitimacy from the process.

Should the review be tailored or generic?

The effectiveness of the board is influenced by a combination of interactions and processes that are dynamic by nature, and which can be difficult to assess. There is no meaningful generic template; strengths and weaknesses are multifaceted and interwoven, and there are a number of dominating factors which impact all reviews, including, inter alia:

DOI: 10.4324/9781003201182-8

Life cycle

- age, stage, size, and complexity
- the clarity of purpose and strategy
- changes in the landscape
- corporate history and culture
- ability to balance value creation, risk taking, and control
- division of strategic and operational issues
- quality of executive leadership and succession planning
- access to resources
- stakeholder pressures

Structure

- Board, committees and executive committee size, composition, and tenure
- clarity of roles, responsibilities, and independence
- the use of formal/informal time and the quality of information

The impact of culture and dynamics

- Executive and non-executive director dynamics and relationships
- speed of decision-making, levels of bureaucracy, and management of conflicts
- Board leadership, individual approach, and contribution.

What should the review cover?

An honest examination of the board's ability to achieve its objectives allows directors to question their approach to, inter alia, the development of strategy, the oversight of risk and control, the management of performance, leadership and succession, and the consideration of shareholder and stakeholder views. It provides an opportunity to explore the influences on the board's culture and dynamics; the quality of its debate; the contribution of individuals and the board as a whole; the impact of leadership roles such as the chair, senior independent director (SID), committee chairs, and CEO; and the board's size and composition. It also encourages an assessment of the board's processes, its calendar and agendas throughout the year, the quality of information, and the strength of its secretariat support.

When should the review be commissioned?

An external review will take more time to organise and conduct than an internal review; both need to be planned within the board calendar. Although there is often pressure to conduct a review around the timetable of the company's published annual report and accounts, it is more important to work backwards from a date during the year when the board will have adequate time to discuss and consider its findings and recommendations.

How long should it take?

Given that this is a snapshot in time, it is useful to conduct the review within a limited and defined period. This enables directors to draw on the same experiences, and refer back to the same occasions, for example, the last board or committee meetings, or strategic awayday.

Whose responsibility is it to commission the review?

Although it is usually the chair who commissions the review (the effectiveness of the board is the chair's responsibility), it is important that all directors are supportive of the process. Good communication with the board regarding the approach and purpose, the process and time commitment, the necessary level of candour, and the feedback methodology will enhance the quality of input and level of engagement.

Experience, skill, and chemistry are critical, and, if external, the board has to be comfortable that an individual or firm will be able to maximise the long-term benefits of the review and satisfied that the reviewer can conduct the work with a sufficiently objective and independent view. The chair may decide to ask a potential reviewer to meet additional directors, such as the SID, and/or the board as a whole, before making the final decision.

What approach should be adopted?

There are a number of different approaches, which vary from the sole use of an online questionnaire to an in-depth psychoanalytical assessment. The approach taken will partly depend on why the review is taking place – to be compliant, to respond to external pressure, to benchmark the board's performance, to facilitate change, or to enhance the board's contribution and long-term effectiveness.

It is important that the chair has the right to choose, in consultation with colleagues, the appropriate methodology for the board, and has the opportunity to assess the skill, experience, and chemistry of the reviewer. Reviewers will have different interpretations of their role, the way in which they conduct the review, what topics will be covered, and what questions will be asked. Some will work with a template, which predetermines the role of the board and best practice for directors; others will design a bespoke review for every company. Some will attend to the historic and/or current effectiveness of the board; others will be forward looking, testing the board's preparation for the future.

A number of methodologies will be focused on tangible, visible outcomes such as board papers, processes, and structures; others will explore less tangible influences such as behaviour, relationships, culture, and dynamics. There are no right or wrong methodologies, but there are different and decisive board needs, levels of engagement, required skills and competencies, and board outcomes.

Specific questions to ask the reviewer include:

- How will the internal or external reviewer interact with directors before, during, and after the review?
- Which board papers and related documents should be disclosed?
- Which participants should be included, and how much time will they need to invest in the review?
- What will the review cost?
- How will we measure the longer impact and value?

What advantages do interviews offer?

A well-conducted interview process is an effective and flexible methodology which can produce high-quality evidence. A thoughtful and relevant interview, which is conducted within a confidential forum, encourages directors to talk openly about issues and concerns on an anonymous basis, to consider answers to questions that may not have been posed by the chair, colleagues, or shareholders, and to continue the consideration of issues after the interview, and often after the review itself has finished.

Interviews work well on a semi-structured basis, where the interviewer has a framework of topics to be covered (and therefore a basis for comparison between directors), but enough flexibility to vary the emphasis. The intimacy of such an interview, and the benefits thereof, depend on the confidence and confidentiality of the reviewer, but should provide a unique opportunity to discuss the performance of the board, its culture and dynamics, and the use of its time.

How much should the interviewer know about the company and the board?

A properly contextualised interview requires substantial forethought; the interviewer should know enough about the company, the external environment within which it is operating (for example, the impact of changing regulation, a fast-moving competitive landscape, or a sector in decline), and the director's background, and role of the director within the board, to be able to maximise the relevance of the questions and understand the context of the answers.

Will directors be open and honest?

An experienced interviewer will help directors feel at ease at the start of the interview, usually by explaining the context of the review, the framework for the discussion, and the parameters of confidentiality and anonymity. The skill of the interviewer is key; the ability to listen to what is said and what is not said, distinguish certainty from uncertainty, and understand the range of factors shaping nuance and interpersonal dynamics is vital if sensitive material and candour are to be handled correctly.

Specific questions for the interviewer include:

- Has the reviewer worked or studied in relevant fields which involve information gathering, analysis, and presentation? In a comprehensive review, a huge amount of evidence is gathered, demanding high-quality analysis and skilled written and verbal presentation.

- Can the reviewer communicate difficult messages in a constructive way? Most boards demonstrate areas of both strength and weakness, and the emergent themes need to be presented in a way which encourages the directors to engage with the issues and agree on resolutions.
- Has the reviewer spent a significant amount of time in board and committee meetings, either as a director, attendee, or an adviser? It is helpful to know that the reviewer understands the context within which they are operating, is knowledgeable about the topics, and can empathise with the issues that arise.
- Is the reviewer independent and objective? Ongoing business relationships with the company, or ties with particular board members, most importantly with the chair, may inhibit directors from candid discussion and influence interpretation of the findings.

Should board observation be allowed?

A comprehensive review should include observation of the board and committee meetings, strategy days, and private sessions; this helps the reviewer observe the board dispassionately (rather than relying solely on personal accounts), triangulate the evidence given during the interviews, and prioritise strengths and weaknesses.

It also facilitates important observations concerning, inter alia, the physical characteristics of the boardroom, the interplay between directors, and the relationship between the quality of information provided to directors in advance of the meetings and the related discussion.

Will the observer change the dynamics in the room?

Occasionally directors are concerned that colleagues will behave differently whilst being observed. This is rare; most board meetings include the presence of external advisers and attendees, and directors are not usually self-conscious or shy. More important is the ability to trust the reviewer with private and often highly sensitive information; confidentiality is paramount, and the chair needs assurance that the information will be used only within the context of the review.

Who will participate in the review?

The majority of information usually comes from the board directors (both executive and non-executive) and the company secretary; this ensures that all the participants have a holistic and comprehensive view of the work and dynamics of the board. However, it can be helpful to include executives below the board, particularly if they have good exposure to the directors. Retiring, newly appointed directors, active shareholders, and regulators, can also offer useful perspectives.

How should the findings be communicated to the board?

Depending on the approach taken, the findings and recommendations from a review can relate to a variety of influences on the board's effectiveness and can be communicated in a number of ways. Written documents, board presentations, individual meetings, collective discussions, and workshops present a variety of opportunities for constructive criticism and objective debate.

What should be disclosed in the annual report?

There are a variety of review methodologies available, which increases the need for reporting clarity and transparency. Part of this disclosure is easily communicated in writing, specifically the name of the individual and/or the firm conducting the review, any existing relationships with the company and the board (and potential conflicts of interest), and a description of the process undertaken; this is often disclosed in both the chair's statement and the corporate governance section.

It is more difficult to describe any confidential or sensitive themes which have emerged, particularly if they relate to individual directors, and the culture and dynamics of the board. The chair and the senior independent director may decide to give major shareholders and regulators a verbal update on these issues, and any agreed changes, when appropriate. Occasionally the reviewer may be asked to contribute to these meetings.

Part II

OFFICERS OF THE COMPANY

8

CHIEF EXECUTIVE SUCCESSION PLANNING

Kit Bingham

Choosing the chief executive is arguably the most important task facing any board of directors. It follows that planning for the moment when one chief executive hands over to their successor is equally critical. A smooth and seamless succession process allows an organisation either to continue executing its strategy without unnecessary distraction or to send a decisive signal that change is underway.

Conversely, a muddied or mishandled succession can undermine the organisation's leadership, rupture key relationships, prompt unhelpful politicking and gossip, and deflect management from other core priorities. So how can boards be sure they get it right?

This chapter seeks to provide a short list of questions that any board should ask themselves as they tackle one of their central responsibilities of hiring the right CEO.

DOI: 10.4324/9781003201182-10

Internal or external?

Question one for any board considering chief executive succession is both straightforward and momentous: do we make an internal promotion or look outside?

In a perfect world, a chief executive hands over to a knowledgeable and trusted lieutenant who has been developed for the role over several years. But business life is seldom perfect, and not every board will have a bench of ready-and-waiting chief executive candidates at hand. The decision to look externally should not be determined solely by whether there is a credible internal successor, however. It is more important to ask what the organisation needs from its next chief executive.

Boards should ask themselves:

- What is our vision for the business? What are our strategic goals, and what skills do we need to deliver them?
- What are the principal business challenges we will face over the short and medium term (for example, managing growth and achieving scale, cutting costs, conducting M&A, engaging in internationalisation, commercialising a new technology, dealing with culture change, and so on)?
- Does our leadership team have the experience to enable them to meet and overcome those challenges?
- What values do we wish to represent as a business, and what kind of character and personality is required to take the business forward?

Much will be determined by the state of the business. A well-performing organisation facing relatively "steady state" markets may be better placed to appoint an internal successor. But if "change" is the organisation's priority, then staff, shareholders, and other stakeholders will be reassured by the appointment of a chief executive from outside.

How do we evaluate the pool of external candidates without destabilising the incumbent chief executive?

Before pulling the trigger on a change of chief executive, boards may wish to establish the breadth and depth of the external candidate pool.

This must be done carefully as any leaks will only undermine the incumbent chief executive. Executive search and recruitment firms can be useful in delivering a "mapping project," namely a desk-based research exercise that provides a broad overview of potential candidates, their track record and notable achievements, informal references, and intelligence about a candidate's willingness to move.

Conducting this type of research professionally ensures that no hares are set running inappropriately, and it reduces the risks of leaks or unhelpful chatter. A map of potential external candidates should be an ongoing "living" document, maintained and updated over months or even years as part of a long-term succession plan.

When do we start?

As James Bond says about a game of golf: "It's never too early to start winning." A thought-through succession plan may evolve over several years; indeed, many chairmen say it begins on the first day of a new chief executive's tenure. A chairman should tell an incoming chief executive that one measure of the success of her tenure will be whether, when she leaves, there is at least one (or preferably more) credible internal successor(s). The same discipline should be applied to annual appraisals. Done well, chief executive succession is a "painting the Forth Bridge" exercise that never really stops.

Do we involve the chief executive?

Yes, but this requires a mixture of tact and toughness from the chairman and the board. A confident chief executive will recognise that succession planning is one of their key responsibilities, and a topic that requires their engagement and input.

More insecure types may fear that any talk of chief executive succession undermines their own position and hastens the day of their departure. This is a further reason why succession planning should be a continuous conversation. If succession is a regular topic for review, then the discussion can occur without heat. Conversely, if chief executive succession is seldom or never discussed, and is then suddenly tabled for debate, even the most self-assured business leader may hazard a guess that the countdown clock on their tenure has just been started. Over-communication of the plan to the chief executive and the cadre of potential successors is vital.

Chairmen should engage in a robust and frank discussion with the chief executive about their strengths and weaknesses, and what the company may require in future. The questions outlined above about strategic direction, the pace of expected change, and the skills needed at the head of the company in the future should be central to this discussion. The incumbent chief executive is arguably better placed than anyone to advise on the strengths and weaknesses of her top team and should be a vital source of intelligence on who is best placed to step up to the top job.

Equally, incumbent chief executives will have a desire to shape their own succession. No leader wishes to see their work undone or undermined by their successor, and it is only human to wish to be followed by an individual who commits to the strategy they have inherited. A wise board will have the common sense to distinguish between the unique insights that an incumbent chief executive can provide versus a natural instinct to shape their own legacy.

How do we ensure we have a strong internal contender?

Large organisations may have a greater range of internal candidates. In a multinational group, it can be easier to retain future chief executives by giving them a substantial division or business unit to run. Smaller companies may find that high-calibre individuals are unwilling to wait for the top job and are therefore more easily poached. Boards should ensure that potential internal candidates are allowed the necessary development to prepare them as much as possible for the top job. One concrete step is to invite that individual on to the board as an executive director. The advantages are clear: it gives an individual access to all aspects of the business, not just their own patch, and immerses them in the realities of working with and through a board. The disadvantages are equally obvious: the modern preference is for smaller boards with fewer executive directors. There may be several internal candidates, and a chairman must either have all of them or create division by selecting only one or two.

Finally, it is not a step that is easily reversed; if an internal candidate does not make the grade as a potential chief executive, then perhaps they are not worth their board seat. Potential future chief executives can have their horizons and abilities stretched in other ways. Regular exposure to the board, by making presentations or attending board dinners, is essential. A formalised one-to-one mentoring relationship with an existing non-executive director can also be useful, as can supporting them to take an external non-executive position. Aspiring chief executives can be given a project outside their normal executive responsibilities, such as leading the integration of an acquisition, overseeing an IT overhaul, or leading entry into a new market.

Internal contenders should also be exposed (if they are not already) to external stakeholders, particularly investors and financial analysts. Giving them a prominent role in an annual general meeting or capital markets day is a good option. In conversations with chief executives, many say the aspect of the top job that most surprised them, was the amount of time spent engaging with investor audiences. Familiarisation with this part of the job is one element in maximising the chances of a new chief executive being successful in the role.

To what extent should we rely on psychometric assessment?

A board may feel it has a good grasp of a candidate's past performance, backed up through interviews, reference taking, and so on. But assessing an individual's leadership "agility," their ability to adapt to new challenges and apply past skills to new problems, is less easily discerned through conventional methods.

This is where targeted psychometrics and assessments should be deployed. These evaluate not only a candidate's past performance but can empirically test their potential to adapt to new situations. This is vital where boards are considering candidates who are stepping up to a bigger role with challenges where they have not been previously tried or tested; or transferring sectors or firms where there are different operating models, stakeholders, or cultural expectations.

If we don't appoint our internal candidate, how can we retain them?

It may not be possible (or even desirable) to retain an unsuccessful internal contender for chief executive. And a board should probably work on the assumption that an unsuccessful internal candidate for chief executive will probably leave to fulfil their ambition elsewhere.

However, a well-planned and executed succession can maximise the chances of retaining valued talent, and also provides room for contingency planning, should internal candidates choose to leave.

People are more likely to stay in an organisation that has offered them opportunities for development, given them every chance to succeed, and made their final judgement based on thorough analysis. A rushed or knee-jerk appointment is a sure means of telling an unsuccessful candidate that they are not valued.

What happens when my succession plan falls apart?

A board of directors can put in place the most seamless and well thought-through succession plan. Sadly, real life intervenes. In the words of Mike Tyson: "Everyone's got a plan until they get punched in the face."

In the somewhat more prosaic phrase of one chairman: "Succession planning only works when you know when someone's going to leave. Everything else is contingency planning." Any good succession plan involves the nomination committee (or similar) regularly asking itself this question: if we needed a new chief executive tomorrow, what would we do? In many cases, the chairman will step in as an interim chief executive or executive chairman, and a wise board will ensure that the chairman has the time and capacity to do so.

The likely requirement to respond to the unexpected underscores the need to have a permanently "live" succession plan, involving both internal and external candidates. At any given point, the board should have a clear view of the strength of internal candidates and their stage of development. And a board that has maintained a regularly updated mapping project will have a sense of how internal candidates stack up against those who may be available externally.

9

CHIEF EXECUTIVE REVIEW

Charlotte Valeur

The relationship between the CEO and the board is key to the overall functioning of any organisation. When that relationship works well, and everyone is aligned, an organisation will generally be able to find solutions to the many challenges that invariably occur in any organisation.

The board and the CEO should put in place and commit to a reciprocal agreement based on a set of principles that will be central to their work together. The following are proposed principles that would work for most organisations:

Values: commitment to uphold the agreed values of the organisation
Transparency: commitment to full transparency on all matters
Risk management: commitment to manage the organisation's risks and foster a risk culture
Stakeholder engagement: commitment to employees, clients, shareholders, wider stakeholders
Ethics: commitment to behave at all times according to generally held core ethical principles such as beneficence (do good), nonmaleficence (do not harm), and justice (fairness).

DOI: 10.4324/9781003201182-11

The agreed principles should then flow into a discussion and agreement to have certain feedback mechanisms in place to get two-way input on how the CEO/board relationship is working. I personally believe it is important that the feedback goes two ways. The board gives feedback on the CEO and the CEO gives feedback on the board. The feedback should be given at least twice yearly. In putting together a feedback questionnaire, the CEO and the board should agree which areas are important to focus on. Once the feedback has been collated, they should identify what needs restoring and the tools and timeline for doing so.

The board should have their own clarity of what kind of CEO is needed for the organisation in its current and future evolution. All organisations have different life cycles and each cycle often needs a different CEO to effectively lead it. It is rare to find a CEO agile and experienced enough to function in any cycle. An unexpected major crisis often sees CEOs out of their depth with a board who either won't or can't see that the CEO needs substantial support or sometimes needs changing to a different kind of CEO. Keeping a CEO in place who is struggling with a rapidly changing situation to the one they were hired for, is a real risk to any organisation. The risk is twofold, the CEO can have a breakdown, leaving the organisation with a gap in their executive management, or they can make the wrong, or no decisions, leaving the organisation drifting in the unknown. Either situation is untenable and the responsibility of the board, not the CEO. Timely moves by the board to address the situation is absolutely key. There will always be early warning signs that should be responded to from the inside before outsiders do.

Early warning signs will be:

- Shift in CEO behaviour such as turning away from the board's guidance, not listening to feedback, not being interested in other people's thoughts.
- Becoming defensive and not offering clear explanations. This can also come with limiting the necessary transparency to the board, leading to everything becoming opaque.
- Disengagement is another red flag for the board to keep an eye on. Feedback loops reduce or disappear; clients, employees and other stakeholder engagements reduce; the CEO defers questions to other

staff, and so on. This will lead to the management team losing focus and board meetings becoming difficult to get clarity in for the board.

Other early signs of a troubled CEO include signs of stress and increased external activity that does not form part of their KPIs, such as serving on other boards, attending or speaking at conferences, and so on. If a CEO spends more than 20–25% of their time not serving their organisation, then that organisation will suffer.

There can be a variety of reasons why the behaviour of a CEO shifts from what the board expects. The agenda of the CEO might have changed with business, home, or health pressures. It can also be a shift in mindset from the effect of having power where they might lose what it took to achieve it.

For listed companies, experiencing an interest from activist investors should be a clear warning sign that something is not right one way or the other. As soon as this happens, the board should investigate why activist investors would be interested, and act to rectify any of the specific concerns aired.

Sometimes a CEO can manage to shift their leadership to conform with the success of the business and create great results. This requires a person who is able to change with the business cycle. Business cycles are inherently unpredictable, and it can be very difficult to see clearly what happens next. CEOs and boards will always have to accept a level of unknown unknowns and create a culture and environment that is agile enough to survive when unknown unknowns happen. That culture should fit around the agreed principles to safeguard anything going too wrong.

Questions to ask when reviewing the CEO:

Personal

- Is the CEO a person of integrity?
- Does the CEO have the respect of their peers?
- Does the CEO set and display high standards?
- Does the CEO have a high level of personal drive and energy?
- Does the CEO say and think "we" rather than "I"?
- Does the CEO demonstrate respect for others?

How does the CEO gather knowledge?

- Shows enthusiasm for what we do
- Is curious about what needs to be done
- Considers what is right for the organisation

How does the CEO handle decisions?

- Develops action plans
- Takes responsibility for decisions taken
- Takes responsibility for communicating
- Has a focus on opportunities
- Demonstrates perseverance
- Stands by own words and standards
- Is approachable to talk about concerns

Leadership

- Does the CEO understand the state of the organisation and the business?
- Does the CEO lead the organisation towards the vision using the mission and values to do so?
- Does the CEO understand and communicate the purpose of the organisation?
- Does the CEO have the right agenda for the organisation?
- Does the CEO exhibit the right leadership skills, style, and practices fitting the current and future needs of the organisation?
- Does the CEO clearly define, communicate, and implement the overall strategy of the organisation?
- Is the CEO supervising, directing, controlling, and managing the organisation's affairs and operations in a sound manner?
- Is the CEO clarifying roles and responsibilities, setting priorities and timelines?
- Is the CEO analysing issues and creating new approaches to them?
- Does the CEO actively promote corporate social responsibility and sustainability within the organisation?

Management

- Does the CEO ensure the organisation has succession planning and talent development?
- Is the CEO actively building the culture of the organisation and inspiring and motivating employees?
- Is the CEO able to lead change in a constructive and efficient manner?
- Does the CEO seek different and innovative approaches to resolve issues and meet opportunities?
- Does the CEO show a high level of resilience, remaining calm and stable when facing difficulties and pressure?

Board relations

- Does the CEO work with the board in developing the organisation's vision, mission, and strategy?
- Does the CEO work with the board in developing appropriate policies and procedures?
- Is the information the CEO provides to the board complete, adequate, and timely?
- Does the information provided about the organisation's performance, risks, and opportunities enable the board to make decisions?
- Does the CEO adhere to the agreed principles of working with the board?
- Does the CEO maintain a good working relationship with the chair and members of the board?

Financials

- Does the CEO have a good understanding of the organisation's financial health?
- Is the CEO supported by a qualified chief financial officer?
- Does the CEO ensure that the organisation's financial records are accurate?

The following questions are for the CEO to use for feedback to the board:

- Do the board members understand the state of our organisation and the business?
- Does the board have an appropriate agenda for the success of the organisation?
- Does the board support the workings of the organisation through exhibiting the right practices?
- Does the board operate based on values and agreed principles?

At the end, it is worthwhile leaving a space for indication of areas of weakness or areas needing improvement both for the CEO and for the board.

10

EQUALITY, DIVERSITY, AND INCLUSION

Marianne Egelund Siig

Evidence for the business case for equality, diversity, and inclusion (ED&I) has accumulated in the last 15–20 years, erasing any doubt that having insight into these matters is salient to most aspects of your business. Whether you consider input, for example, attracting capital, talents, or customers; the efficiency in production, processes, and interactions internally; or the output/impact of your organization and its branding, products, customer relations, or effect on society, diversity, and inclusion, ED&I has become an organisational imperative. Consequently, it is something that is now on the radar for many, if not all, stakeholders.

- Investors, suppliers, and partners have a stake in the organisation and cannot ignore the importance of your focus on these matters. Likewise, the organisation is affected by the success of the entities in which you have a stake.
- Effective risk management is also dependent on the awareness and understanding of equality and discrimination dynamics. From disruption to legislation, a diversified and inclusive organisation is essential

DOI: 10.4324/9781003201182-12

- for ensuring the robustness, stability, and collective intelligence to withstand and prosper.
- As one would expect, ED&I is crucial in working with your people and culture. Being able to recognize, attract, develop, and retain diverse talent requires solid ED&I competencies and efforts.
- ED&I reaches way beyond human resources (HR), however. Establishing significant diversity intelligence all throughout the core business, from research and development (R&D) to communications to product development and customer relations, will help you see more opportunities, reach more customer segments, increase customer satisfaction, and avoid pitfalls.

The importance of equality, diversity, and inclusion goes beyond the mere business case. There is an increasing demand for organisations to operate responsibly and sustainably. The expectations for transparency and engagement that today's organisations are faced with go far beyond traditional corporate social responsibility (CSR) efforts. Mere compliance is far from sufficient; organisations must be ethical in all they do, and their contributions must be meaningful, making a positive difference, but also avoiding the loss of brand value and customer loyalty when intended or unintended discriminatory practices become public.

There are increased demands for diversity-intelligent marketing and products, and the backlash companies encounter when failing stakeholders in this respect has become more far-reaching.

Heightening the diversity intelligence in a company will serve as a lever for your business, unfolding the full potential and operating in the world as a good role model showing the way for others. ED&I strategies are not only the right thing to do but also the smart thing to do. The questions in this chapter represent by no means a comprehensive list but are meant to inspire discussions and enrich the ED&I strategies in the company you serve as a board member.

Essential questions

- Am I, together with my governing and managerial colleagues, aware of the business case for ED&I and the overwhelming body of scientific evidence supporting it?

- What kind of role model is the board for equality, diversity/inclusive behaviours? (For example, is there awareness of micro-behaviours and subconscious bias, how they affect decision-making, and what should be done to counteract them?)
- Do we have gender balance (50/50 or 40/60) in our board, C-suite, and on the VP level? If not, why not and what are we doing to get there?
- Do we have diversity on a broad scale (different backgrounds, ages, skin colours, nationalities, cultures, religious beliefs, sexual orientations, genders, values, personalities, physical abilities, and so on) in our board, C-suite, and on the VP level (for example, that no majority should exceed 70%)? If not, why not and what are we doing to get there?
- Do we have an inclusive culture in which all employees can be the whole human beings they are, valued for their uniqueness and included both socially and in decision-making situations? And do our organisational structures and processes support an inclusive culture in which historical discriminatory practices are no longer reproduced?
- What would be the benefits be of seeing gender balances, equality, and D&I as a part of our business imperative? What would it require to get there?
- Who are our "role-model" companies when it comes to ED&I, and what would we like our company to be recognized for when it comes to ED&I?
- How many talented individuals do the board members/the CEO/the executive team each know in the organisation that at least on three characteristics are different from yourselves (gender, ethnical, sexual orientation, religious belief, age, and so on)?
- If you trust in the business case for ED&I, how much does it cost your company not to have the necessary, for example, gender balance, every year?

Investors, suppliers, partners

- How do diversity and equality considerations affect our (policy for) choice of suppliers?
- How do we ensure that our supply chain is discrimination "free"?
- What expectations regarding our diversity management efforts do our stakeholders have?

Legislation, risk, and transparency

- How do we ensure that we are compliant with current national/regional/supranational legislation concerning matters of equality and discrimination and that we stay up to date with new requirements?
- Have we conducted a risk assessment of factors pertaining to diversity and equality-related threats (for example, litigation costs from lawsuits, leaking of talent pipeline/inability to attract the best talent, inability to respond to [changing] customer demographics, the launching of new products that are racially/genderly, or otherwise lopsided)?
- Are we fully utilizing people analytics to create transparency concerning and guiding the ED&I agenda (for example, splitting our people data into genders, age, and so on)? And how can we use new technologies to further advance these insights?
- How do we ensure that we offer equal pay?
- How are equality and discrimination concerns integrated into our organizational policies (for example, code of conduct, HR/people policies on harassment/employee well-being and safety, and so on)? For example, do people feel that they can safely raise their voices/opinions throughout our organisation? And do they have an easy, safe, confidential place to go if they do experience backlash/harassment/bullying/micro-aggressions?
- What measures are we taking to eliminate gender-based (and other) discrimination already existent in our policies (for example, differences in maternity/paternity allowances, incentive- and compensation systems, and so on)?

People, talent, and culture

- When we recruit, do we look for a "good fit," or for someone who will bring something "different" or "complementary," to the table/team?
- What kind of diversity management measures have been implemented in our recruitment and talent management units (for example, analysis of where and how the pipeline is leaking, employer branding efforts to attract a diverse pool of talents, the neutralizing of gender bias in job advertisements and job descriptions, neutral job applications without

name and photo, promotion of our company as an inclusive workplace, affirmative/positive action recruitment policies, the minimizing of bias in screening and interview situations)?
- Are we aware of the current diversity and equality trends in society – locally and abroad? (For example, are our organizational structures, processes, and culture ready to meet the demands of our future workforce, for example millennials?)
- What is our official corporate language? Our unofficial language? Do our corporate languages facilitate or impede inclusion?
- Do we offer any employee benefits supporting a gender equal workplace?
- What constitutes the "norm" in our organization, and do people who diverge from that norm feel included and valued? And do they have equal access to power and decision-making fora?
- How are we incentivizing our leaders to help us further the ED&I agenda (for example, key performance indicators, incentives, bonus schemes, honouring, and so on)?
- How are we as board members/an organisation supporting our leaders/specialists/HR professionals/individual contributors in fostering a gender-balanced, diverse, and inclusive workplace and environment (for example, employee resource groups, unconscious bias training)?

Core business and communication

- How are we working with the ED&I agenda in other areas of our business than HR (for example, marketing/branding, packaging, R&D, design, business and product development, customer service, partnerships, CSR)?
- Do we consider matters of equality, diversity, and difference in our product development and testing processes?
- How are matters of equality, diversity, and inclusion relevant to our core business areas?
- Is there any bias to be found in our branding and communication visuals and/or wordings (commercials, photos, videos, websites, catalogues/folders/flyers)? Are the heads of communications and branding/marketing sufficiently "diversity competent"? Are their staff?

Customers, community, and market growth

- How well do our staff mirror our customer base/the society?
- How are we engaged in advancing equality in our communities (for example, sponsoring science camps for girls, lobbying for equal rights to parental leave, partnering with universities to solve the problem of the skewed pipeline, partnering with NGOs and public institutions to increase employment rates of people from minority and immigrant groups and so on)?
- How are we considering equality, diversity, and difference when we generate and use our customer/client analytics?
- Do we fully appreciate how a diversified company staff can contribute to gaining access to new customer segments (for example, via cultural insights, language competencies, networks, and so on)?

Acknowledgement

I would like to thank Sofie Skovbo Gottlieb for her help in the preparation of this chapter.

11

HEALTH AND WELL-BEING

Alison Charles

You are surrounded by many challenges: digital transformation and the benefits and threats that they bring to your business and to your position in the market. Are your competitors hunting you down? What are your economic challenges? As a director, you are facing all of these things – and these are the easy topics to focus on. However, are you neglecting your most valuable resource, missing the biggest lever for your success as a business – your people? Do you have a strong employer brand, or do you struggle to attract and retain the right people?

When there is no active well-being strategy, the likelihood is you are losing productivity and impacting your bottom line. That is without even considering the moral imperative. A strategic well-being policy enables you (the board) to discharge your responsibilities and comply with regulatory and legal obligations. It also enables you to have healthy, happy, productive staff.

Employees are being squeezed between the need to work smarter and do more with less. The pressure of the "always on" lifestyle of modern technology brings with it the digital integration between workplace and home. There is tremendous uncertainty in the current work climate, and employee health and well-being have never been more important. The way people are managed and engaged are now bottom-line issues, with a need for all organisations to create cultures that enhance well-being and help people thrive.

As well as benefiting individuals, improved employee engagement and well-being build business resilience, performance, and productivity. Strategic health and well-being programmes require a significant degree of planning from the outset. Alignment with the organisation's broader business plan is critical for success. Board involvement/direction/backing/vision is vital for embedding the health and well-being strategy in corporate culture. It needs a long-term, sustained culture-change programme until it becomes the normal way of doing business.

Strategy and return on investment

- What steps does the board take to discover the well-being challenges of the organisation?
- Does the organisation have a well-being strategy?
- What is the reputational impact (risk) of not having a well-being strategy?
- How do you link the health and well-being of the workforce to the success of the business?
- How do you demonstrate ROI and value?
- What is your well-being spend and how is it structured? Is it fragmented?
- How do you shift the company away from reactive spending, on managing problems like absenteeism, to proactive spending on supporting and engaging all employees?
- What do you report to shareholders and investors, and what is important to them?

Measuring return on investment (ROI) should be relatively easy. Employee engagement, employee turnover, absenteeism, exit interviews, new employee training, who is performing well, and the impact on the organisation are all measures you could use. All the data should be readily available if you just join it up.

By developing a health and well-being strategy, rather than just a collection of benefits, you can ensure that what you're offering your employees helps support the company's wider business objectives. For example, if your business is looking to reduce employee absenteeism through sickness by 25%, you could ensure that your benefits focus on helping employees stay healthy, or return to work more quickly if they have been struck down by an illness. Alternatively, if you want to improve staff retention, you should research what benefits would appeal to your staff the most and incorporate those into your strategy.

By linking the well-being strategy to the company's objectives, it also enables you to set key performance indicators, showing how the strategy can improve these areas. This in turn could help achieve senior management buy-in. Publicly reporting people measures, including well-being-related ones like absenteeism, flexible working, parental leave take-up, and staff satisfaction, are important to your shareholders and investors. It also helps your reputation, recruitment, and retention, and in a talent war makes you the employer of choice. The cost of dealing with absenteeism, lost productivity, and staff turnover is disproportionately high and only focuses on a proportion of the workforce. Wouldn't you rather pay less, channelling the funds to engage with every employee more effectively?

Employee engagement

- Do you claim that employee mental health and well-being is a priority in the workplace?
- How do your employees believe/know you care about their well-being?
- How do you keep relevant and sustain engagement?
- How do you know the company is using the most effective means to engage all employees?
- What are you doing to directly remove the stigma of talking about mental health issues?
- Do you understand what is important to your employees?

The most effective strategy is a holistic approach to well-being, in which mental health, physical health, training, and personal development are the essential building blocks to help employees fulfil their potential and be resilient.

There is a whole generation sandwiched between the need to look after their children and their parents at the same time, while holding down a job or making a career. There is a younger generation that will be retiring much later, if at all, who can't afford to get on the property ladder. The modern-day Employee Value Proposition (Benefits) has to provide different people, at different stages in their life, with what they need. It is not just about the amount of remuneration you offer. Truly engaged employees who feel the company really cares about their well-being are productive, healthy, and happy and are the advocates of your business.

Benchmarking

- What are you doing to strengthen and measure employee engagement activity relative to the competition?
- How do you or will you benchmark your well-being policy?
- Will you/what will you publicly report?
- Is benchmarking simply a cosmetic exercise, or does it express genuine willingness to adopt a powerful well-being strategy?

Recent research[1] based on FTSE 100 companies, found a positive/significant link between strong people management and organisational performance. Those that have robust arrangements for reporting on employee engagement and well-being outperform the rest of the FTSE 100 by 10%.

Business structure

A coherent well-being strategy can only be developed by the board linking together HR, health and safety, and occupational health.

- Are the business functions organised in such a way well-being can be managed in a cohesive manner?
- How is the well-being strategy and policy managed?
- How are managers supported and trained? How do you know the support and training is appropriate and effective?
- Do you share your own stories and encourage others to do the same?

---

1 Research by Business in the Community (BITC) Workwell, 2019

The well-being policy is derived from the well-being strategy. Typically, this is managed by an HR professional or a similarly suitable role. Well-being must be linked to business objectives, such as the organisation's creativity and innovation, and be able to report back on these metrics.

In conclusion

For the majority of employees, mental health is still a no-go area, a subject that cannot be discussed with colleagues or managers for fear of discrimination and victimisation. It is time to take break the culture of silence and take action to make your company the employer of choice. Unless the board is actively promoting and seen to be promoting well-being in every level of the business, the strategies and policies that are developed will count for nothing.

- Does the board truly understand the threat of the well-being crisis on the business's objectives or the upside potential when every employee is actively engaged?
- Are you throwing opportunities away?

12

HUMAN RESOURCES

Reena Dayal

Executives will agree that managing the human capital of any company is critical to the delivery of its business vision and strategy. Most executives will also "get it" that human capital has the potential to turn a challenge into an opportunity and resurrect a failing business. Yet, weak human resources (HR) actions and a failing HR strategy are the number one reason which directly or indirectly impacts the downfall of every company that we know of in history. Where are executives going wrong, and what can boards do differently? I suggest we take a slightly different approach in answering this question.

To begin with, I invite you to take a step back with me as I review the evolution of HR over the past 50 years and share emerging trends. By doing so, not only will we offer a context to why questions need to change at board level but also begin to unpack why executive teams and boards belonging to different age generations are in conflict. Armed with this understanding, board members can better guide, challenge, support, and empower this function and strengthen their contributions and the overall HR mandate.

DOI: 10.4324/9781003201182-14

The rise of human resources

The HR function in organisations was born at the time of the Industrial Revolution and in the 1970s and 1980s it was popularly known as personnel management. The personnel management role was to induct new people who joined, manage their work rota, disburse salaries, help employees and engage with worker unions. In fact, the term "personnel management" arose from the military. The personnel management department helped the organisation function more efficiently by managing a resource that needed direction. There was no real need to retain them – most people joined a company and retired from the same one. Promotions were linked with tenure and so was compensation.

Board papers and reports included new union demands, manpower numbers, tenure awards, ISO 9000 and Sigma certifications, statutory reporting, and salary percentage increases versus budgets. Boards rarely asked questions on HR matters unless it was something extraordinary, and when they were asked, these were discussed with the CEO or finance director.

By the end of the 1990s, this function was being renamed HR. With the changing dynamics of a global economy, a mobile talent workforce and the technology sector beginning to raise its head, we recognised that employees had a choice of where they worked and with whom. With choice came the inevitable need for companies to attract the best and then ensure they were being "retained." The HR function responded with creative solutions such as targeted talent acquisition strategies (often called headhunting with sign-up fees), culture-vision-values programmes, leadership development through global secondments, employee trainings beyond processes and functional expertise, ESOP-like[1] compensation schemes with exciting incentives, and career/succession planning programmes. Companies and HR teams were responding to a "resource" which was becoming more demanding and key emerging skills as scarce.

Questions asked by boards were on themes including: How do we attract the best talent from around the world (especially in key positions)? How are we aligning leaders to deliver the organisation's vision and enhance stakeholder value? Which best practices can we implement that encourage

---

1   ESOP, Employee Stock Ownership Plan

employee engagement and retention whilst enhancing the organisation's ranking on "Best Places to Work" surveys? These questions were often answered by the CEO and sometimes the HR director. With the changing times, the stance of the board was also seen to change.

The 2000s radically shifted the role of HR, and by the 2010s it was demanding its place at the decision-making table. Fuelled by the war of talent across geographies, exponential growth of disruptive companies entering the market, global recession and Generation X entering the workspace, the time had come to upskill and empower this function. The mandate was becoming complex, and what was becoming essential basics was best-in-class talent attraction, engagement, and retention solutions. What made companies stand out were their ability to offer global mobility and high-powered roles to emerging talent, radical incentives, intelligent HR analytics, and delivery of a robust employee value proposition (EVP). It was a time to treat employees as an equal. They were in the driver's seat of their personal growth, career journey, and job choices, and the technology era was signalling massive disruptions.

Questions asked by boards pushed HR functions to be more strategic – How can we think globally, act locally through the deployment of HR strategies? Which analytics will help us identify levers that will help us win not just the talent war but also become future proof? what is our unique EVP and what do our people think of it? How do we develop leaders to define/lead an unknown future? What more can HR tell us about workplace and workforce design as we get ready to embrace the future workplace? These questions were often answered by an HR champion on the board or, the HR leader. HR was now occupying a "seat" at the top table.

Looking forward

As we power into what is being acknowledged as the unpredictable 2020s, HR as a concept and function is in a state of flux and is expected to change in more ways than one. It is expected that out of the three quadrants of who is responsible for HR, how are HR strategies deployed, and what are the outcomes, two will change. This will determine the questions board members ask and the answers they receive.

The quadrant that will remain the same is "the what" or outcomes. The HR function and mandate remain to ensure that the talent acquisition, development, engagement, and retention strategy helps deliver short-term goals and long-term growth whilst maximising stakeholder value. The "how we meet these outcomes" changes dramatically because of the other two quadrants that will change, that is, who is responsible for HR and how strategies are being deployed. Traditional responses would point to the HR function being responsible; however, with the evolution that we have seen in the past few decades, and as we look forward into the future, we expect to see radical shifts.

HR outcomes will require the collective ownership and response of HR practitioners, non-HR business executives or department heads, and employees, whether these stakeholders are currently employed by your company or are past alumni or are future potential recruits. This is a triple matrix where not just the stakeholders widen but also the time lapse of when they engage with the organisation expands. Let us take one example of talent acquisition to explain this triple matrix.

How will employees deliver on talent acquisition? Envision a scenario where potential employees will engage with your company at apprenticeship or higher education level, making a choice if you are the company they will choose to work with. Envision newly hired employees who act as magnets, pulling excellent talent from previous companies and networks with them. Envision current employees visible on social media and at public events who directly or indirectly "recruit" and attract potential talent. Envision employees who have exited your organisation and with whom your organisation has created bonds through extended community projects; whose exit terms have been so well managed and forward looking that they act as strong alumni ambassadors and/or "comeback" employees.

Let us stay with talent acquisition and move on to senior leaders: Tesla and Elon Musk. Without wishing to be caught up in the controversy of Musk's leadership brand, the emerging fact is a CEO's personal brand might just have more talent-attraction power than the company brand. Envision external thought leaders partnering with your company leaders in sponsored forums, choosing to join your company based on networks that you help create. Envision ex-leaders engaged as strategic mentors to on-board new talent or who are on your alumni talent recommendation panels. Radical, maybe. Possible, yes.

Staying within the remit of talent acquisition, and as you begin to see where we are going with this triple matrix, I invite you to reflect on how the HR function contributes with these stakeholders. By championing intuitive processes, artificial intelligence-supported data analytics, influencer employee brand stories, talent forum sponsorships, apprenticeship schemes, outreach programmes, alumni schemes, portfolio roles, and other flexible solutions, they begin to create multiple opportunities and infrastructure that empower all stakeholders to be involved in talent acquisition without any compromise on governance. Such an HR function will have the potential to not just maximise human capital but to redefine the business landscape.

With this context in mind, I offer 20 questions boards can ask about human resources. They range from the statutory to open-ended questions. Many of the statutory questions are often asked given the traditional approach of boards – robustness in reviewing these is essential. For the others, the opportunity is to ask questions in a manner and intent which reveal new insights, hidden challenges, and emerging opportunities – which ensures that human capital potential is being maximised with the collective efforts of all stakeholders.

Questions to ask

- Is the board clear on how the HR strategy is supporting the organisation's vision and goals?
- Is the board clear on how the HR strategy is embedding organisational culture, diversity and inclusion initiatives, and transformation programmes?
- Who else is the board listening to on HR matters across the organisation stakeholder map – customers, employees, future talent, competition, broader leadership teams?
- What HR outcomes and metrics are we tracking?
- What talent metrics or HR key performance indicators are included in the goals of business leaders and HR? How are we performing on those and how are they linked to promotion and rewards?
- Is the board sufficiently comfortable with the planning/readiness levels to move to alternative workforce models in response to changing business landscape or disaster scenarios?
- What HR and workplace trends present risks and opportunities to our vision and strategy?

- Can the executive share with the board what is intended for HR analytics and employee feedback?
- What is our employee value proposition (EVP) and how are we delivering on it through policies, processes, practices, and initiatives?
- Does the board know how the EVP drives business strategy?
- How are we measuring and strengthening current leadership capabilities and capacities – C-suite and two or three levels beneath C-suite?
- Can the executives share what strategies we are putting in place now to sustain our leadership talent pipeline?
- What is the retention rate of our high performers based on current and future business needs?
- What is the succession pipeline for hierarchy agnostic key roles within the organisation? What is our stand-by back-up plan for key positions?
- What capabilities must we invest in to drive future growth and how are we investing in these?
- What statutory obligations and legal duties must the board be responsible for, monitor, and review with reference to human resources?
- How is our reward and recognition strategy delivering on our value proposition?
- Does the board have line of sight on executive pay and criteria for disbursement?
- What actions can board members take individually and collectively to deliver the HR mandate?
- How can board capabilities be strengthened? What is the pipeline strategy?

13

REMUNERATION FOR EXECUTIVES AND MANAGEMENT

Brian Kearney

Executive remuneration that is well structured and clearly linked to the strategic objectives of the organisation is important for long-term stability and growth. Executive directors who contribute to the long-term success of that organisation should be rewarded appropriately and on a transparent basis as stakeholders want to see remuneration being used effectively to attract and incentivise executives as well as fostering a culture for sustainable growth.

Not all organisations will have a remuneration committee (RemCom) in place; however, the work of this committee is integral to achieving the board-approved objectives. People play an enormous role in achieving those objectives, and it is vitally necessary that how they are remunerated supports the achievement of those objectives and does not conflict with them. Aside from the performance of executive directors and senior management at board meetings and presentations (non-executive) directors have their most insightful view of their management teams as a result of being on their remuneration committee.

DOI: 10.4324/9781003201182-15

It is important that when the RemCom is part of the organisation's structure, that it has a complete, appropriate, and regularly reviewed terms of reference (ToR). For these cases it has been assumed in the following that the RemCom ToR empowers the RemCom to make any awards under board-approved incentive/bonus plans. For those organisations without a RemCom, this work becomes part of the general board of directors' remit. So given the above, what should directors be asking about executive remuneration?

Early in the strategy cycle

In many ways this is probably the most critical stage as it can set the tone and parameters for all aspects of executive remuneration. Fundamental errors and/or misunderstandings at this stage can have lasting effects on the organisation's performance and stakeholder relations, particularly for shareholders and employees.

- Has the RemCom been asked for its views on the capabilities and appropriateness of the executive team (Execs) to be charged with developing and presenting the new/updated strategy for the organisation?
- How do the execs' remuneration packages and their structure compare with comparable businesses in your sector, and in particular those at a similar stage in the strategy cycle (even if historically)?
- In what respects do the historic incentivisation awards for the execs suggest they are achievers and capable of delivering the strategy, including significant change if required?
- How has the RemCom aligned the execs' incentivisation with the achievement of the strategy objectives?
- How has the RemCom assessed whether the incentivisation elements are sufficient – if awarded – to make a difference to the relevant execs?
- How well distributed are the packages at the various senior levels – CEO, C-suite, and senior management, and reflective of the likely contributors to success in achieving the strategy?
- Do the incentive plans encourage teamwork or individual contribution or initiative, and which or what combination does the RemCom consider most appropriate for the strategy under consideration?

Development and implementation of long-term incentive plans (LTIPs)

There is a wide range of considerations involved in designing and implementing an effective LTIP with implications for all the organisation's stakeholders. Many organisations use external expertise to help them develop their LTIPs, and the RemCom would be well advised to have access to the appropriate expertise on design, market norms, taxation, and employee contracts. The resulting LTIP needs to be appropriate to the specific needs of your particular organisation and not blindly follow your adviser's advice, however expert.

- How does the LTIP support the organisation's strategy?
- Can the LTIP support variation in that strategy?
- How does the LTIP align executives' interests with those of shareholders and the wider environmental, social, and governance (ESG) stakeholders?
- What compromises have been made in having regard to these – sometimes competing – interests, to arrive at a practical and effective LTIP?
- How has the senior management been involved in the design of the LTIP?
- Are the timescales and duration of the LTIP compatible with the successful implementation of the organisation's strategy?
- At the end of the LTIP life, how can the RemCom show that potential awards to management will be fair in the context of shareholder rewards and the organisation's ESG commitments?

Start of budget cycle

While of relatively short duration, the budget period is hopefully a further step forward in the achievement of the organisation's strategy. Inevitably there will be many things to be achieved in the next 12 months, but it is part of the RemCom's role to ensure the remuneration packages of the senior team help keep that team focused on achieving the longer-term goal that this budget is a step towards. Although pay rises or other pay adjustments may be set out in board-approved budgets, there should not be an automatic process to grant such remuneration changes but rather prior proper consideration.

- Relative to success in achieving last year's targets, which members of the management team appear capable of delivering the coming year's targets?
- Relative to the budget targets, how reasonable do the changes in targets look relative to performance targets set for individual team members?
- What apparent contradictions or inconsistencies are there between the execs' targets for the year and those set out in the organisation's strategy?
- Do any of the exec team's personal targets suggest their skill base may need to be enhanced, or even may need to be replaced in the short term?
- Are the proposed packages for execs appropriate, rational, and have they had some degree of market validation?

Annual incentivisation awards

Hopefully, there is sufficient interaction between the chair of the RemCom, the CEO, and the board chair so that the RemCom is not dealing with major surprises. In particular, it is not helpful if the outcome of this RemCom meeting comes as a major surprise to the board or the senior employees. The CEO should be able to support the recommendation for awards for their direct reports, and such other executives as has been agreed. These recommendations should be consistent with the non-executive director's knowledge of the individual's performance during the year. It goes without saying that the CEO, while it is reasonable to put forward their case for their own bonus, should not be present for the discussion around approval or otherwise of their award.

- How have awards been distributed over the various senior levels?
- Why have any particular levels been disproportionately rewarded or penalised?
- Have there been significant amendments made by the RemCom to the CEO's award recommendations in respect of the CEO's direct reports?
- To what extent has the RemCom amended awards which might have been made on the basis of measurable metrics alone?

- What is the proportion of achievable bonuses that have been awarded at the various levels, and how has the RemCom rationalised that in the context of the organisation's performance?
- Has the RemCom had appropriate opportunity to discuss the CEO's proposed award in their absence (and that of an executive chairman) if relevant?

Vesting of long-term incentivisation awards

In theory, having put an effective LTIP in place, it should then be a simple matter for the RemCom to formally approve occurrence of the individual's accrued right to the award. However, virtually all LTIP schemes give the RemCom varying degrees of discretion over the actual awards, both as regards timing and quantum. Equally, during the life of the scheme, the makeup of execs may change and/or beneficiaries may move from one category to another. RemCom decisions are just as relevant now to ensure that strategy and LTIP objectives can continue to be achieved and appropriate individuals make up the executive team. Even if there has been no change in the make-up of the team, the RemCom should ask itself periodically whether that executive team still has the skills and capabilities needed to achieve those objectives. If not, the RemCom should bring it to the attention of the board, if necessary without executives present, with such recommendations as it believes necessary.

- In what respects and to what extent has the RemCom exercised its discretion on vesting of the LTIP?
- How has the RemCom shown that the objectives of the LTIP have been achieved?
- Does the executive team continue to be appropriate?
- How do the organisation's various remuneration schemes ensure that it does not now face a potential critical loss of skills and experience with the finalisation of the LTIP?

14

SUCCESSION PLANNING FOR EXECUTIVES

Tim Drake

Succession planning is a key part of a board's responsibilities. Often perceived as just an human resources "box ticking" process, succession planning is essential to ensure an organisation is able to continue with its purpose in the event of unexpected disruption. It requires the commitment of the full senior leadership team and board to identify business-critical roles, the skills and attributes required to succeed in them, and to develop and nurture talent to ensure they can step into those roles successfully. Done well, good succession planning will ensure the legacy of any board for years to come. Done poorly, or not at all, organisations risk a backward slide at the loss of just one key player.

At its most fundamental, succession planning requires a board to anticipate the needs of the business and identify the roles that are integral to its continued success. Establishing the skills and attributes required to fulfil those roles is then the starting point of a process to build a talent pipeline which extends through the business in order to ensure a steady supply of future leaders. Some key questions for a board, particularly at the start of a succession planning process, include:

- Where are we at risk of business failures in the event of an unexpected disruption?
- Do we have a formal succession plan in place?
- What are the key roles in the business?
- Do we have profiles/outlines for key roles to understand the attributes needed in successors?
- If the entire SLT was replaced, what would our legacy be?

Keeping one eye forward

As well as looking at current incumbents and considering what may be required to fill those roles, the board also needs to keep one eye forward, anticipating how the needs of the business may change. Not only should succession planning identify business-critical roles, and establish those skills and attributes needed for successors, but it is vital the board also looks to the future and considers the likely changes in skills needed – perhaps as a result of changing regulation, consumer habits, or technological advances. These changes will mean that the skills needed to fulfil roles will need to adapt over time, making it vital that succession planning be a continual, ongoing process.

- What changes and trends are we anticipating, and what impact will that have on the skills and attributes the business needs?
- How often are we reviewing our key role profiles to ensure they match the changing long-term needs of the business?
- How will we combat high demand for specific skills and attributes in the future?

Embedding success into your culture

The best succession planning is integral to the culture of a business. It is essential the board leads by example and embraces a mindset that is geared towards talent development and pipelining. Done properly, this will ensure that your carefully nurtured talent will remain in the business despite temptations from elsewhere. The best leaders strive to develop their successors to be better than they are, rather than viewing them as the competition. It is no surprise that businesses where the drive for talent development is authentic have the highest rates of retention. The board must ensure that their commitment to good succession planning is echoed through the senior leadership team and embedded into the culture of the business. This will also ensure that succession planning is embraced as an ongoing process, rather than a simple once-a-year tick box exercise. Some key questions for boards to ask themselves might be:

- Who are the owners of our succession plan? And how are the owners of our succession plan demonstrating their ownership?
- How would I know that we have a formal succession plan in place that lives and breathes our culture?
- What are members of the senior leadership team doing to demonstrate support and involvement in our talent development process?
- How would we describe our "talent development" mindset?
- What are we doing to engage and attract talent down the pipeline to develop the leaders of tomorrow?

Growing the leaders of tomorrow

We have discussed the importance of the involvement of the board and senior leadership team in the successful succession-planning process, but the engagement of employees is also key. The board's role here is to ensure the process is objective to engage the support and trust of those in the talent pipeline. The board should seek to understand how talent is identified, against what criteria they are assessed, and how they are developed. External assessments, such as psychometric testing, can offer a useful, objective perspective for understanding skills, attributes, strengths, and weaknesses, at both an individual and collective level.

Individual development is not a one-size-fits-all process, so it should be understood that techniques which suit one individual (coaching; 1:1 mentoring; assessments; courses and so on) may not suit another. It is essential to get this right, as without the engagement of the employee in their own development, the pipeline will inevitably fail. The board must ensure that the process of assessment and development is objective and measurable, so that the best talent is being attracted and retained, and the process is carried out with the needs of the business foremost, to prevent bias from creeping in. While retaining internal talent has many obvious benefits, there are times when fresh blood would be useful, so the board should also challenge itself and the senior leadership team to consider whether this would be beneficial and complementary to the existing team.

- How confident are we that we have the talent that we will need in our pipeline?
- What measures are in place to ensure we are retaining our talent?
- Would a fresh perspective (from external talent) be useful to the business?
- What are we doing to validate our beliefs and assumptions of our people in order to do the best for them and us?
- How are we developing our people to be better than our current incumbents?
- What skills should we be looking to develop to ensure we are able to fulfil our key roles in the future?
- Are we ensuring our talent is given suitable development opportunities?
- What are the best techniques to nurture talent and ensure we retain our best employees? Are we using them?

Creating a balanced and effective team

While it is of course critical to ensure that individuals in the pipeline have the skills and attributes needed to take on a specific role, it is also important to consider the broader profiles of the team they will work with. Assessment techniques, as mentioned above, can also be used to map out the profiles of a team collectively to identify those attributes which are missing. Teams which have been together for a long time can often develop well-worn thought patterns, become stale, and lack the ability to solve problems creatively – they can become "stuck in a rut." To work effectively, the best teams have an optimum blend of skills and attributes, quite often with diversity of thought and background to challenge and offer a fresh perspective. These attributes can be quite separate to the specific skills required to carry out a role, but can be critical in order to ensure a team functions in an efficient and balanced manner.

- How long has the senior leadership team been working together?

- Are we confident that the senior leadership team members are regularly challenging their assumptions and considering new perspectives?
- How do we know the team is functioning effectively?
- At a collective level, what attributes does the senior leadership team display? Are there attributes they are missing?
- Has the existing team become safe and complacent? How would we know if they have?

Setting up for success

As well as ensuring the continued existence and growth of an organisation, succession planning should also take into account the individuals and roles within that organisation. Boards can take advantage of their position to take a strategic overview of the succession planning, recruitment, and development processes within their business, and consider which elements have worked, and which have not. Setting your people up for success is a continual process which requires regular reviews to ensure that processes are continuing to deliver the leaders your business will need for the future. Objectively reviewing previous appointments to understand where they succeeded – or failed – is one way of understanding what makes an appointment – and a succession plan – successful. There are a few others:

- How confident are we that our planned successors would be successful if they moved into the role tomorrow? If not, why not? What can we do to ensure this?
- How do we set up our people for success in their roles, either pre- or post-appointment?
- What would success look like for each role and each successor?
- How successful have our internal appointments been?
- How successful have our external appointments been?
- Do we have at least two potential candidates for each organisational-critical role? Or are we reliant on a handful of "rising stars" to be slotted in "in case of emergency"?

Part III

LEADERSHIP

15

LEADERSHIP IN THE BOARDROOM

Dr Randall S. Peterson

Leadership matters – it matters whether the leadership in question is of a small team, a large organisation, or a board. Research consistently shows a strong connection between the quality of leadership and better outcomes. But what is effective leadership? How do you know it when you see it? If you ask most managers or investors, they will typically talk about the style of individual leaders and mention ideas such as charisma or authenticity. But what does this mean for boards? Does it mean that we need effective chairs who understand how to lead in the boardroom? The short answer is yes, and much more. Business schools have been studying boards and senior executive team dynamics and what makes for better outcomes for decades. It is not an exact science, but it does give us some clear ideas about what matters, the how and why of leadership success in the boardroom, and things to look for to increase your chances of positive outcomes for your organisation.

Everyone matters

When we focus on successful leadership in the boardroom, most observers overfocus on the chair. Yes, every great board has a great chair who can facilitate effective conversation, who enforces norms of rigour, and who brings out the best in each board member. A bad chair can undo the hard work of many good individual directors. However, especially in the boardroom, each and every director is a leader in their own right. If individual directors refuse to tolerate bad behaviour or ignore bad news in the boardroom, it is extremely difficult for others, including the chair, to continue to ignore these important issues. Each individual director has an obligation to raise concerns and questions when they see ill-advised practice. Indeed, this is the point of a board at the helm of most organisations globally as the collective responsibility of a board should be better at identifying questions, concerns, and risks than any one individual or executive. This is the original reason why boards exist.

Collective responsibility

Building on the point that every individual director matters is the important truth that every individual around the board table is individually and collectively responsible for the decision(s) made as a board. This means that no one director can ever use the excuse that they are not responsible because, for example, they were outvoted. If the decision is fundamentally wrong (i.e. unethical, disastrous and so on), there is an obligation on the part of the individual director to continue to challenge the board. That is not to suggest that every individual will fully agree with every action the board takes, but when the decision crosses over from a judgement of better or worse into just plain wrong, that is an important distinction. It is why most effective boards rarely need to resort to voting, but instead operate on the principle of qualified consensus – where any director can stop any decision, but only if one believes it is fundamentally misplaced.

The coordination challenge

Collective responsibility is an excellent mechanism for identifying and avoiding mistakes, but also makes it highly unlikely that the board will identify or achieve the best possible solution(s). The reason is that boards and all groups are notoriously bad at sharing full information, learning from each other, and coordinating their individual efforts. Rather, in an effort to meet the collective responsibility challenge, boards and other groups often stop once they reach the first acceptable solution where everyone agrees on a resolution or action. Effective leadership and governance deals with this problem by prioritising learning over winning in the boardroom. Boards collectively make their best decisions when the individual directors are open to the possibilities in understanding the business better rather than being concerned about not making a mistake.

What follows are 20 evidence-based questions that will help you assess the leadership culture of your board and ensure you have the best chances for success. Each of these questions is associated with research-backed support[1] for positive answers predicting board success (in no particular order).

- To what extent are directors highly attuned to their environment and major changes occurring around them?
- Does the board adjust failing policies in a timely fashion (i.e. the board recognises shortcomings and attempts to cut its losses by making midcourse changes)?
- Is criticism of ideas and individuals in private meetings not only acceptable but also actively encouraged as a way of improving decision-making?
- Does the board accept that painful and divisive choices cannot be avoided (that is, that it will not be possible to achieve everything on their wish list)?

---

1 S. Boivie, M. K. Bednar, R. V. Aguilera, and J. L. Andrus (2016). "Are boards designed to fail? The implausibility of effective board monitoring" *The Academy of Management Annals*, https://doi.org/10.1080/19416520.2016.1120957;

H. K. Gardner and R. S. Peterson (2019). "Back channels in the boardroom" *Harvard Business Review*, September/October Issue, 104–111;

R. S. Peterson (2018). "It's time to vote majority rule off the company board listen to the specialists on your board and adopt "qualified consensus" for decision making." *Organizations & People*, October 24, 2018. https://www.strategy-business.com/article/Its-Time-to-Vote-Majority-Rule-Off-the-Company-Board

R. S. Peterson (1997). "A directive leadership style in group decision making is both virtue and vice: Evidence from elite and experimental groups" *Journal of Personality and Social Psychology*, 72, 1107–1121. https://doi.org/10.1037/0022-3514.72.5.1107;

R. S. Peterson, P. D. Owens, and P. V. Martorana (1999). "The group dynamics q-sort in organizational research: A new method for studying familiar problems" *Organizational Research Methods*, 2, 107–136.

- Does the board demonstrate a capacity for "double-loop learning" (that is, the capacity not just to monitor performance with respect to established indicators, but also to undertake periodic reassessments of performance indicators to ensure that they are measuring the right things)?
- Does the board accept that most policy and strategy decisions require a fluid process, weighing competing values and making subtle trade-off judgments (that is, decisions are made in many ways depending on the circumstances)?
- Can the board act decisively in emergencies?
- Does the board have formidable problem-solving skills and is it adept at improvising solutions to unexpected events?
- Do directors assume that they share a "common fate" (that is, either they will succeed together or fail together), and not have individual, functional, or divisional agendas?
- Does the board show strong team spirit?
- Are the directors intolerant of gamesmanship, their focus instead being on achieving shared goals rather than political games (for example, claiming expensive perks, redefining criteria for success and so on)?
- Are directors remarkably open and candid in their dealings with one another (that is, no false appearances and deceptive manipulations)?
- Is there a genuine common commitment to solving problems confronting the board (that is, a no-nonsense task-oriented feeling to the group)?
- Does the chair make clear his/her policy preferences (that is, so that directors are not constantly in doubt as to where the chair stands on important issues)?
- Do individual directors believe in self-sacrifice for the greater good, and are they willing to have their ideas "lose" if the rest of the board disagrees with them?
- Are individual directors open, confident people who are willing to consider that they might be wrong?
- Is there an atmosphere of trust and mutual support within the board?
- Are there clear rules of engagement for how members should engage with one another (for example, norms of civility, constructive challenge and so on)?

- Does the board prioritise continuous learning for each and every director?
- Does the board appreciate the value in diverse, even conflicting perspectives on the problems they discuss?

16

TONE FROM THE TOP

Sir John Parker

The organisational "tone from the top" is driven by the integrity, honesty, and professionalism of the leadership team and each board member. The board must set the remit and drumbeat for the behavioural expectations of directors and management, and it is important that every individual consistently lives out the organisation's values in their interface with all stakeholders.

It should not be forgotten that it is a privilege to serve in a boardroom – large or small. It is also a great honour to be chosen to lead; to lead teams, to lead companies, to develop them, and to get the best out of them. It took me some time on my boardroom journey to fully appreciate the extent to which the leader can really influence and shape events and the future. As the leaders of today and of tomorrow, you should never underestimate the power you have to change things for the better.

Leadership in corporate life

From early days in management, I was also taught that in each leadership role performed, one should endeavour to always "leave things better

DOI: 10.4324/9781003201182-19

than you found them." I was also taught to believe in "deeds not words." We who have the privilege of leadership must take ownership – and the responsibility and authority that go with it.

- Do you take ownership for the board's collective and individual actions?
- Do you lead confidently with integrity and honesty, communicating clearly your expectations and the unambiguous goals you want all of your team to aim for whilst avoiding intensity?
- Do you as the leader also have some fun and not neglect the power of good humour?
- Have you learnt the difference between being liked and being respected, and do you worry about the things you can really influence and not about those you can't?
- Do you leave your ego at home?

Whatever leadership role you find yourself in, it will be one of constant discovery about your own capabilities and potential and about the potential of the people you work with. All good leaders are on a journey, inspiring, building, and developing their teams as they go. However, it can also be a lonely place where you can feel isolated and alone.

- Do you demonstrate courage and calmness when faced with a very tough situation, especially one that has arisen without any warning?
- Do you exude a quiet confidence that "you can find the way through crises" – if all the team will rally around and give their support?

I came to the conclusion in my early days as a leader that you must never lie awake – since you can't solve much in the middle of the night and if you don't get your sleep you'll not be fit to handle tomorrow's challenges.

- Have you as leader learned to relax, set work aside, and get time for mental refreshment?
- Have you found your ideal work-life balance?

In the midst of tough challenges, you can be sure you will get a new perspective from resting the mind and giving it something entirely different to think about. All work and no play or no renewal of the soul is not good for us human beings. There are so many lessons to learn about leadership and having a balance in life. There is no point wrestling with a difficult issue for 24 hours in the day – you need to find a work-life balance.

Quality leadership

The word "leader" comes from a root meaning a path, a roadway or the course of a ship at sea, and quality leadership is critical to the success of any organisation. It is critically important in the boardroom, which creates the drumbeat for the executive and sets the tone for all that an organisation stands for as well as all that it aims to do for its shareholders, its employees, and the communities in which it operates.

The greatest bulwark against the destruction of shareholder value is a high-quality board comprising a wide bandwidth of skills and experience. I take considerable care and derive great satisfaction from building quality boards that create a professional openness and culture of transparency and respect to challenge. You can get such wise collective advice and steerage from a highly professional board team. We all need to be reminded that "None of us are as smart as all of us." As chairmen, we must also seek constant improvement in all our board management and administrative processes with the aim of keeping at the forefront of best boardroom practice.

- Does the board take ownership of the strategy, debate, and stress test it?
- Does the board empower the CEO and the executive to execute it and deliver the strategy?
- Does the board hold management accountable for the strategy?

Leadership is vitally important in the CEO and in each executive director. Together they release the day-to-day energy and direction into the business. They see to it that the board decisions, not only on strategy but on major policy, are implemented and together with management, they lead the organisation on the "journey" to be the best and to be at the forefront. As a chairman, your most important task is to ensure the company is led by a quality CEO.

Restless leaders

Some readers will be familiar with the Japanese word "kaizen." It captures the philosophy of constant improvement. Leaders need to be "restless" in seeking out ways to do things "better tomorrow than we did them today." The journey of constant improvement, leaving things better than we found them, to be the best, has to be at the heart of leadership thinking. Great human talent is what makes great companies.

- Do you ensure that you and your key people are developed to the maximum of their potential?

All of you as leaders are unique as individuals. You are, in fact, a special individual with the capacity to achieve great things. And so you need to work to ensure you develop to the maximum of your potential – you, as an individual leader, need to seek to discover your inner strengths and perform at exceptional levels. But many leaders, many managers, like many people, never exploit their unique abilities or discover their true potential as a leader.

Finally, here are some further characteristics that over the years I have come to associate with a good organisational leader:

Do you communicate effectively the board's agreed strategy?

It is critical when the strategy and the overall plan is agreed for the leader to gain the commitment of the management team and employees by layers of continuous communication. You need to set out to grab the attention of the people.

Do you have the ability to inspire and build up the team to believe in the plan and to be confident about its execution?

The leader must be visible, let people make some mistakes, but be there to give support and guidance when required. He or she is there to make people feel warm and confident and part of a great team and company.

Do you empower your people, giving them clear authority with well-defined responsibilities?

The good leader holds people accountable for delivery, rewards, and celebrates success with them. I am sure you will agree that part of the thrill of leadership is to see others, either as individuals or as a team, grow and master something they have not achieved before.

Do you listen and learn?

Listening with great care is a respectful thing to do with colleagues. It is not only valuable, it's vital.

Are you decisive?

"Paralysis through analysis" can be a disastrous trait.

Are you courageous and do you sometimes rely on instinct?

Sometimes as a leader you are confronted with the totally unexpected – there is no time to study options – you are faced with making an instant decision and you will have to rely on innate good judgement and on your instinctive feel for what is right. So there are times when you must act without too much analysis, based on instinct and gut feel. Certain unexpected events call for decisive action within a short window of time.

Finally, are you consistent in your behaviour – do you live out your words? As our American cousins would say, "Do you walk the talk"?

Do not as a leader sign up to behavioural codes or value statements if you are not going to be consistent. I can think of no greater risk to a leader's credibility than not living out these words.

17

CULTURE

Charlotte Valeur

Any experienced executive has an understanding that a good strategy delivered by a poor culture is a failure waiting to happen, just as a good culture with a poor strategy would be. In my view culture and strategy are completely interlinked. Both are key for an organisation to be able to achieve success. Success depends upon not just a vision and strategy but also the people who carry out that vision.

Culture is the product of an organisation's values, which in turn should be the bedrock underneath the surface. An organisation's values should not change easily, but the culture (and strategy) might. Culture is more akin to a shifting landscape that sits on top of the values. Both are important foundational aspects of any organisation. Organisational culture (and behaviours) is a shared experience that is expressed within the organisation and in the wider world. Many people describe it as "The way we do things around here."

Culture will impact on performance both positively and negatively. The relationship between an organisation's culture and performance is easy to see if we understand that outperformance is realised when strategy, structure, and culture are aligned. It is then that employees know where they

DOI: 10.4324/9781003201182-20

are going (strategy), understand their roles and responsibilities (structure), and behave based on the values that give the foundational basis for working together (culture).

Culture also carries substantial risks and opportunities, potentially impacting not just performance but the well-being of employees too and at all levels. Organisations with toxic cultures where there is little respect, honesty, and transparency will have no internal trust. Self-agendas and egos can run amok in such cultures, eventually being detrimental to the organisation as a whole. Organisations with a culture of collaboration, honesty, and transparency however will tend to have high degrees of trust. Culture is visible and a lived experience to all stakeholders, directly impacting how they interact with the organisation, which in turn impacts the bottom line.

In many ways the cultural tone is set from the top as it follows from the defining values of the organisation. If leadership lives by strong values that are fully aligned with the organisational values, then this will flow down through the organisation, encouraging a strong culture throughout the organisation. Culture should not be left to evolve on its own, however. It needs to be consciously worked on from the leadership level down, to ensure the organisation does not experience a culture drift. The culture can easily shift from the starting values and work practices as a result of poor leadership. Any organisation ignoring the changes in client demands and expectations or the changing needs of their workforce will likely experience difficulties, and the culture needs to be able to adapt to meet the different demands whilst retaining the same underlying values. Cultural agility comes to the fore especially when an organisation is looking to digitalise. Digital change needs to be combined with a focus on cultural change in order to be successful.

Many organisations have impressive written value statements, but it is only when the organisation embeds these values into everything that is said and done that culture becomes something employees can see, hear, and feel in their everyday work. This is when it becomes possible to develop a solid positive culture where employees are happy and feel safe. It is this that in turn increases the possibility of organisations being able to deliver superior performance all round.

Culture manifests itself in many different places and in many different ways, and the boardroom is the natural place where these threads come together. The habitual ways an organisation and its employees approach problems and issues are a clear indicator of the culture that exists. For example, if the board is discouraged or even blocked from investigating issues of concern in depth, it is a big red flag that a culture of transparency and openness does not exist. This in turn poses a risk to the organisation as a whole and thus to its shareholders and wider stakeholders.

The culture of the board itself is also worth monitoring. Boards with a healthy culture can more easily set the tone from the top by taking their own culture seriously and ensuring the overall culture of the organisation is also healthy. A healthy board cultural outlook starts by asking the following questions:

- Does the board have the right board composition?
- Do the board members have clarity of what board culture is desired?
- Do the board members consider how they are contributing to the culture?
- Are we structuring the agenda to focus on the right issues?
- Do the board and committee members display the desired board culture?

A healthy board culture can be recognised by board members:

- Acknowledging the importance of culture
- Being role models of values and the culture
- Frequently discussing culture and values at board meetings
- Integrating values and culture in strategic discussions and decisions
- Encouraging management to embed positive behaviours and values
- Ensuring that regular culture surveys are conducted
- Spending time out of the boardroom speaking with and listening to employees and other stakeholders.

Questions to ask

- Has the board established clarity on the values and culture of the organisation?
- Is culture assessed on a regular basis? If yes, how?
- Does the culture serve as a unifying force and reinforce the elements of the strategy and business model in a productive way?

- Is culture part of overall risk oversight?
- How is culture oversight embedded into the ongoing work of the board?
- Does the board review the culture of the board and its key committees on a regular basis?
- Is culture an integrated part of the board's ongoing discussions with management about strategy, risk, and performance?
- Does the regular assessment of culture include both qualitative and quantitative information, and incorporate data from sources outside the organisation?
- Is culture an explicit part of the selection and evaluation of the CEO?
- Do the CEO and senior leadership use culture as part of their own leadership development?
- How do the company's key performance indicators (including compensation, promotion decisions, and other rewards) reinforce the desired culture and avoid unintended outcomes that could undermine culture?
- Do shareholder and stakeholder communications include a description of how the board carries out its responsibility for overseeing the organisation's culture?
- Is culture seen as a corporate asset?
- What are the collective behaviours, norms, and values of the organisation and among the employees?
- Is there alignment between organisational culture, purpose, values, strategy, and the business model?
- How does the design of policies such as the code of conduct and internal controls, directly support the organisation's culture?
- Does the board influence culture?
- Does the board take collective responsibility for actively monitoring culture?

18

ETHICS AND WHY THEY MATTER

Knut N. Kjaer

Board members are responsible for setting the strategic priorities of the organisation and guiding the executives towards those goals. As such, boards are in charge of value creation and of ensuring that the business model is sustainable over time.

This means that managing risk is a key priority for the board. Equity owners (and increasingly wider stakeholders) want to be assured that profit created today is repeatable in the future within a tolerable amount of risk. Capital markets price risk in real time, so even risks years ahead may be reflected in the value of the firm today. The dominant risk when we consider performance and value over time is the lack of integrity in top management and the wider corporate culture.

The tone from the top (and the associated values, ethical behavioural standards, or Codes of Conduct), is set in the boardroom. The board is responsible for having in place a top management that is trustworthy and who act with integrity. It is responsible for the corporate culture being sound and healthy. To be on top of this, the board itself needs to have a clear common understanding on why such values are important for the risk-controlled future performance, what basic values need to be in place, and how the board must work to follow this up.

Are we as the board in control of the main risk factors of the company?

Running a business is mainly about managing risk, and organisations need to have in place an active system for this. The board must have ultimate ownership of this enterprise risk management (ERM) system and not just passively respond to risk management reports. Below are suggested some long-term non-financial risk factors that can be discussed in the boardroom. My reasoning is that it is the sustainability of performance over time that really requires sound ethical principles in an organisation. Over the shorter haul a corrupt management can fool the market and also the board. Good numbers don't necessary say much about the repeatability of the business model. Also, some boards run the risk of being preoccupied with short-term performance, quarterly and annual reporting, and so on. and not serving the role of managing risk and safeguarding longer-term value creation. So, from time to time we need to take a step back and ask:

What risk factors stick out when we apply a medium- to long-term horizon?

One such risk is poor management of the broad group of stakeholders. It is important to remember that value creation does not take place in a vacuum but is 100% dependent on the social and environmental context the organisation operates within.

- What is this context and how does the management of stakeholder relations impose risks (and opportunities) on the organisation?
- Who are our stakeholders in the broadest sense? On my list is customers, own employees, governments and regulators, societies at large, and also the environment.
- How do stakeholder relations affect the risks of our operations?
- What key performance indicators (KPIs) do we use to ensure that we manage relations with our customers well? Net promoter scores (NPS) and so on.

- What KPIs do we apply to monitor the motivation of our employees? NPS, turnover, sick leave, and so on.

All these aspects are important as it is the board's role to monitor the trends and ask the right questions – why is this happening? what can we do? It is also the board's role to monitor the quality of stakeholder management and the risks related to long-term value creation. These key factors are all related to the **governance** of the organisation.

- Do we have the right quality of leadership, do they have the right incentives, do we as a board provide sufficient strategic leadership and inspiration as well as the ongoing checks and balances?
- Do we have sufficient trust in the top management?
- Do they operate in an environment of strong values and sound principles of being open and honest?

As board members, we are extremely dependent on the top management. If we don't have reason to trust the team in place, we have no chance of being on top of the risk management of the company and of taking the responsibility the owners have put on us. Ultimately, the board is in control of hiring and firing the top leaders, and in this context, is often seen as being too slow to react.

How do we control the risk of fraud inside our firm?

Fraud impacts not just the finances of an organisation but also its brand and reputation, and is a growing problem for organisations as the trend for digitalisation continues apace. Most fraud can be caught by internal controls or audit processes; however, people commit fraud for a range of reasons. Senior management teams therefore need to remain alert to changes in behaviour as prevention of fraud should always be the priority. Organisations should follow and report on the success of schemes that enable better understanding of stakeholders, such as: know your employees, know your customers, know your suppliers, and know your assets. Unfortunately, many corporate tragedies are self-inflicted, and had there been a positive "pre-loss" approach in place, the outcome would have potentially been very different.

How do we control the risk of government actions against our firm?

A growing example of government action taken against businesses and industries would be in the realm of climate ethics and justice. There will be times where governments around the world will have to take firm action to make the necessary change in behaviours happen. The best way to control those risks, as a firm and/or an industry, is to embrace and implement the changes needed to reduce climate change. When firms and industries operate ethically, they reduce the risk and impact of actions from government, not just with regard to climate change.

Do we as a board understand the values underpinning long-term stakeholder relations?

I have already mentioned two such values: openness and honesty. Several more can be added: acting with integrity; having a moral compass; acting in the interest of the defined objectives and not self-interest; demonstrating loyalty, fairness, and concern for others; showing respect for others and being law abiding; and so on. All of these can be boiled down to: integrity.

- How does the board work to develop a common understanding of the right values for the business and set the right tone from the top?
- What is our key message on values that will uphold the right organisational behaviours and ethical standards?

Do we understand why this is important?

There is no doubt that enterprise behaviours and ethical standards are important for viability as well as the long-term sustainability of our organisations. Without these being in place, the board cannot act in the interest of long-term risk-controlled value creation, and as previously mentioned, we cannot be in control if the senior management can't be trusted.

- How has the organisation determined its actual ethical risks?
- What information on company ethics should the board receive?
- Is the CEO the ultimate "chief ethics officer"?

- Boards should receive information on management's assessment of the organisation's ethical risk exposure.

Questions to ask

- Does the board have awareness of previous breakdowns in ethical behaviour?
- How do we ensure that our top management and corporate culture are ingrained with integrity?
- Does the organisation have all the legally required ethical guidelines in place? (whistle-blower policy and so on)
- Has the company identified the most relevant ethical topics for its operations, so it knows what to focus resources on? If so, how? (risk mapping, impact/materiality assessment, and so on)
- Does the organisation have an appropriate code of conduct (CoC) in place? How is this distributed and adopted by all managers?
- Does the board do an annual review of the CoC – to capture best practice and learning?
- Are the organisation's ethical guidelines publicly available?
- How do top management and the board act when there are breaches against the CoC?
- Does the company have a plan for continuous improvement in the implementation of the ethical guidelines?
- Have both board members and employees received ethics training? Is this a regular event?
- Is ethics a regular agenda item in board meetings?
- Is someone in both the board (political) and management of the company (operational) appointed as responsible for developing, monitoring and controlling ethics/CoC? If yes, do they have both required competence and impact on decision-making?
- Are incentive schemes linked to ethical behaviours (generally and/or specifically)?
- What system do we have in place for pursuing identity checks?
- How does the board monitor and follow corporate values and culture?
- How is the whistle-blower policy implemented and how does it work? What has been the experience and learning so far?
- Does the organisation discuss ethics within its value chain? Is there a supply chain CoC in place?

Part IV

STRATEGY

19

PURPOSE

R. "Bob" Garratt

What is a company for in the future?

The combined consequences of the long-term disruptions of the Western financial crisis of 2009, and more recently the Covid-19 pandemic, have forced all organisations to consider why they are here, whether they can exist in future, and if so, what their long-term purpose is.

The simplistic idea proposed 50 years ago by Milton Friedman, and widely accepted internationally by businesses, governments, and even many not-for-profits, was that companies were independent entities whose main purpose must be on maximising profits for "the owners," specifically by creating "shareholder value," without regard to their social and environmental contexts and impacts. This was heavily underpinned by the concept that striving for monopoly was always good.

This belief has been eroded greatly by the growing public realisation that all companies exist only with the consent of mutually supporting community ecosystems, for example, customers, suppliers, local communities, funders, and governments at local, national, and international levels. Companies can no longer be seen by their boards as divorced from their social, environmental, economic, and political environments. Their focus is primarily to ensure the long-term survival of their business through their entrepreneurship. But they can no longer prioritise profit maximisation at the expense of other members of their ecosystems. Boards will increasingly need to balance all of these in their decision-taking. The previous notion that businesses must always strive to become a monopoly is dying.

Consequently, new board mindsets are needed to best use this new context of increasingly mutually supportive players, and their consequent and ever more explicit rights and duties as cooperating parties. It is from such board acceptance that their future business purpose needs to be evolved. The practical and intellectual challenge for future directors was summed up neatly by F. Scott Fitzgerald:[1]

> The test of a first-rate intelligence is the ability to hold two opposed ideas in mind at the same time and still retain the ability to function.

This applies to all of our organisations, whether small or large businesses, not-for-profits, mutual or state-owned enterprises. In my work across five continents, I see a growing acceptance of a basic structure for effective corporate governance regardless of the national legal system or political ideology. The legal basis is growing from common law, which, as it is persuasive of the 54 countries of the Commonwealth, the USA, and is seen to be growing in China out of Hong Kong, is becoming the exemplar for the world.

Back to basics

Creating a company is a very human and emotionally powerful activity, not a purely impersonal financial or legal one. The word "company" originally signified the human coming together to break bread and give companionship. Humans realised that cooperation by combining diverse skills, attitudes, and knowledge would allow them to create more goods and services than any individual ever could. The resulting "commonwealth," social, environmental, and financial, flowed to the benefit initially of all members of a small, founding group. However, as these groups became larger and

---

1 F. Scott Fitzgerald "The Crack-Up" 1936, February, *Esquire*.

the surpluses bigger, the distribution of such wealth became distorted. The necessity to balance equality of inputs and outputs "fairly," and so govern the creation and distribution of environmental, social, and financial wealth, was eroded over the centuries and so clarity of purpose was skewed.

This distortion was reinforced by the received wisdom about the creation and "natural" distribution of power in our organisations. Industrialisation reinforced this distortion with its mechanical hierarchies and generated the creation of "them and us" binary thinking and behaviours. This has led to many of the public's criticisms of current businesses and their underlying profit-fixated purpose. Key amongst these criticisms is the public's feeling of deliberate exclusion from the development of the policies and strategies of most businesses, and the consequent lack of concern of the company's impact on local environment and communities. We have lost the common wealth idea; however, one of the few recent positive developments has been to give humanity a golden opportunity and the time to reconsider the future purpose of all of their enterprises, and to debate the willingness for all parties to commit to this. We can begin to see the movement from a divisive "either/or" mindset to a more creative "both/and" – one far beyond the current thinking of many boards and politicians. This book is a major step in this direction.

Future purpose

I am privileged in working on five continents and can observe the evolution of major international trends that are shaping fast future business' purpose regardless of whether they are in the private, public, or not-for-profit sectors. I identify two for particular consideration here. First, the growth of the concept of a business needing a publicly agreed, fixed term "licence to operate" in a specific geographic area. Previously, the willingness of a major international business simply to invest in a factory, mine, or IT processing plant was usually sufficient to allow the investor a form of local droit de seigneur. They could do what they wanted, led by a distant headquarters with often locally unhelpful policies and purpose. They assumed that the local workers, suppliers, and tax officials should just be grateful that the company had graced them with their continuing presence. They rarely were, even though the locals needed the employment.

Indeed, Adam Smith warned us in 1776 that, although the creation of the modern joint stock company was a brilliant intellectual breakthrough that dramatically opened up world commerce, it gave these new joint stock companies four worrying and unregulated strengths – unlimited life, unlimited licence, unlimited size, and so unlimited powers. The growing international public criticism of most companies has been about the increasing need to regulate all four of these unlimited powers.

Some smaller countries have governments that are questioning these unlimited powers and demanding that, if you operate within their domain, you agree a time-limited Licence to Operate. They want specified performance criteria in terms of, for example, physical asset usage, employment creation, development of the local community, sustainability, and local taxation. It is this sort of "both/and" thinking that is now also permeating the West in a bottom-up process driven by a disenchanted public questioning the very purpose of their organisations.

What can a board do?

The initial purpose of an organisation is defined when a group of humans come together to offer others through trade a combination of unique goods, services, and information. They will have an integrating vision of what their offering will be, and have strong emotional ownership, rather than just property ownership, of their new business. They are heavily customer (and profit) focused. What is often not appreciated at this early stage is their need to simultaneously identify and build mutual trust with the other players in their eco-system – suppliers, regulators, public services, and communities. Such trust and consequent loyalty within this ecosystem is built by the consistent delivery of quality product, fair prices, and timely service. This is as true of not-for-profits and state-owned enterprises as any business.

From this founding purpose, the reason that we exist, flows a vision of the company's future role and meaning in the medium and long term; the organisation's strategy as to how most effectively to deploy broadly its scarce resources to achieve its purpose; its operational mission as to how efficiently to use on a daily basis those resources; the development of a set of values that bond and develop and assess performance levels for every individual whether board member or part-time security guard. Over time, this creates a deep culture for an organisation that can range from a positive "pride in everything we do" through to the negativity of "what we do when no one is looking." Without a positive culture, an organisation becomes purpose-less.

For a board to agree merely that it should be seen as "a good corporate citizen" defined by a corporate social responsibility statement, was never a sufficient purpose because the statement was too waffly. The necessary metrics were not developed. However, there is more hope now of achieving a more integrated purpose caused by the convergence of two trends. First, the international move away from equity share-based funding, and its often short-term mindset; and towards more medium- and long-term funding seen recently through the exploration of performance bonds. This process is evolving quickly into the development of performance metrics for environmental and social impact bonds, including financial bonuses for overperformance. Second, such performance bonds are beginning to combine with new board mindsets based around medium- and long-term ESG impacts (environment, social, and governance consequences of board decisions). However, the current rush into ESG funding is dangerous. It tends to avoid the entrepreneurial base of our businesses. So, I suggest that such future funding will not be ESG but "EES+G" – funding based on entrepreneurship, environmental, and social impact overseen by effective corporate governance. This seems to be a very attractive concept for many businesses, especially in the "developing world."

In future, boards will have to rise above merely basic financial performance metrics to embrace the new EES+G community-based demands. To balance these new demands, they will need to invest time for personal director and board development. This means agreeing internationally entry-level minimum knowledge, attitudes, and skills to become a recognised director. This sets them on the track to become a "learning board" where their entrepreneurial decision-making ensures that their rate of learning will be equal to, or more than, this increased rate of environmental change. They will have to develop new rapid feedback systems so that their operational performance balances social and environmental impacts to ensure that it regularly reviews its commitment to its new purpose.

The angry public, the stressed physical environment, local communities, and future generations demand this.

Questions to ask

- Does your board have a rigorous process for determining its purpose?
- If so, does its thinking stretch beyond financial performance and into social and environmental impacts? Is its rate of learning up to the rate of change in its external environment?
- Does it have the governance systems to track and develop the board and executives both leading into an uncertain future, and yet ensuring prudent control of the present?
- Does it budget time and money to develop individual directors and the board as a whole to ensure the continual delivery of its purpose?

20

STRATEGY

Jean Pousson

All too often, strategy is difficult to define. There is plenty of evidence out there to suggest that directors, when asked, are unable to articulate the strategy simply without deferring to wordy mission statements. Similarly, when looking at conducting a comprehensive strategic review, whether conducted due to a change in leadership or financial crisis, very divergent results can arise.

Strategy however is not the same thing as vision or mission. The mission should lead and be intelligently aligned with the vision; however, not everyone understands the differences and nuances between the two. The vision should be a collective view based on solid strategic analysis rather than being decided by the ambition (dare I say ego?) of one or a few. The vision should be sufficiently ambitious, different, well understood, and supported. Values should be sufficiently decomposed to clarify their true meaning and be regularly tested. Variables like honesty, professionalism, and so on are never in dispute. However, does everyone fully understand how these relate to their organisational world? Do the values support the vision and purpose of the organisation?

DOI: 10.4324/9781003201182-24

Strategic decision-making

People: Has the chair got a good strategic antenna? That is, does she or he facilitate the strategic discussions well and not allow drift into operational matters? Is there good contribution from all the directors? Do the non-executive directors have voice? Do they challenge constructively? Do all directors make regular contributions outside their sphere of competence? Do you make hard strategic decisions? Can you recall the last one(s) you made? How often have you deferred to more research or external consultants instead?

Tools: There are many tools out there to assist in strategic conversations, for example, PESTLE, 5 Forces analysis, and so on. Were any used? Were the tools used intelligently with good facilitation? Was the analysis appropriate? That is, did the findings from the tools inform the end decisions? Was the thread established from all of them?

Process: Are you happy with the process that you went through to arrive at your final choice of strategic option(s)? Does the process stand up to scrutiny? How many were involved? Are you comfortable about the authenticity of the data on which your assumptions would have been based? Next time around, would you repeat the same process?

Capabilities: Is everyone on the board sufficiently strategic? A successful functional director may not necessarily have the personal capabilities required to be a good strategist. What developmental activities are the directors (and the board) going through in this area? Experience is great as long as the future resembles the past.

Learnings: How was the learning captured from previous periods? That is, what did you get wrong? A really good question to ask yourself and the board is just that. Looking back over the past 12 months or so, what has surprised you? Should you have been surprised? How did you react to unexpected events? How quickly did you react? If the pace of change on the outside is faster than the pace of change on the inside, you are in big trouble. Is the business model still relevant?

External Environment: Are you comfortable about the quality of that analysis, particularly as it pertains to your organisation? Who was involved in this? Was any external professional advice sought? What are the potential high-impact changes? Has the thinking on that analysis been sufficiently creative, or was it carried out by the same population?

- **Industry specific analysis:** What might this industry look like five years from now? Ten years from now? Will the current major players be the same? Please do bear in mind that in many instances industry boundaries have become very blurred. Is the industry growing, stagnant, or declining? Is the industry profitable? What have been the major drivers of change? How might this be further changed going forward?
- **Stakeholders matter:** Not all stakeholders have the same level of interest, influence, power, or urgency. They are not all equal, so are you happy that the level of engagement with the respective different stakeholders is apt? How has that balance changed over time? Will it remain the same going forward? How will stakeholders' levels of interest and power shift? Might there be new stakeholders on the horizon? Stakeholders can sometimes react very negatively to a change in direction and obstruct what the board thinks is a sensible strategic choice.
- **Competitors:** How solid is the analysis? Can you easily identify your main competitors' source of competitive advantage and intent? Who are the new competitors? Who could be new competitors? How different are you to your competitors or would be competitors?
- **SWOT analysis**: What were this year's findings compared with last year's? Under each topic were the items prioritised? Are the strengths real capabilities that can be leveraged to produce advantage? Have you analysed your capabilities? Could competitors emulate? Have you tracked the opportunities going back a few years? That is, are identified opportunities followed through? If something was identified as an opportunity for the last five years, why is it still in the SWOT analysis? What action has been taken (if any)? Have the strengths been cross-matched with the key success factors? That is, are you good at things that are strategically important?
- **Customers:** You cannot please everybody all of the time – so have you decided where to compete? And by implication where not to compete? Why do customers buy from you? Why do customers stay with you? Frequency of purchase doesn't necessarily imply brand loyalty. Customers can get lazy as well and don't bother looking around. What percentage of your revenues and profits are attributable to new customers? A business that cannot attract new customers worries me, and it should worry you as well.

Generating strategic options: Are you happy with the process of generating options? How many were presented for discussions? What methodology did you apply for the ultimate selection? As this is an important consideration, find below key questions to ask in respect of making that choice:

- In line with the vision? In line with purpose? Do the values complement?
- Is the choice in line with all strategic analysis? That is, PESTLE, SWOT, and so on.
- Will all stakeholders be on board?
- How will the strategy be communicated? Who will communicate to stakeholders and when?
- How might competitors react? Will it differentiate you from your competitors?
- Will it create competitive advantage? Will it create shareholder value?
- Was the choice driven by solid all-round analysis and not merely financial considerations?
- Is it genuinely strategic or merely tactical? For example, cost-cutting in itself is not a strategy, as important as it may be.
- Is there visibility beyond the immediate time frame?
- Are you clear about the market(s) that you will attack?
- Once you decided on a strategic option, were you able to (very quickly) determine the business objectives that would support that choice?
- Do you have the capabilities? If not, how will you acquire them?
- Are there any constraints? Financial or otherwise?
- Are we clear as to how we compete? That is, price, service, and so on.
- Have you had a deep enough discussion about the final choice?
- Can you confidently explain why you have discounted the others?
- Have you considered the "What if we win" situation? That is, what if you exceed your most optimistic forecast? Have you considered that position?
- What needs to change to support that choice? Is there any investment required?

- Will the prevailing culture support? Is the current structure adequate?
- Are implementation procedures well in place?
- How will the review take place? Who will carry out any reviews?
- Have the risks been fully understood?
- Have the STRATEGIC risks been fully understood? For example, what if competitors/suppliers engaged in mergers and acquisitions that could change the landscape? What if some of your competitors had a change of intent and direction?

Status quo: Sometimes this can be the final choice (that is, we stay as we are). Are you sure that all other options have been well discussed? Has the board become lazy as the financial visibility looks good? A well-performing share price is not always vindication of a good strategic choice! Did the strategic analysis drive the financial targets or the other way round?

Diversification: When this is touted as an option, ask yourself this question: "If we are struggling in a market that we know, what hope do we have in a market that we do not know?"

Acquisition seduction: This can be proposed as a sure and quick way to grow in a manner that organic progress would not match. Corporate strategy drives acquisition strategy – not the other way round. Who is driving the acquisitions? Why? Have you done this before? Who is advising you? Please do remember that external professional advisers get paid on completion and not success.

Implementation: Are you comfortable that the strategic intent has been translated into a set of intelligent key performance indicators and objectives? Have the financial forecasting and budgetary activities taken into account the strategic assumptions? Can you recognise the strategy in the forecast numbers? Does the board dashboard have a healthy mix of financial and non-financial data? Is the dashboard sufficient to give you a quick handle on strategic progress?

Ongoing review: Are there plans for regular future discussions? Who will drive these discussions? Will they go beyond financial and other chosen key performance indicators?

21

VALUEISM

Paul Barnett

Where boards fall short

Few people would disagree that the first duty of a company director is to ensure the organisation's long-term success. The law[1] states, a director must act in the way he or she considers, in good faith, would be most likely to promote the success of the company for the benefit of its members as a whole, and in doing so have regard (amongst other matters) to the likely consequences of any decision in the long term.

In this most basic duty directors are often failing. That was the view of Dominic Barton, former global managing director of McKinsey & Company, and Mark Wiseman, president and CEO of the Canada Pension Plan Investment Board. In their article[2] "Where Boards Fall Short," it was stated, "most boards aren't delivering on their core mission: providing strong oversight and strategic support for management's efforts to create long-term value," adding "this isn't just our opinion. Directors also believe boards are

---

1 UK Companies Act 2006 Section 172
2 https://hbr.org/2015/01/where-boards-fall-short

falling short." Based on their survey of 772 directors in 2015, they found only 34% agreed that boards on which they served fully comprehended their companies' strategies. Only 22% said their boards were completely aware of how their firms created value, and just 16% claimed that their boards had a strong understanding of the dynamics of their firms' industries. Has anything much changed since then?

The link with strategy

Over the last few years, I have spoken with senior executives, institutional investors, policymakers, analysts, business journalists, and directors about this, and the consensus view is that nothing has changed. In fact, the real situation is much worse than the McKinsey findings suggest.

When I have presented this research to senior executives, they always confirm they do not believe the board knows how the organisation creates value. In the vast majority of cases they struggle to answer the question themselves.

In my view three fundamental questions that any strategy should be able to answer are: What value are we creating? Who are we creating value for? And how do we create that value?

It is only through the creation of value that the long-term success of the business can be assured. So, the strategy also needs to answer the related future-focused questions: What value will we create in the future? Who will we create it for? And how will we create it? This will drive the change and innovation decisions in a process that needs to be continuous and iterative. But the future-focused question and plans cannot be addressed if there is no understanding of how the status quo is being achieved.

Directors need to be able to monitor performance in relation to the execution of the strategy and hold the executive to account. The board must ensure the firm is accountable to investors and other stakeholders through its reporting. That also requires measuring and reporting based on the factors considered material to the future value-creation potential of the organisation.

In whose interests?

The situation is made more complicated by the debate over whose interests the business needs to focus on. One school of thought, based on the Milton

Friedman logic, is that shareholder value should be the primary focus. It has been a long-held dominant view, until the announcements by the Business Roundtable and the World Economic Forum two years ago, that business must primarily concern itself with the interests of all stakeholders.

In his book,[3] Arie de Geus, a former senior executive at Royal Dutch/Shell for 38 years, notes that if the purpose of business is

> †to survive and thrive in the long run, then the priorities in managing such a company are very different than the values set forth in most of the modern academic business literature. Such a purpose also contradicts the views held by many managers and shareholders.

He makes clear that "It does not exist solely to provide customers with goods, or to return investment to shareholders." Instead, it "exists primarily for its own survival and improvement: to fulfil its potential and to become as great as it can be."

De Geus's thinking stemmed from research on the lifespan of businesses that were at least as old and as successful as Shell. They learned what strategies would assist directors in fulfilling their duty, to act in the ways most likely to promote the success of the organisation for the benefit of its members as a whole, decisions being made with due regard for the likely consequences of any decision in the long term.

Making such decisions in a way that ensures sustainable value creation and the protection of it over the long term, is impossible if directors and executives lack a shared understanding of what value they are trying to create, who they are creating it for, and how they will create it.

On this point De Geus says,

> Financial analysts, shareholders and many executives tell us that corporations exist primarily to provide financial returns. Some economists offer a rather broader sense of purpose. Companies, they say, exist to provide products and services, and therefore to make human life more comfortable and desirable. "Customer orientation" and other management fashions have translated this imperative into the idea that corporations exist to serve customers. Politicians, meanwhile, seem to believe that corporations exist to provide for the public good: to create jobs and to ensure a stable economic platform

---

3 *The Living Company: Growth, Learning and Longevity in Business* (Nicholas Brealey Publishing, 1997).

for all the "stakeholders" of society. But from the point of view of the organisation itself – the point of view which allows organisations to survive and thrive – all these purposes are secondary.

To what ends?

In the last sentence of the passage quoted above, I think he should have said, "all these purposes *should* be secondary." But that does not mean they are unimportant. Creating value for all these groups is the means to the end, which is the long-term success of the organisation. Today we have a situation in which the means are seen as the ends, and maximising shareholder returns became the most important of these. This situation is made even worse in the case of publicly listed companies where share price is used as a proxy for shareholder value and has become the value that firms focus on creating, managing, and manipulating.

It is this focus on market value that makes the conversation about "what value do we create" so important. The right focus is not market value, but value for customers and all the stakeholders upon whom the business depends to achieve long-term success. Those stakeholders will include, but not be limited to, shareholders. They include employees and suppliers. They also include the society that grants the firm a licence to operate and create a profit under the terms of its social contract.

Introducing valueism and the value scheme

The focus on shareholder value maximisation, and market value as a proxy for that, has led to a system geared to value extraction by rent seekers, not value creation. The balance needs to be shifted back to a focus on value creation that will sustain the long-term success of a business. To distinguish this approach from the dominant logic, I call the value creation focused approach valueism.

Valueism includes the concept of the value scheme, a business's unique scheme, or model, for creating value for all stakeholders in a way that is designed to ensure the long-term success of the organisation. Importantly, it is not limited to financial value.

A scheme is "a plan, design, or program of action to be followed; a project." A value scheme is based on a design process that understands what value means from the perspective of each stakeholder group, in both financial and non-financial terms. Once mapped, the aim is to ensure all stakeholders' interests are met in a fairly and balanced way over time. This is in the belief such an approach is the best way to achieve and sustain long-term success. By taking account of more than just financial value, it is possible to avoid the trade-offs that are wrongly assumed to be unavoidable by many.

The risks become clear

By thinking of value in these terms, and by creating a value scheme to deliver sustainable long-term value creation, the strategic risks also become clear. The importance of this should not be underestimated. Today, given that directors and executives have such a poor understanding of what value the firm creates, for whom and by what means, it hardly needs to be stated that their ability to understand and manage risks well must be close to zero. This almost certainly explains why they expect to have to deal with a major crisis every two years on average, or annually in the case of larger businesses. The evidence of this can be found in the PwC Global Crisis Survey 2019[4].

Questions to ask

On the topic of value creation and preservation, the questions that should be being asked in the boardroom can be structured in the way they might be asked in the process of starting to map the firm's existing value scheme:

- Who are our customers (by segment)?
- Do we know what value we create for them, as seen from their perspective?
- Who do we depend on to create that value?
- What value do those we depend on expect in return, as seen from their perspective?
- Do we know what the appropriate key performance indicators (KPIs) are for all of the above?

---

4 hwww.pwc.com/gx/en/forensics/global-crisis-survey/pdf/pwc-global-crisis-survey-2019.pdf.

- How do they compare to the KPIs we use today?
- Do we have the ability to ensure we understand how we perform in relation to the above?
- Can we be more transparent about our performance?
- Do we need to rethink our reporting approach in relation to the above?
- Can we map our value creation scheme to see how it operates as a system?
- Are there ways to improve this existing system?
- How long do we expect our current value scheme to remain relevant?
- Do we know what risks we are exposed to?

The board and executive might then collaborate to develop designs for a future value creation scheme, to ensure it drives strategic thinking, innovation, and any change/transformation plans, resource allocation decisions, and the development of new competencies and capabilities. Related questions might include:

- How long can we expect our current value scheme to achieve our goals?
- What might our performance look like in the short, medium, and long term without changes?
- What needs to change and when?
- Should we be making strategic choices now?
- Are incremental improvements going to sustain us, or is transformational change needed?
- Can we create a permanent value creation-focused innovation system?
- Does the firm have the capabilities and capacities it needs now, and will need, to execute future plans?
- How well are we communicating our future value-creation potential and plans internally and externally?

All the questions should consider financial and non-financial value. At regular intervals it makes sense to ask the "what if?" and "what needs to be true?" questions that expose related risks, and to design risk mitigation approaches.

22

INTELLECTUAL PROPERTY

Dr Janice Denoncourt

An enterprise's assets may broadly be divided into two categories: physical assets and intangible assets.[1] Certain corporate intangibles may be protected as forms of intellectual property rights (IPRs), giving rise to potentially valuable and powerful legally constructed monopolies over technology. Intangible IPRs exist even in simple machines, relying on a range of corporate-controlled and owned IPRs – from patents to designs and trademarks – in order to compete in the marketplace. Corporate IPRs ownership has become a central feature of modern economies because they assist companies in overcoming the problem of copycats, reduce the risk of competition, and stimulate investors to purchase company shares, raising capital for the firm. Further, IPRs enable numerous possibilities for creating new products and services that may give rise to modern business models to deliver future organisational value (both financial and reputational).

Directors are collectively responsible for optimising the firm's investment in its portfolio of IPRs to promote the success of the company. As

---

1 J. Denoncourt, *Intellectual Property, Finance and Corporate Governance* (2018) Routledge-Taylor Francis, p. 3.

the corporate law domain is increasingly crossing over to deal with IP law domain, directors have to manage the accountability aspect of their role in shaping an organisation's IPR portfolio, activities, technology, strategy, actions, values, and ethics. Directors need to consider the role and impact of entity-owned IPRs on their stake.

Composition of the board and oversight of technology and IP rights

As a matter of best practice, the composition of the board of an IP-centric entity should reflect its R&D, innovation, technology, IPRs, and business model. In line with their legal obligations, both executive and non-executive directors, as individuals and collectively, should possess a reasonable ability to engage with and be prepared to make decisions regarding corporate technology and IPR assets, seeking expert advice as necessary.

Corporate law has now expressly addressed "technology" and "IP" in its "soft law" 2018 Corporate Governance Code[2] and Guidance on Board Effectiveness for large and listed companies.[3] For large and listed corporate boards to be effectual, they will be able to:

(1) explain the main trends and factors affecting the long-term success and future viability of their company – for example, technological change or environmental impacts, and how these and the company's principal risks and uncertainties have been addressed; and
(2) understand how *intangible* sources of value are developed, managed, and sustained – for example, a highly trained workforce, IP, or brand recognition.

Questions for directors

The best way for directors to manage complex technology and IPR issues is to ask questions. The IP landscape is sophisticated and complex, giving rise

---

2 Revised Corporate Governance Code (18 July 2018) UK Financial Reporting Council.
3 See FRC at www.frc.org.uk/getattachment/61232f60-a338-471b-ba5a-bfed25219147/2018-Guidance-on-Board-Effectiveness-FINAL.PDF, accessed on 2 February 2019.

to significant opportunities and risks, particularly if businesses fail to implement an IP strategy appropriate for the company's business model. Creating and following an IP strategy will help de-risk the company's business activities. It can also support revenue generation through a licensing or royalty programme with third parties or partner organisations.

What do we invent and how do we create?

- What registered (patent, trademarks, designs) and unregistered (copyright, trade secrets) IPRs does the company own and control?
- What technology does the company own and control?
- Does the company employ researchers, inventors, and creators? If so, is there a company IP policy?
- Who are the company's KEY personnel responsible for innovation and creation?
- Is their contribution to the success of the company acknowledged and appropriately rewarded in accordance with the law?[4]
- Who is responsible for managing and coordinating corporate technology and IPRs internally?
- Who are the appointed IPR external advisers and are they appropriately qualified?
- When was the last corporate IP audit undertaken to locate and understand the company's existing portfolio of IPRs?
- How and where are key IP records and documents stored and shared?
- Do company employees have the necessary level of IP awareness to protect corporate IP?
- When employees leave the company, is their exit managed in an "IP aware" manner?

---

4 Since the introduction of the UK Patent Act 1977, employee inventors are entitled under s 40 to statutory compensation for certain inventions owned by the owner-company. For example, according to CMS Employee Inventor Reward Survey (2014), 82% of respondents indicated that they offer rewards to employee inventors in Europe, see https://cms.law/en/Media/Local/CMS-CMNO/../Employee-Inventor-Rewards-Survey, accessed on 30 May 2019.

Corporate technology and IP strategy

- Is the company's business model dependent on technology and monopoly IPR protection?
- To what extent does the company's portfolio of IPRs protect the technology? In other words, does the company have "freedom to operate," or does it need to obtain permission from another IP owner?
- What is the technology readiness level[5] (TRL) of the new or core technologies?
- who are the company's competitors, and do we have intelligence on their activities?
- How does the company's IP position complete with its peers?
- Who are collaborators or potential collaborators?
- What new innovations and creations merit investment and human resources to develop?

IP value

- How and how much does the company's technology and IP contribute in terms of value?
- What is the current financial status of the technology and portfolio of IPRs?
- How should the company track the investment in and performance of its technology and IPRs over time (metrics and performance indicators)?

De-risking corporate IP rights management

- What risks does our IP, or lack of IP, rights expose the company to?
- Is the company's technology at risk of obsolescence?
- What principle risks and uncertainties are associated with the technology and key IPRs (for example, expiration, infringement, or enforcement litigation, licensing and so on)?

---

5 The TRL system is a well-established method of estimating the maturity of critical technology developments on a scale of one to nine, with nine being the most mature technology. It was originally developed by the US National Aeronautics and Space Agency (NASA) in the 1980s.

- Are existing IP management plans being followed? Does the company need to probe further to uncover issues and/or to address red flags? Loss of key inventors and creators?

Values and IP ethics

- Is continued investment in technology and IPRs sustainable and socially responsible?
- Are the company's technology and IP-related activities, actions, and ethics in line with company culture and able to withstand regulatory and public scrutiny?

Accountability, transparency, and mandated corporate reporting

- Does the company need to specifically report the value of our corporate intangible IPRs in line with International Accounting Standard 38 Intangibles, include additional notes to the financial accounts, and deal with technology and IP rights in our narrative reporting?

In conclusion, this series of questions provides a good starting point to support directors to identify corporate IP and relevant human capital, and then begin to analyse more complex technology and IPR strategy and risk issues. Ultimately, the goal is to deploy corporate IPRs, create value for the company, and improve corporate performance, management oversight, and behaviours in line with their duty as fiduciaries.

23

DATA ETHICS

Tony Fish

Data ethics centres on how to make better decisions and ensure ethical outcomes. Data ethics is a broad topic encapsulating data and ethical decisions, data-based judgement, bias, the ethics of collecting and analysing data, and the ethics of automation created by data. The data we collected in 2010 could paint a low-quality, black and white, abstract picture of our world, and the data could be used to inform, frame, or guide. In 2020, the data collected can describe our world in high-definition colour, and is being used to mould, form, and shape actions in complicated environments. We are accelerating our collection and use of data. Boards need to get deep and dirty with data and the ethics of judgement based on data. It is complex and often requires new skills.

Professional bias

Boards are biased towards professionals who represent experience in finance, legal, operations, marketing, and sales. These "core functions" are supported by professionals with information, innovation, technology, and human resources expertise. Boards will typically have a deep appreciation

DOI: 10.4324/9781003201182-27

of the expertise in each of the core functions and will have their own experience in each core area to draw on as a reference point. Members feel comfortable understanding and questioning strategy, ratios, metrics, margins, and returns. Often the supporting functions are represented by a single professional and there is little broader expertise amongst the other board members. When data and ethics enter the room, most members feel uncomfortable. Still, there is a chorus of opinions backed from well-known academic institutes, leading consultancies, articles, and journals, but little practical grounding. This paragraph is an observation on the current status and not a criticism. Data, ethics, and data ethics are new, and this chapter details questions we should be reflecting on and asking, as data is now fundamentally a core function.

Data and statistics

"Lies, damned lies and statistics"[1] is an unattributed quote but helpful in the context of discussing data and ethics. The use of statistics to bolster weak arguments is now followed by the use of data to create the outcome you want. Like statistics, which can back any opinion, data can be found to support any recommendation. The most fundamental question a board needs to wrestle with: "How do we know if the decision we are being asked to approve is only based on data that creates that recommendation?" Data is no different to any question a board has been asked to approve previously; however, according to McKinsey, 95% of decisions made in business are based on financial data, which represents, according to Google, 3% of the data available. We accept that there is bias in the data that gets presented in such a board paper derived from this 3% of data, but as the remaining 97% of data becomes available to the board for decision-making, it is not going to get any easier to unpick (to carefully analyse the different elements) if we are being asked to make the right "ethical" decision. It is worth noting that data is not easy to understand, and in many situations, is not understood even by experts and professionals. Data is not oil, sunshine, time, labour, or any other of the analogies, which all fail. Data is data.[2] Data is closer to the discovery of a new element or quantum particle,

---

1 "Lies, damned lies and statistics" https://en.wikipedia.org/wiki/Lies,_damned_lies,_and_statistics.
2 "Data is Data" https://medium.com/@tonyfish/data-is-data-90ba0b803178.

which has its own unique characteristics. Data itself creates data, and everything is data. Insight, knowledge, and wisdom built on data just create more data. Decisions are just more data. Data means that bias is amplified, which can hide ethical problems. Our systems are built on discrimination.

Ethics

Like data, ethics is equally not easy to understand, and in many situations is not understood. However, as we study and gain a better understanding of human behaviour from more data, it becomes increasingly evident that determining an ethical outcome for two people is complicated, for society it is complex, and for everyone it is impossible. We must be able to explain and justify the rationale for any decisions which affects others. However, linking our judgement and decision-making to a framework that our ethics or culture can be applied to at scale, is a delusional claim. We have to get comfortable that our judgement and decisions, based on any ethical code, hold us to a standard by which we must be prepared to be judged. If we are deemed to be lacking by professional standard, law, or society, directors must be willing to accept the consequences.

Governing data

Data in this context is all data. All data embraces data that comes from the market, customers, partners, supply chain, and internal data from all systems, as shown in the Figure 23.1 below. Data is collected and stored, analysed, and this creates value, insights, and margin, which we observe as an outcome. More data comes from understanding how our actions, which are measured outcomes, impact each of the data collection points. Governance and oversight encompass how we manage the entire system and process from the collection of data to understanding how our decisions impact outcomes. Data enables a leadership team to qualify and quantify new risks beyond the obvious of data security, cyberattacks, and poor processes. Data enables leadership to enquire about any and every aspect of the business that can be measured, which means that whilst once we were unable to determine the impact of a decision, a board can now receive direct feedback from the data that supported a decision, to the outcome, and determine if the delta needs to be addressed.

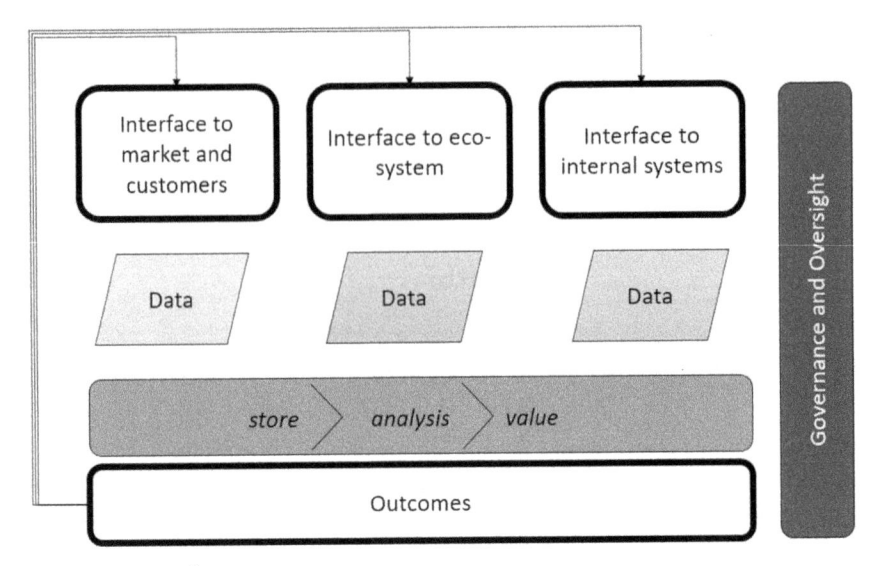

Figure 23.1 Interface to ecosystem

Schools of thought

Essentially all ethical and moral thinking has the same goal, and there are several diverse ways to help reach a positive impact by considering what is best for others and seeking mutual benefit. Selecting a model for a specific context increases the chances of a successful outcome, which is a positive impact. There are numerous books in which moral philosophy and philosophers are categorised; however, there are three core schools: virtue ethics, consequentialist ethics, and deontological or duty-based ethics (Table 23.1). Each approach provides a different way to understand ethics and has implications for the decision-making process. If I asked the question "What is the best way to achieve a healthy life?" you could respond with one of three approaches: good nutrition, through exercise, or through spiritual discipline. Each is vital but inadequate by itself. It is in bringing these and other strategies together that we can create better outcomes from a complex decision. In ethics, no one school answers all the issues, concerns, and problems raised by a diverse society; therefore, many schools need to be considered to reach an ethical decision.

Data ethics

- Do we have a data ontology and/or data dictionary? What standard does it meet?
- What confidence do we have in the lineage and provenance of data?
- What bias could be in the data, what bias is in the data set, what are the implications?
- What data do you get from third parties, what is their model, and have you asked q2 and q3 of the sources of external data?
- Do you need the data you have, is the data valid, how have you determined that the data is useful?
- What data is being used to support human and automated decision-making?

Ethics and data

- Which framework (from the Table 23.1) are individual leaders using, and are we applying all frameworks equally?
- What framework does our company and our values align to and why?
- Whose ethics are we guided by, and how do we know?
- Who is accountable for the outcome of our ethical choice?
- What level of transparency are we using, and is it working for us?

Algorithms and automation based on data ethics

- Do we know the true origin of the algorithms used in our company?
- Do we know what data was used to create/determine the algorithms?
- How are we sure that the data set used would apply today?
- How are we made aware of the unintended/unimagined consequences?
- What process and procedures do we have in place to test and qualify algorithms and automated decision-making, and are these biased towards certain re-enforcing conformational outcomes?

Table 23.1 Ethics and philosophy

	Virtue Ethics	Consequentialist Ethics	Deontological Ethics
Overall-philosophy	How to Live Your Life?	Is It Good?	Is It Right?
Summary	What kind of person/company do I/we want to be in the current situation/context?	What impact is my/our behaviour having on the world?	What are my ethical principles telling me, we should do?
Key Questions Informing Ethical Decisions:	What virtues bring me/us closer to my/our goal; which vices prevent me/us from achieving it?	Am I/we doing more good or harm by my/our behaviour?	What duties do I/we owe and how do I/we decide between conflicting duties?
	Is my/our behaviour consistent with being a moral person?	Is my/our behaviour making the world a better place?	What does reason require of me/us regarding my/our treatment of others? Are my/our reasons consistent and coherent?
Key guiding principles	Aspiring to a set of virtues and avoiding a set of vices.	Actions aim at bringing about the greatest good for the most significant number of people.	Having a duty to others based on ethical principles.
	Integrity is a primary value and finding the right balance within and between values.	Benevolence is a primary value.	Respecting the autonomy of others is a primary value.
Original Philosophers	Aristotle (384–322 BCE) Alasdair MacIntyre (1929)	David Hume (1711–1776) Jeremy Bentham (1748–1832) John Stuart Mill (1806–1873)	John Locke (1632–1704) Immanuel Kant (1724–1804)

Analysis and insights based on data ethics

- What tools are we using to create analysis and insights based on data?
- Are our tools part of the system or independent of the system?
- Who is checking the analysis and insights, and how are they being checked?

- What happens to analysis and insight that does not align to decisions, strategy, outcomes, or rewards?
- Who controls and determines the process by which the analysis and insight is conducted and presented?

Governance and oversight for data ethics

- Do we have diverse data ethics skills and experience on this board?
- Is data ethics working for us?
- Who is "us" in this context?
- Whom are we asking about data ethics, bias, and outcomes?
- How do we know if the decision we are being asked to approve is based on data that could only create that recommendation?
- What checks and balances do we have in place to understand and determine the filters and direction we are being guided towards?
- What delegated authority is there that enables ethical questions to be asked and decided on outside of our visibility, especially regarding marketing, sales, privacy, terms, model, and the use of data?
- How are we sure, and reassured, our decisions based on data have a positive impact on our customers, partners, and society?
- Are we willing to be judged by a professional standard, law, or society, and do we accept the consequences?

It is critical that we can explain and justify the rationale for decisions which affect others made with data. We must be comfortable that our judgement and decisions, based on our chosen ethical code, hold us to a standard by which we must be prepared to be judged. If we are thought to be lacking by professional standard, law, or society, we must be willing to accept the consequences.

Part V

SUSTAINABILITY

24

ENVIRONMENTAL, SOCIAL, AND GOVERNANCE

Sir Mark Moody-Stuart

Environmental, social, and governance (ESG) refers to the three categories that enable businesses to measure the real sustainable and societal impact of their outputs. Any business thrives on making or providing goods or services which society needs or wants. The first step towards a socially responsible business is to make sure that there is clarity on this purpose of the company. It is then possible to develop measurements as to how efficiently this is done, not just in terms of cost and quality, but also in the use of natural resources, and to examine whether in addition to the positive elements of the purpose there are negative side effects for society or the environment which need to be mitigated.

Just as important as the underlying purpose is how this purpose is delivered. It is useful to view this in terms of the major Conventions of the United Nations on human rights, working conditions, the environment, and anti-corruption, such as are reflected in the Ten Principles of the UN Global Compact[1].

---

1 www.unglobalcompact.org/what-is-gc/mission/principles.

In 2015, the General Assembly of the United Nations unanimously approved 17 Sustainable Development Goals (SDGs), each with subsidiary indicators. These SDGs provide an important checklist for identifying where and to what extent the organisation's purpose contributes to these globally agreed goals. This is not corporate philanthropy; it involves a focus on areas where the company has skills related to its core purpose and business which can be channelled for the wider benefit of society.

Priorities vary in relation to different stakeholders, whether workers in the organisation or its supply chain, consumers of its products, its shareholders, or the national priorities of the countries where it operates, and includes global priorities. All are important, but the emphasis will vary depending on the nature and spread of an organisation's business. Making sure that the company is effectively considering, addressing, and reporting on its social and environmental responsibilities and performance is very important to the success of a company and to building the trust with different elements of society on which such success ultimately depends.

Questions to ask

- Has the purpose of the organisation's business and its overall contribution to society been established through discussion widely within the organisation and taking into account the views of external stakeholders?
- Has this purpose been discussed and agreed with the board and is it clear?
- Have all groups touched or impacted by the organisation's activities in delivering its purpose been identified – workers, supply chain, consumers, operational neighbours, shareholders, and governments?
- Have both the positive and negative impacts of the organisation's activities been identified?
- Have the organisation's activities, both its core purpose and activities to deliver this, been mapped against the UN SDGs?
- Has the organisation identified those SDGs to which its core purpose has particular relevance, in addition to those SDGs to which every organisation should be making a contribution?
- Are there modifications which could be made to the organisation's activities, and even its purpose, which could increase alignment with the SDGs without significantly impacting other objectives negatively?

- To what extent has a similar analysis been made for its supply chain?
- Have adequate steps been taken to encourage and ensure that suppliers are living up to their own responsibilities?
- Are all material impacts measured, using for example indicators of the Global Reporting Initiative?[2]
- Are the trends in these indicators positive or negative, and how do they benchmark against others in the industry?
- Have targets been set, with clear time frames for delivery?
- Is attention paid not just to the delivery of targets but to how they are delivered?
- Is the delivery in line with the company's stated values?
- Is the delivery undertaken in line with principles such as those of the UN Global Compact, in line with the major UN Conventions on human rights, the environment, working conditions, and anti-corruption?
- Is the organisation reporting publicly in an integrated and transparent way on its performance, so that stakeholders can see how the corporate purpose is being delivered, positive impacts enhanced, and negative impacts ameliorated?
- Are these public reports transparent on both positive and negative impacts of the organisation's activities?
- Does the organisation undertake special efforts to explain to different stakeholders, including shareholders, how an integrated approach is in the long-term interest of all stakeholders and hence to the health of the company?
- Does the organisation undertake regular surveys of stakeholders, both internal and external, to evaluate the alignment of performance both with the company's stated values and with stakeholder needs and aspirations?
- In such surveys, is there appropriate use of independent third parties, including civil society organisations, to ensure frank responses?
- Is the organisation taking full advantage of the work done by other companies and civil society organisations in developing voluntary standards and practical guidance in many areas and the lessons that can be learned from these (for example, the UN Guiding Principles on Business and Human Rights, the Extractive Industries Transparency

2 www.globalreporting.org/.

Initiative, principles for sustainable trade in various commodities, the Voluntary Principles for Security and Human Rights, and other elements of the World Bank/International Finance Corporation Performance Standards)?
- When dealing with communities neighbouring the organisation's operations, has an independent civil society partner been used to check on their community priorities rather than what might appear to executives to be most needed?
- Has the same civil society partner worked to ensure that the community is aligned in their views and that the governance structures in the community are such that views expressed are not just from one part of the community, for example, an unrepresentative leadership?
- Is the organisation transparent about payment of taxes and whether tax is paid in each country aligns with work actually done?
- Have the financial flows of the organisation in each country of operation been analysed and reported on in terms of revenue generated, investment and dividend flows, taxes paid, employment generated, and so on, and does the distribution of these flows appear to fairly reflect activities and use of resources?
- Does leadership meet and openly engage with critics and try and understand the basis for their criticism, and not just dismiss views as ill-informed?
- Does leadership make efforts to join with others in business and civil society to assist governments to build fiscal and regulatory frameworks which are in the interests of society as a whole and not merely influenced by individual corporate or industry interests?
- While pure philanthropy is not and should not be the driving force for the organisation's approach to social responsibility, does the budget allow for local operations to contribute to local citizenship activities which build local community relationships although they may be unrelated to global programmes?
- Does the organisation support and encourage individual or collective voluntary activities by employees, in particular but not exclusively, using their professional skills and abilities?

25

CLIMATE CHANGE

Dr Geoff Kendall and Martin Rich

Today's economy is not fit for purpose. Two hundred fifty years ago, there were fewer than one billion people on Earth. Back then, Earth's resources – and its resilience in the face of our demand for them – must have seemed limitless. So it should come as no surprise that classical economics – which dates from that period – did not consider the fact that we live in a finite, resource-constrained world. That belief set the tone for the way we have done business for generations: producing, consuming, and disposing of ever more stuff, without weighing up the long-term consequences.

Decades of industrialisation powered by cheap fossil fuels, rapid population growth, and widespread encroachment on the natural world have taken their toll. Ever-more extreme weather events, coupled with a huge drop in soil fertility due to intensive agriculture, are affecting crop yields around the globe. Fresh water is scarce in many areas. Many natural resources that were once plentiful are now harder and costlier to obtain. The long-lasting effects of these climatic changes are often felt first by those who are financially and physically vulnerable. But their shockwaves – in the form of economic migration, supply chain disruptions, and the rise of populism, to name a few – impact us all. There are now around 7.5 billion people on the planet, and two billion more are set to join us by 2050. If everyone is to have the opportunity and capacity to lead a fulfilling life, things need to change fast.

A global response: the SDGs

Recognizing the extent of the challenges facing humanity, world governments came together in 2015 to launch the UN Sustainable Development Goals (SDGs). The SDGs – which were co-created with academic experts, business leaders, and civil society advocates – are a rallying call for everyone, from nation states to corporations. There are 17 SDGs in total, underpinned by 169 targets which all UN member states have committed to reaching by 2030. They offer all economic actors something that has been sorely lacking: a shared vision for the problems we must solve, and a common vocabulary for directing and describing progress. Yet five years on from their launch, bold ambition has translated only into modest action.

Enter the novel coronavirus: an unexpected opportunity

Covid-19 created a rare peacetime opportunity to challenge many of our unquestioned assumptions about the roles of business and government. Our collective response to the crisis, while far from over, shone a spotlight on the limitations inherent in our current socioeconomic system – and there is much we can learn from as we seek to build back better. Clearly, we have not been adequately valuing everything that should be valued. The pandemic surfaced a disconnect between what really matters (essential needs) and what doesn't (non-essential wants), and much of our economic activity suddenly started to appear frivolous.

We aren't well equipped to understand systemic risks

When the pandemic hit, it quickly surfaced that experts had been warning global governments for many years about the inevitability of such an event. Yet those in power did not grasp the systemic nature of the pandemic risk – and therefore the full extent of the disruption it would cause. Even in debates on national responses to the pandemic, people can be heard arguing about whether to pay more attention to the health crisis or the economic crisis, as if they are separable. In an increasingly volatile, uncertain, complex, and ambiguous world, we need to get better at understanding the interdependent systemic contexts we operate within.

There is no going back

To avoid this level of economic disruption again – be it due to another virus, failed harvests, extreme weather, or myriad other events – a new course needs to be charted: one which regenerates Earth's natural systems, rebuilds our social fabric, and in so doing increases our resilience to future shocks. Climate change responses should therefore be enriching our system intelligence, valuing what really matters, and pursuing extra-financial success.

Enriching our systems intelligence

Businesses need better systems intelligence if they are to effectively anticipate, prepare for, and respond to future shocks. The confluence of societal, environmental, and technological macro-level forces, as described below, is already disrupting entire industries.

- Societal pressures: Social norms and people's needs are shifting, in response to factors as diverse as mass economic migration and workforce automation – all exacerbated by a rapidly growing and ageing population.
- Environmental pressures: These range from more intense and frequent droughts and flooding brought on by the climate crisis, to the build-up of pollutants in nature, and increasing competition for natural resources.
- Technological pressures: A number of emerging technologies – artificial intelligence, 3D printing, and gene therapy, to name a few – are making it possible to meet societal needs in completely new and far less impactful ways.

Every twenty-first-century business would be wise to embrace this new perspective, to enrich its systems intelligence and thereby increase its chances of success.

Valuing what really matters

Today the global economy focuses almost exclusively on growth of production and consumption. As money changes hands when goods and services are bought and sold, our economic system has evolved to treat financial returns and value creation as one and the same thing. This evolution has been a consequence of the fact that every major nation on Earth has sought to maximise GDP since soon after the Second World War. This is why central banks and governments expend so much effort tweaking interest rates and other factors trying to adjust borrowing and spending patterns in pursuit of never-ending growth. It is also why companies seek out the cheapest, legally acceptable route to getting something done. If that route results in generating waste, overharvesting raw materials, using creative approaches to pay less tax, or outsourcing work to regions with less progressive labour standards, so be it.

Such negative impacts occur not because decisions makers are blind to social and environmental concerns, but because the economic context within which they are operating is not adequately driving the right kinds of outcome. As long as our economic system pursues GDP alone, restorative outcomes will remain the exception rather than the norm.

Pursuing extra-financial success

Companies that focus on extra-financial success in the years ahead will increase their own resilience and that of society as a whole. Social and environmental issues are extra-financial, because enduring financial success today depends on the degree to which we can find new ways to meet societal needs while restoring the natural world and our social fabric.

We end this chapter with some simple questions which business leaders should ask themselves, to start embracing and operationalising this new mindset.

Resilient versus efficient

One of the most common ways for companies to improve their financial bottom line is through efficiency drives. When it comes to resource use, this makes complete sense. Reducing the amount of materials used in products and packaging prevents waste. Reducing water use – particularly in water-stressed regions – eases the burden on a public resource everybody needs. However, efficiency measures undermine resilience if they reduce the capacity of a business to cope with unforeseen circumstances.

- How resilient is our business to external shocks?
- What steps can we take to help us as a board, and our business activities, become more resilient?
- How can we ensure that our activities are creating value for society as a whole in the long term?
- How can we reduce our greenhouse gas (GHG) emissions to zero – decreasing risk and benefiting society – throughout our supply chain, operations, and products?
- Can we go beyond zero and use product inputs, design operational processes, or produce products that draw down GHGs from the atmosphere?

Competitive versus compliant

It is bad for business and bad for society when environmental, social, and governance issues are seen as matters of legal compliance.

For one thing, regulations relating to environmental and social protection almost invariably lag behind what science tells us is required. So merely obeying the law, on issues ranging from toxic waste to working conditions, rarely equates to causing no harm. Secondly, it can be more expensive for a business to continuously monitor and gradually adapt to changes in legislation than to eliminate the risk entirely through preventative action. Any company which has eliminated its greenhouse gas emissions, for example, is immune to any future carbon tax.

Getting ahead of environmental and social issues is about competitiveness, not compliance. Progressive companies do what society actually needs, rather than what laws currently demand. And they leverage that fact – lobbying for more progressive legislation, knowing that they will benefit reputationally from doing so, while increasing pressure on their peers to step up.

- What response will both serve society and give us a competitive edge?
- Do we know what need we are serving, or are we just selling things?
- What can we do better in order to increase our support to succeed?
- How can we prove that our actions are authentic, not just green-washing?
- Can we lobby government and regulators to demand progressive legislation, requiring our industry as a whole to take climate action?

Holistic versus defensive or selective

Even though the SDGs have been described as a crowd-sourced "purchase order from the future,"[1] most companies have not yet adequately answered their call to action. Many current responses seek to defend the status quo, by building a narrative around what a business is already doing. However, this does not reflect reality as every business decision is in fact a trade-off (either negative or positive). If we take a systems approach – by looking at all interactions between the company and its suppliers, its customers, other socioeconomic actors, and the environment – it is possible to identify otherwise unforeseen issues. Negative trade-offs can then be anticipated and avoided – or at the very least mitigated.

This systemic approach to managing extra-financial performance is crucial, because positive and negative impacts almost never cancel each other out. Gradual gains in one area, at the expense of exacerbating problems elsewhere, aren't going to fix things. We must eliminate – and eventually reverse – all of the damage done to our natural systems and social fabric, and that means striving to maximise the good while working consciously and continuously to eliminate the bad. Such a holistic response is essential if we are to make the SDGs a reality. We can think of this third way as creating not just shareholder value, or even shared value, but system value.

- Is our SDG response holistic? And if not, what would that take?
- Are we clear on our organisational systemic interdependencies?

---

1 "Breakthrough Business Models" by Volans and the Business and Sustainable Development Commission (http://businesscommission.org/our-work/paper-new-breakthrough-business-models-needed).

- How might we redeploy our core competencies, existing assets, and know-how in completely new ways to make money in service of the SDGs?
- Are we doing everything possible to eliminate our own negative impact, throughout our value web, with respect to climate change?
- Are we doing everything possible to increase our own positive impact, or to help others eliminate their negative and increase their positive impacts, with respect to climate change?

That's the way to build a twenty-first-century business that people will really want to work for, buy from, and invest in.

26

SUSTAINABILITY

Sara Lovisolo

The focus of investors and policymakers on the transition to a low-carbon and sustainable economy means not only that a company has to be aware of its impacts on society and the environment, but it has to assess and mitigate the impacts that a changing business and regulatory environment – in response to the climate emergency and other sustainability considerations – can have on the company's business model and bottom line in the short and long term. This is the emerging notion of "double materiality" in sustainability. As regulators and consumers put pressure on investors, banks, and companies to become part of the solution to dramatic environmental and societal issues, and as technologies and markets evolve, sustainability can pose a threat to the long-term viability of a business.

While the corporate social responsibility/environmental, social, governance (ESG) chapter of this book looked at the impacts that a business can have on its stakeholders, here we are taking the outside-in view. Furthermore, we are not only looking at the operations of a company, but also at how its business model and product offering can seize the opportunities deriving from the transition to a low-carbon and sustainable economy. As consumers change their preferences in response to their sustainability concerns, and as new market opportunities present themselves, it's imperative that companies reflect on whether they are positioned well to benefit early on from these developments. This requires that the strategy department, the risk function, and the product development teams across a company's divisions cooperate to achieve a shared view of the sustainability risks and opportunities – and the resulting changing competitive landscape – that the company is faced with. Depending on the sector a company is operating in, some of these risks and opportunities will be more obvious, others more elusive and difficult to assess and quantify. It's important however to understand that a company's competitors will be struggling with the same challenges, and getting started in this journey – by asking the right questions – is more important than having all the answers to hand.

The context for the sustainability assessment of the company is provided by global policies and trends. First and foremost, the Paris Agreement on Climate, signed in December 2015, sets the ambitions of governments to avoid the disastrous effects of runaway climate change by limiting the rise in average global temperature well below two degrees Celsius compared to pre-industrial levels, by the second half of the century. This ambition is turned into national commitments (Nationally Determined Contributions or NDCs) set out in terms of absolute reductions in the greenhouse gas emissions of their economies, often identifying the specific strategies they are going to follow (for example, energy efficiency, renewable energy, afforestation and so on). Based on their NDCs, states have been developing local policies aimed at ensuring that their commitments are achieved.

Secondly, often in response to the climate challenge, technological innovation is leading the charge of the transition to a low-carbon economy by changing the way energy is produced, people move around, food is grown, and consumer goods are distributed and consumed. Technological innovation – and the associated change in markets and consumer behaviours – can pose a threat to the business models of companies which do not anticipate or adapt to these changes. Small to medium-sized enterprises are not exempt from these risks but are also in general better placed than larger companies to take advantage of the corresponding opportunities, because technological innovation is usually delivered by start-ups and smaller companies. Scenario analysis is a formalised approach to take account of the changing business context. It is based on the creation of states of the economy, regulation, and technology in the distant future. Scenarios are narratives about possible future situations. Companies can create their own scenarios, or they can use scenarios made available by research bodies such as the International Energy Agency (IEA) or the UN climate research body, the Intergovernmental Panel on Climate Change. Scenario analysis consists in figuring out the impact of a specific scenario on a company's business model, profitability, competitive position, and ultimately its chances of surviving and thriving in different business environments and states of the world.

Questions to ask

- Is the company taking into account sustainability risks in its approach to enterprise risk management?
- Do the company's principal risks address any material environmental, social, and governance issues?
- Are the mitigation plans put forward by the company to address its principal ESG risks robust?
- Does the company perform scenario analysis with regard to its climate-related risks? Does the company have any plans to get scenario analysis done soon?
- Is the company aligning its greenhouse gas emissions with a trajectory compatible with the objectives of the Paris Agreement?
- What benchmarks is the company using to assess its progress on the sustainability agenda?
- How does the company compare to its competitors in the way it manages its sustainability risks and opportunities?
- Does the company provide any products or services that enable it to take advantage of the opportunities arising from the transition to a low-carbon and sustainable economy?
- Is the company making any investments (for example, R&D) now that will enable it to take advantage of the opportunities deriving from the transition to a sustainable and low-carbon economy in the future?
- Are the company's competitors moving faster in developing a product offering that incorporates sustainability considerations?
- What are the most promising markets or product lines for the company to develop a profitable sustainability offering?

- How sophisticated is the company's market intelligence with regard to sustainability risks and opportunities?
- Has the company developed an "equity story" or business narrative that incorporates sustainability considerations?
- Is the company able to explain in an effective and credible way to its investors – and providers of capital more broadly – how its strategy incorporates sustainability considerations?
- Can a robust sustainability strategy open the doors to new sustainability-focused investors and providers of capital, thus helping to diversify the company's sources of funding?
- Are there any reputational risks associated with the company's own positioning around sustainability, such as greenwashing?
- Is the company's policy engagement or lobbying activity consistent with its sustainability positioning?
- Is the company considering its compliance requirements – in terms of reporting and performance – as mere costs, or as investments to be leveraged?
- Is the company aware of its potential for market leadership in the space of sustainability?
- If the company is not a leader in sustainability yet, does it have a road map to achieve leadership over a defined period?

27

SOCIAL IMPACT

Oonagh Harpur

Social impact is the way any organisation affects the communities in which it operates. An organisation which does not consider its social impacts and social values risks compromising its sustained long-term success. This chapter provides a toolkit for the board's leadership and governance of social impact.

What are social impacts? Social impacts include those which simply protect an organisation's basic licence to operate – paying fair taxes, meeting minimum standards for wages, ensuring human rights and healthy and safe working conditions – and those which confer a licence to lead – actively contributing to social mobility in recruitment, remuneration and promotion, paying a living wage promoting and supporting mental health and well-being, adopting science-based targets[1] for carbon reduction, setting targets for procurement spent on small and medium-sized businesses in supply chains, removing unconscious biases from machine learning/artificial intelligence systems.

Social impact matters to society and all the communities in which an organisation operates: from the communities producing the raw materials

1 https://sciencebasedtargets.org/companies-taking-action/.

used in products and services through to the way those products and services are consumed and waste is disposed of. Organisations support and enable the livelihoods and success of every individual and organisation with which they are involved. Their collective success enables a society's success. Social impact is not incremental or incidental to it. Societal impact is integral to business and organisations whether it is recognised or not. Businesses can only provide returns over the medium and long term if the societies in which they operate prosper.

The social impact of any organisation matters and can be a risk or an opportunity. The risks include reputational risk, regulatory threat, and financial performance. The opportunities include strengthening reputation, brand, market share, and sustainable and profitable growth by meeting the growing expectations of different stakeholder groups.

The close interrelationship between business and society and their respective health becomes particularly clear at times of crisis. During the 2020/21 lockdowns of communities due to the coronavirus pandemic, people needed reliable and safe local food supplies, deliveries, and accessible healthcare. Nice-to-haves and luxuries became just that, and staying overnight or flying to another country was largely no longer possible. The status of certain workers became "essential," no longer just "unskilled." Many people lost their livelihoods; most economies went into recession, and sociopolitical and geopolitical tensions increased. Thousands of businesses failed, while thousands of lives were lost.

It is the responsibility of the board to lead on social impact and to assure investors and wider society about progress with managing the risks and opportunities from the social impact of the organisation. In 2013, Tomorrow's Company and the City Values Forum developed a guide and toolkit for boards of financial services companies.[2] This publication drew on the lessons learned from the financial crisis of 2008. It was revised and republished in 2016 as "Governing Culture" for the Financial Reporting Council's Culture Coalition. What follows applies the Guide's Toolkit to the board's leadership and governance of social impact.[3]

2 "Governing Values: A Guide for Boards of Financial Services Companies." www.tomorrowscompany.com/wp-content/uploads/2016/05/Governing_Values_a_guide_for_boards_of_financial_services_companies_L_53c3dae25207e.pdf.
3 "Governing Culture: Risk and Opportunity. A Guide to Board Leadership in purpose, values and culture." www.tomorrowscompany.com/publication/governing-culture/.

Leading boards focus their agenda on six priorities

1. Inspiring with social purpose and values
2. Aligning strategy with social purpose and values
3. Promoting and embodying social purpose and values through board leadership and composition
4. Guiding decisions with social purpose and values
5. Encouraging and rewarding desired behaviours
6. Ensuring that progress is being achieved

Here is a set of questions for each priority area for the board to consider in relation to its organisation's social impact:

Inspiring with social purpose and values

It starts with purpose. Purpose is an expression of why an organisation exists. In this chapter, purpose is renamed "social purpose" simply for emphasis.

The best organisations have only one purpose and it is a purpose that answers the questions "Why do we exist?" and "What value do we create for society that justifies our licence to operate?" Purpose includes the social impact the organisation wants to have on the lives of everyone in its ecosystem. A clear, inspiring social purpose gives meaning to people and their work. It improves morale and decision-making throughout the business. By anchoring behaviours and communication in this social purpose, businesses can build trust and loyalty with key stakeholders and over the long term provide investors with a financial return.

- What is our shared understanding of the social impact of our business?
- What are the risks and opportunities?
- What does, or might, our business do that benefits society or protects society from harm in the communities in which we do business?
- How might the UN's Sustainable Development Goals[4] help us identify our social impacts?
- How well does our purpose describe the way we wish to create value for and protect society? Which different stakeholder views have been taken

4   www.unglobalcompact.org/sdgs/about.

into account in setting the social purpose? Have these been considered in the round? How satisfied are we that the value we are promising to society meets its reasonable expectations?
- How do our values support our social purpose and the long-term sustainability of our business? Whom do we value – individuals, local communities, governments, other businesses, especially our suppliers and distributors – in our business operations and who gets left out?
- How authentic, aspirational, and inspiring is our purpose to attract and retain the people we need for our future success? How clear are we in our narrative about any current or future vulnerabilities which could undermine the narrative? What about our suppliers, customers and investors now and in the future? How well do our purpose and narrative inspire trust and loyalty?
- How are we monitoring society's changing expectations of our business, our sector, and the wider business community?

Aligning strategy with social purpose and values

Boards set the direction. In doing so, they seek to use strategy as a galvanising force to align everyone around purpose and commercial goals. Strategies succeed when supported by aligned behaviours, culture, and values. As Peter Drucker, the management guru, is reputed to have said, "Culture eats strategy for breakfast."

- To what extent are our strategy and commercial goals consistent with our social purpose and values? What are the barriers, enablers, risks, and opportunities?
- How might we adapt our strategy to create greater shared value between the people and communities we impact and our investors?
- What are the values and culture we will need to ensure everyone in our business works towards the strategy consistent with our social purpose?
- What resources, capabilities, and consistent behaviours does our business need to deliver our strategy? What opportunities are there to reskill and develop our people and strategy instead of making people redundant? What training and development would help our people behave more consistently with our social purpose and values?

- What are the strategic goals, social impacts, and timelines against which the board can measure progress towards our strategy consistent with our social purpose and values?

Promoting and embodying social purpose and values through board leadership and composition

Social impact starts with leadership from the boardroom. As was seen in the UK Brexit referendum, most boards and senior leaders lived in a social bubble and were out of touch with the experiences of wider society. It is the responsibility of the board to ensure it is listening to and responding to the reasonable expectations of all stakeholders on social impact, including investors. The "Social Board,"[5] a paper by Acre Resources, offers a menu for board directors to connect with society:

- Who leads on social impact in the boardroom and owns it across the business? What roles do the chair and CEO play in promoting and embedding our social purpose and values?
- How well does the board reflect wider society? How does the board listen to the voices in the different communities in which we operate? How does the board collectively and individually engage with the communities in which we operate?
- Have we explored the added value of a public interest non-exec, a stakeholder advisory board, a next-generation shadow?
- What are we doing to ensure there is a pipeline of diverse talent from senior leadership through the executive board to the board?
- How well does each director understand the needs and expectations of our people and the communities we work within? When did the board last review employee engagement, customers or suppliers' attitudes, or those of the wider communities we work within?
- What values and behaviours are most commonly exhibited in our boardroom meetings and in the communication of our decisions? How safe is it for anyone to raise any issues relating to our social purpose or values in the boardroom or throughout the organisation?

5 www.acre.com/thought-leadership/the-social-board.

Guiding decision with social purpose and values

Everyone in a business – employees and contractors – makes decisions every day that can detract from, or add to, our social impact and shareholder value

- How do we ensure that board decisions are consistent with our social purpose and values as well as our strategy?
- How do we make sure that the right people are taking critical decisions across the organisation at the right level, at the right time, and consistently with our strategy, social purpose, and values?
- Where does ownership of social impact sit across the organisation? How well is it owned by every colleague who makes those critical decisions?
- How do we help our people use our social purpose and values to guide their decision-making? How do we test the resilience of their decision-making when faced with conflicting interests? What training and development might be needed especially for new recruits, newly promoted employees, and new contractors?
- How confident are we that our people will speak up when those around them do not make decisions consistent with our social purpose and values? How confident are we that our "Speak Up" channels are working effectively?

Encouraging and rewarding desired behaviours

This is really the "brass tacks" of social impact. How does social impact show up in all the processes, policies, and routines of the business operations?

- How do we encourage and reward behaviour aligned with our social purpose and values? Are relevant key performance indicators built into performance review processes from the chair to the most junior employee and contractor?
- Do the other directors and I practice what we preach? Do our actions and communications reinforce our leadership on social purpose and values. For example, do we promote volunteering days throughout the organisation – and how do board members get involved?

- When I walk out of this board meeting, could I explain the social impact of our decisions to any one of the people I know in the business, to our clients and suppliers, or to my friends and family? What will my board colleagues say? Will our formal communication be consistent?
- Who gets hired and promoted, and who gets left behind? How well does our remuneration system reward those who proactively contribute to achieving our social purpose and strategy?
- What sanctions do we use when behaviour is not aligned?

Ensuring that progress is being achieved

The key theme is transparency – businesses need to be honest and truthful about their impact, and describe not just what they're doing right but also what they're learning and what needs to change. They need to be clear about where progress isn't sufficient and what they're going to do about it. Historically, businesses have focused on telling only the positive story and demonstrating compliance.

Transparency around impact can have big impact on trust. Boards not only lead on the social purpose, culture, and values of a business and set the direction through the strategy; they also have a responsibility to assure themselves on behalf of investors and society that the business is walking its talk.

The expectations of business are changing rapidly towards greater transparency around environmental, social, and governance reporting; impact investing demands for specific SDG-related measures; and government legislation and regulations around specific social impacts such as human rights, bribery and corruption, and minimum wages.

There are proposals in the UK for boards to produce a public interest statement and to report annually on progress with assurance of its achievements through an external auditor.

- How do we ensure that all the people on whom the business relies to create value, inside and outside the organisation, are making decisions aligned with our social purpose and values?
- How does the organisation measure and report on its social impact? What about goals and ensuring that progress is being achieved?

- How far might external or internal audits be helpful to provide external assurance?
- Where insufficient progress is being made, how is this addressed?
- Where social impact risks are expected, what mitigating actions can be taken?

"Governing Culture: Risk & Opportunity," City Values Forum and Tomorrow's Company 2016. It was prepared for the FRC's culture coalition to provide a guide to board leadership on purpose, values, and culture.

Part VI

BOARD MEETINGS

28

ROLE AND RESPONSIBILITIES OF THE BOARD

Natalie Sykes

The main role and responsibility of the board is the overall management and oversight of the organisation, providing leadership within a framework of good governance and controls with careful risk management, at all times.

At the outset, the board provides continuity for the organisation by setting up the legal entity and representing the organisation, its products, and services, in front of its stakeholders.

A board's responsibilities will include determining the long-term aims of the organisation, providing leadership to achieve these aims, and establishing a supervisory process to ensure that the management of the organisation is effective as well as being accountable to its stakeholders.

Setting the direction

Once up and running, the board is responsible for setting the policies and direction of the organisation. It is responsible for setting the vision, mission, and values of the organisation as well as reviewing and evaluating opportunities and threats, and helping management determine the strategy and strategic options to be pursued.

The board is charged with overseeing the development of goals and strategy as well as the implementation process in order to address any problems the organisation may have in growing within its competitive environment. The board should drive the organisation's strategy forward, ensuring that the organisation and its financial resources are properly applied in order to successfully implement the chosen strategic priorities. The directors are expected to lead by example and ensure that good standards of behaviour permeate throughout all levels of the organisation.

The board governs the overarching policies of the organisation, and any changes to these policies are subject to board approval and agreement. Changes in policies are formulated and agreed by the CEO and employees, often driven through a commitment to continuous improvement of the organisation.

The right resources

The board is responsible for ensuring that there are sufficient financial resources in order for the strategic priorities to be implemented and delivered. The board also has a responsibility to make sure there are the requisite skills and experience within the board and executive team in order to oversee and execute strategy delivery. A large part of this obligation rests with the careful selection, appointment, and ongoing performance evaluation of the CEO as well as the careful ongoing evaluation that the board directors' skills are those required to bring strategic success to the organisation.

The way in which the board governs its relationship with the CEO is an important part of the overall governance of the organisation, which is also directed and set by the board. The dynamics between the chair and CEO are vital to board functionality, and it is important that these roles are separated, usually two different individuals with complementary skill sets. The chair leads the board, whilst the CEO leads the organisation. In unusual circumstances, the chair may become an executive chair with executive powers for a defined period of time.

Stakeholders are placing increased importance on delivery of long-term economic success while at the same time developing an appropriate working culture, so that in times of stress, the organisation can be relied upon to maintain a resilient performance. The board and executive management must ensure that decisions around value creation and the organisation's value system and culture are fully integrated.

Board oversight

The board is responsible for identifying the nature and extent of the risks facing the organisation in achieving its strategic aims and the risks to its long-term viability. The board is tasked with overseeing the risk management process, information system, and appropriate internal controls to facilitate the proper functioning of the organisation. The directors should monitor the organisation's risk management and internal control system and carry out periodic reviews of their effectiveness.

The board also has a fiduciary duty to protect the organisation's assets and ensure they are in good order with appropriate measures being taken to safeguard these by having full awareness of threats, opportunities, weaknesses, and challenges. This is extremely important as each director has equal and shared liability should this duty not be appropriately discharged.

The board is also responsible for the appointment of auditors and for ensuring that the audit is performed in a timely manner each year while demonstrating that the organisation is a going concern and operating within the insolvency laws.

Board operations

The board also ensures that the organisation's obligations to its shareholders, investors, members, and all other stakeholders are widely understood and managed accordingly. The directors are tasked with providing information to give stakeholders a clear and broad view of solvency and liquidity, the company's risk management approach, and the long-term viability of the business. The board needs to ensure that communications to and from stakeholders are relevant, effective, and take into account their interests. Boards continually need to monitor and improve their own performance. This can be achieved through board evaluation and effectiveness reviews, which provide a powerful and valuable feedback mechanism for improving the functioning of the board, maximising strengths, and highlighting areas for further development.

A survey of 1,100 directors from consultants McKinsey,[1] revealed that of the three dimensions of board operations the survey covered, effective processes emerged as the most challenging. In comparing board dynamics between the executives and the board, dynamics within the board itself, and board processes, the directors stated that the biggest struggle was with establishing effective processes. The quality of induction training and ongoing access to development opportunities were also named as real areas for improvement.

Looking forward, no organisation is immune to the effects of pandemics, cybersecurity, digitisation, and geopolitical risks, so these topics should be part and parcel of every board's discussions. Because businesses evolve and potential disruptions can arise at any time, it is important that boards maintain an agile and flexible approach to their operations.

Questions to ask

Setting the direction

- Is the board determining the organisation's vision, mission, and values?
- Does the board support the vision, mission, and values?
- Is the strategic plan developed by executives and approved and adopted by the board?
- Does the board ensure the budget reflects the strategic priorities?
- How does the board measure the implementation of the strategy?

Resources

- Does the board ensure that the board composition reflects the strategic needs of the organisation?
- Does the board ensure the executive team has the necessary skills to execute the strategy?
- Does the board ensure the financial position is adequate to be able to execute the strategy?
- How does the board select, appoint, and terminate directors?

---

1 www.mckinsey.com/business-functions/strategy-and-corporate-finance/our-insights/a-time-for-boards-to-act#.

- How would the board deal with an underperforming CEO?
- Does the board encourage challenge and constructive discussion prior to decisions?

Board oversight

- Does the board oversee the execution of a strategic plan?
- Does the board have procedures and policies in place for good financial oversight?
- Has the board appointed a well-functioning audit committee that manages the relationship with the external auditor?
- Does the board ensure a risk management policy is in place for the board to be able to perform risk oversight?
- Has the board adopted a conflict of interest policy?
- Does the board ensure good compliance with laws and regulations and regular compliance reporting to the board?
- Does the board ensure stakeholder engagement, management, and communications planning is in place?
- Does the board ensure that all stakeholders are mapped effectively?
- Does the board measure the organisation's social impact?
- Does the board performance manage executives?

Board operations

- Is the board focused on governance, not executive management?
- How does the board demonstrate its commitment to good governance?
- Does the board have clear roles and responsibilities between board and executives?
- Does the board have a committee structure in place to accommodate the organisational needs?
- How does the board decide what the delegated powers of authority should be?
- Does the board conduct board reviews on a regular basis?
- How does the performance of board members get evaluated?
- How is their underperformance addressed?

29

BOARD MEETINGS AND THE AGENDA

Dineshi Ramesh

The board's remit is vast, yet it has limited time at its disposal. The best board meetings move an organisation closer towards its goals whilst giving directors confidence that they are discharging their duties well.

Effective board meetings do not happen by chance. There is extensive planning behind the scenes, and a careful balance needs to be struck between structuring the meeting well and human interaction. A great conversation is what you're aiming for, as Theodore Zeldin[1] explains,

> When minds meet, they don't just exchange facts: they draw different implications from them; engage in new trains of thought. Conversation doesn't just reshuffle the cards; it creates new cards.

The challenge

The challenge is how to ensure the board meeting focuses on what matters most. What are the conversations the board needs to be having and how do

1 *Conversation: How Talk Can Change Our Lives* Theodore Zeldin, Mahwah, NJ: HiddenSpring, ©2000.

DOI: 10.4324/9781003201182-35

you ensure vital topics do not get crowded out? Board intelligence in collaboration with the Cambridge Judge Business School conducted research that shows that boards typically spend too much time in one of two areas: governance (a pronounced concern in financial services) and in the "weeds" of operational performance.

Most boards say they want to be spending more time on strategy and looking at how the organisation is progressing towards its long-term goals. The reality can be weighed down by firefighting or operational issues. By designing a forward-looking calendar built around the board's priorities, the balance can be redressed.

Purpose and the agenda

The foundation of an effective board meeting is the agenda. Most chairs design their board agenda in consultation with their company secretary and chief executive. The starting point tends to be the list of "must do" items – be they statutory, administrative, or routine in nature. They are easy to recall, and they often fall into the "boring but important" category of meeting items.

However, the board agenda should start with the important topics, which are sometimes harder to identify. Figuring out the conversations the board should be having is the starting point for any good agenda. Let's look at this in three steps.

Step 1 – what are the board's priorities?

A good starting point is to answer two essential questions for the coming 12–18 months:

- What are the big decisions this forum will take or shape (steering)?
- What are the big items this forum should monitor (supervising)?

To ensure you cover the right bases, consider these two questions across three areas: strategy, performance, and governance. Try to phrase your responses in the form of questions to help drive specificity and avoid ambiguity. For example, rather than an item on "culture," be specific: "how well have we embedded our culture?" Rather than an agenda item on "growth," specify "what is the right mix of acquisitive and organic growth for 202x?"

By posing these issues as questions, it becomes clear whether the style of conversation being prompted is steering or supervising in nature. This in turn, signals to the board to get ready to make a decision or to challenge performance.

By agreeing the board's priorities, there will be:

- A shared sense of purpose – the board will be united in their understanding of the issues that matter most in the coming year. This reduces the risk of misaligned expectations between members and makes it easier to chair the forum.
- Clarity for the executive – the remit of the board on each topic is clear. The executive can decide how to prepare great information to support the board's priorities and if there are other priorities that should remain the preserve of management.

Step 2 – how to construct the forward calendar?

Translating these priorities into the forward calendar is the next step in shaping the board agenda. Consider the appropriate timing or frequency:

- When should the steering priorities come to the board? Allocate a month.
- How often should the supervising priorities come to the board? For example, monthly, quarterly, or just the once. Supervising is about providing assurance that activity is on track, so the topic may need to come to the board more than once.

In practice, there are other considerations, especially if the organisation's governance structure is more complex than a single board and executive committee. The key here is to coordinate the board calendar with the governance structure it operates within. Once you've done this, you'll have an outline of the board's forward calendar of meetings.

Step 3 – how can you design an agenda that drives a better conversation?

The challenge is how to make best use of everyone's time: the order of matters, the time given to each item, how to regulate energy and concentration, and how to make it is easy for participants to switch between different modes of thinking.

Here are some of the hallmarks of a great agenda:

I. Open the meeting with the chair's remarks and the CEO's report, rather than an administrative item, for example, the minutes. This sets the scene.
II. Allow for fewer but deeper conversations about the most important topics. This is what board members prefer; time to get to the heart of the matter.
III. Group items that require similar modes of thinking together – steering (decision-making) versus supervising (monitoring). Cognitively, this reduces strain.
IV. Consider "zero timing" items. A neat way of dealing with papers that require no discussion, they are purely for note and need not consume agenda time.
V. Build in ample breaks. A tired board is not an effective one.

Now the foundation of the meeting is in place (its purpose and agenda). Let's look at the other drivers of a great meeting.

Meeting effectiveness

One of the most effective ways of helping boards improve their meetings is to self-assess how well the meeting is working (or not!). Unpacking the drivers of a great meeting improves the board's understanding of what it takes to have a more effective meeting. Repeating the exercise will prompt changes to be made from one meeting to the next. Here are five drivers to consider:

- Purpose and Agenda – covered above
- Information and security

- People and place
- Behaviours
- Decisions and progress

Within each driver there is a series of questions that help demystify what makes for a great meeting.[2]

Questions to ask

Purpose and agenda

- Is the purpose of the forum clear?
- Is meeting time being spent on the right topics?
- Do we have the right number of meetings to discharge our duties?
- Is there a forward calendar outlining the forum's priorities?
- Is the agenda well structured with clarity on items for decision versus supervision?

Information and security

- Is high-quality information provided as a pre-read?
- Are there systems and processes in place to support secure, electronic distribution of papers that facilitate collaboration?
- Is the "ask" of the reader clear for each paper?
- Are papers unvarnished, forward-looking, and insightful?
- Is information quality-assured by sponsors with audit trails for key decisions?

People and Place

- Do members represent ample diversity of thought?
- Do we have the right number of members with the required skills (not too many/few)?
- Does the physical set-up and timing support participants' energy?
- Do members adequately represent our key stakeholders?

2 Smart Meeting Score © Board Intelligence.

- Does the set-up of the meeting (physical or virtual) facilitate collaboration (pre- and during the meeting)?

Behaviours

- Does the chair encourage an atmosphere of trust?
- Does the forum contribute effectively (making decisions where required, providing challenge/support depending on under-/overperformance)?
- Is the meeting chaired effectively (kept on agenda/to time)?
- Are conversations constructive (open-minded, upholding the forum's purpose)?
- Does the discussion build on thinking (injecting ideas, solutions) rather than being disjointed/inconclusive?

Decisions and progress

- Does the meeting drive the organisation forward?
- Do we seek to improve our meetings?
- How effective is decision-making?
- Do decisions consider the impact on the long term, the environment, and all relevant stakeholders?
- Are attempts made to ensure decision-making is not skewed by cognitive bias?

These questions have been tested in the field through observation of real board and executive committee meetings, and though not exhaustive, they tend to be the ones that move the dial when it comes to making meetings better. The questions are most powerful when answered by the board as a whole and the results amalgamated. If completed anonymously, you'll get the truest picture of what your board really thinks. Use the results as a calibration point from which you can begin to have better meetings, better conversations, and ultimately move both your organisation and its role in society forward, in the most positive way.

30

BOARD SUPPORT

Siobhan Lavery

Boardrooms are the domain of a stellar cast of people representing many varied and important roles, such as chair, executive director, non-executive director (NED), chief financial officer, investment manager, chief information officer, legal counsel, and auditor, to name but a few. Amongst this ensemble the company secretary can be overlooked and erroneously deemed by some to play only a minor role operating in the shadows; however, the role of the company secretary is fundamental to the smooth and efficient running of the board and in turn the organisation.

No two boards are the same, and even those of a similar size, operating in a similar sector, with a similar structure will have different boardroom dynamics. This means that the demands on the company secretary and the variety of functions they may undertake will vary accordingly; however, the importance of the role is unchanged. The company secretary is often a trusted adviser with key responsibility for ensuring compliance with laws and regulation.

Who fulfils the role of company secretary can also be diverse. It may be undertaken by the legal counsel, may comprise of an in-house team

DOI: 10.4324/9781003201182-36

of individuals, may be outsourced to a third-party provider, or the duties may even be undertaken by a director of the organisation. However, for the purposes of this chapter it is assumed that the board has appointed an appropriately qualified company secretary who is conversant in the rules and regulations that apply to the organisation, sector, and jurisdiction.

The vast majority of a company's secretary's work is undertaken behind the scenes, outside of the boardroom. A good company secretary will make the organisation and completion of various tasks appear seamless, belying the hard work that has been required. The corollary is that, as the focus of a board is rarely fully on a company secretary and the majority of their workload is completed in the background, if there are any deficiencies with that workload being carried out, they can take a long time to come to the board's attention.

Qualified company secretaries have undertaken years of study and passed numerous exams to obtain their qualification. By their nature they should be dedicated and intent on acting with integrity. Following are some characteristics and questions that should apply to all company secretaries, regardless of the organisation or sector in which they work.

Archivist

It has often been said that the company secretary is the "conscience of the company"; however, in fact a key function of a company secretary is to act as the memory of the company by maintaining and storing all the company documents. These range from those required under law (statutory registers), to those required for compliance with regulation and the smooth running of the organisation (policies and procedures), to those that are useful to keep for corporate memory (general correspondence).

For a NED, the company secretary is usually the only source of this material; therefore, it is vitally important to obtain comfort that the documents are being maintained and kept up to date in a proper, efficient, and easily accessible manner.

Questions to Ask:

- Are all applicable statutory registers being maintained and being kept up to date?
- What policies and procedures are in place?

- Does the organisation have in place all the policies and procedures which it is required by law or regulation, or best practice, to have in place?
- How are key documents stored and what measures have been put in place to avoid their accidental destruction (that is, the use of a fireproof safe for hard copy documents, regular back-up of soft copy documents, IT security measures of the system on which on the documents are stored)?

Coordinator extraordinaire

A fundamental function of the company secretary is the coordination of board meetings. As mentioned, a boardroom comprises a variety of people, and a board meeting requires not only the alignment of the diaries of a cast of many, but the practical arrangements of the meeting itself (booking a room, arranging for catering, obtaining any necessary IT equipment), and the timely provision and distribution of papers ahead of the meeting. This requires key planning and multitasking skills, and must be completed to a high standard to ensure the effective and efficient running of the board meeting.

When coordinating with a number of different parties, there are many things that are outside of a company secretary's control – the director who asks for a board meeting time or date or even venue to be changed at the last minute, an adviser who does not provide their papers for the board pack until after the deadline provided, the piece of IT equipment that suddenly fails. Therefore, the company secretary should always be methodically planning ahead.

- Are the board meetings scheduled with sufficient notice and sufficient frequency?
- Have calendar invitations been sent to all participants, and are the details contained in the invitation up to date?
- Has the agenda been circulated for comment sufficiently in advance of the meeting?
- Have the timings of the agenda items and attendees been agreed in advance with the chair and communicated to the appropriate parties?

- Are the board papers and other documents requiring board review distributed in a timely manner?

Another aspect of coordination that often falls within the purview of the company secretary is the submission of various legal and regulatory returns and completion of organisation-specific tasks within set deadlines. These can be numerous, and the failure to meet them can often incur fines or possibly reputational damage. Further, in a world of continual ever-changing laws and regulations, it often falls to the company secretary to bring these to the attention of the board and to coordinate with other advisers to ensure the organisation's compliance with any new requirements.

- Is there a schedule tracking the deadlines the board and organisation must comply with throughout the year, and who is responsible for the completion of those tasks?
- Who is responsible for keeping up to date with regulatory or other changes which may impact the organisation during the course of the year?

Diplomat

A boardroom can contain challenging and demanding characters. An effective company secretary needs to know how to interact with all personalities diplomatically to ensure that they are always viewed as professional, accessible, and impartial by all directors and stakeholders.

- Is the company secretary deemed to be accessible and impartial by all directors and stakeholders?

Scribe

The most well-known function of a company secretary's role is that of minute-taker. Under law, minutes are deemed to be evidence of the proceedings at the meeting, and various court cases have highlighted the vital importance of accurate minutes. Whilst every board will spend time at each meeting discussing minutes, poor practices such as minutes not being circulated for review sufficiently in advance, comments not being provided in a timely manner, and finalised minutes not being signed, can result in an incomplete minute book.

- Are the minutes accurate and of high quality?
- Are the minutes circulated within an appropriate time period after the meeting?
- Does the final version of the minutes tabled for signing contain all directors' comments and amendments?
- Has the final version been signed and returned to the company secretary and filed appropriately?

Succession

There has rightly been much focus on boards devising and implementing orderly succession plans; however, there is rarely any focus on the succession plan for the company secretary. As previously noted, there is great diversity in who fulfils the role of company secretary; however, often the function is carried out by just one individual, which can lead to a significant risk for an organisation in the event of a resignation or injury or simply a lack of efficient communication.

- Who will undertake the company secretarial duties in the event of a sudden absence/departure of the current company secretary?
- Is the replacement company secretary sufficiently experienced and knowledgeable about the organisation and its requirements?
- Does the replacement company secretary have the requisite resources and support to step into the role?

31

THIRD-PARTY PROVIDERS

Charlotte Valeur

Most organisations rely on third parties to save costs, improve services, give an independent view, and help on flexibility and competitiveness. Using third parties therefore has become a natural part of an organisation's everyday operations.

A third party is an organisation, supplier, agent, individual, or vendor that interacts on behalf of or with the organisation. Third-party providers provide all kinds of services from legal and accounts to IT, lobbying, or joint ventures. One of the big challenges facing boards and organisations is gaining an understanding of the full extent of their third-party relationships and how to manage the inherent risks associated with them.

Third parties can create risks as well as opportunities which can impact on areas such as reputation and brand value, or potentially give rise to financial and legal risks. This means that organisations need to conduct careful due diligence up front as well as throughout the relationship in order to appropriately monitor third-party risks. This monitoring can be carried out through a combination of on-site visits and the completing of questionnaires. The frequency of the monitoring depends on the risk rating of each third party and should be part of the contractual arrangement.

Having an efficient and effective third-party management system in place is key to ensuring that all risks are being properly monitored and addressed on an ongoing basis.

Why is third-party management and risk oversight a board matter?

Increasingly boards need to ensure they have proper oversight of third-party providers. Some organisations can have thousands of different providers, all with different risk profiles. In a world of cyber risks, data protection, corruption, and new levels of transparency through technology, boards cannot sit idle with regards to which third-party providers their organisations use and the risk management of same. In many countries there are anti-corruption laws, bribery acts, and similar legislation, where organisations are increasingly being found liable for illegal activities or unethical behaviour of their third-party providers. In addition, customers generally don't make the differential between an organisation and its third-party providers and will hold the organisation accountable to any problems that occur, even if that problem lies solely with a third-party provider. This means that organisations today should ensure their oversight of third-party providers is broad enough to capture health and safety, environmental practices, compliance with laws and regulations, use of intellectual property, corruption, bribery, and many more.

Organisations should also ensure that their ethical standards and codes of conduct applies to all their third-party providers as well. All processes concerning ethics, including training and workshops, should include the organisation's third-party providers, particularly those related to employee standards, health and safety, working conditions, legal and regulative behaviours, and environmental, social, governance measures.

Some organisations have interconnected systems with their third-party providers, which makes it necessary to assure that they have appropriate data security and cyber risk systems in place.

The board should have a clear role in providing oversight and ensuring that executive management has a process in place to manage third-party risks. It should also ensure that contract compliance is being monitored on a regular basis and that adequate resources are available to do this. The objective of the board's ensuring that the organisation has full knowledge and understanding of its third-party exposure, should be to mitigate risks whilst improving quality and reliability of the third-party relationship.

Questions about third parties

- What are the roles and responsibilities for board members and senior management in overseeing third-party risks and opportunities?
- What are the roles and responsibilities for line functions?
- Are there adequate resources to properly manage third parties?
- How often does management update the board on its assessment of third-party risks?
- Are the updates of appropriate timeliness and level of detail?
- Do we have a complete list of all third-party relationships the organisation has?
- Do we have policies and procedures in place for appointing and managing third parties?
- Do our own ethical standards and codes of conduct apply to third-party providers?
- Which third parties can significantly impact the organisation's ability to achieve its strategic goals?
- Should we consider diversifying or consolidating some third-party relationships to reduce risks?
- What approach does the organisation take to perform due diligence on its third parties?
- What are the parameters of oversight of third parties?
- Is internal audit involved with the process?
- How do we ensure all new third parties go through the approval process?
- Does the organisation have robust third-party risk management?
- How often is the risk management matrix updated?
- What controls are in place to mitigate the risks posed by third parties?
- How are problems with third parties identified and addressed?
- Are any significant third-party contracts up for renewal within the next 12 months?
- Do we have a specific third-party risk matrix that is updated on a regular basis?

- Do we have a tech-enabled infrastructure to support the risk management of third parties?
- Do we perform regular third-party due diligence/review?
- Do we have a heightened reputational risk with any of our third parties?
- Do we ensure that our third parties operate according to best practice and our values/ethical values?
- What questions do we ask in third-party reviews?

Third-party review questionnaires should cover a number of relevant questions that can give the board assurances that key third parties to the organisation are fit and proper. The board should ensure they have enough information to gain an understanding of the full extent of the organisation's third-party relationships and associated risks. The third-party monitoring and due diligence should be readily available for boards to inspect.

Questions for third parties

- What is the date of appointment and terms of the contract?
- Have there been any significant or material changes in the ownership structure during the period?
- Have there been any material changes to the team connected to the organisation in the period?
- Has the organisation experienced any operational difficulties during the period?
- What is their internal control framework?
- Have there been any third-party reviews conducted during the period?
- Has the organisation experienced any operational incidents and/or complaints during the period?
- Does the organisation have a disaster recovery and business continuity process plan in place?
- If so, is it available for inspection upon request?
- For information security, does the organisation hold a certification, ISO27001 or similar?
- If not, can you provide confirmation that suitable technology investment and related processes are in place to maintain information security and client confidentiality?

- Have the organisation's information/cybersecurity controls operated effectively during the period?
- Has the organisation experienced any data breaches in the period?
- If yes, please outline any incidents detailing nature, cause, impact, and future mitigation.
- Does the organisation have a testing regime covering PEN tests, social engineering reviews, and business continuity tests?
- Can you provide details of the cybersecurity insurance in place?
- Can you provide details on the level of PI insurance in place?
- Are there anti-bribery, corruption (ABC) and anti-money laundering (AML) policies and procedures in place within the organisation?
- Is the organisation a regulated business?
- If so, can you confirm that it has operated in accordance with its regulatory permits?
- Has the organisation been subject to any regulatory investigation or enforcement in the period?
- Does the organisation outsource any part of its services? If yes, please provide details of such outsourcing.
- Can you confirm that the organisation complies with labour laws and other regulatory requirements?
- Does the organisation use intellectual property appropriately?
- Does the organisation have a diversity policy?
- Does the organisation have policies and appropriate oversight of health and safety?
- Does the organisation monitor environmental impact/emissions?

32

BOARD COMMITTEES

PURPOSE, TASKS, AND VALUE

Jenny Simnett, Filipe Morais, and Andrew Kakabadse

Board committees have grown in importance in corporate governance regimes across the UK, USA, and Europe. Yet how exactly they operate, their role and contribution to good governance and sustainable company performance remain insufficiently discussed and researched topics. A 50% increase in committee activities and meeting frequency has been documented over the last 15 years amongst S&P1500 companies.[1] The expanding role and responsibilities of committees in corporate governance are due in part to more tasks being designated to them, but is due also to the financial crisis of 2008 and subsequent increasing pressure from regulation.

There are many types of committees, but our focus will be on audit, remuneration, and nomination committees as mandated by the UK Corporate Governance Code. Other committees are often established to monitor specific areas of company operation or to control areas of special interest,

---

1   K. D. Kolev, D. B. Wangrow, V. L. Barker, and D. J. Schepker 2019. "Board Committees in Corporate Governance: A Cross Disciplinary Review & Agenda for the Future." *Journal of Management Studies*, 56(6): 1138–1193.

DOI: 10.4324/9781003201182-38

for example, governance, strategic planning, environmental, technology, public affairs, diversity, political contribution, culture, treasury, compliance, and sustainability. The two most common additional committees are corporate social responsibility and risk.[2] Ethics committees are often set up by businesses to guide and control their development and use of artificial intelligence.

In the UK, the impetus for board committees was initiated with the 1992 *Cadbury Report*[3] which mandated the formation of these three committees of the board. This was seen to be a way of perfecting checks and balances and better protecting and serving shareholder interest. The *Cadbury Report* laid out a dual function of committees to "lead" and "control." Today, there is 90% compliance, with the majority of FTSE350 companies having the three core committees.[4]

The three main committees, audit, remuneration, and nomination, are recommended to be "standing" committees, that is, with regular and frequent scheduled meetings. Terms of reference should exist for each committee which explain the role of the committee and the scope of authority as assigned by the main board. Committees set their own agendas, and both inform and educate the board on the depth and breadth of specific areas of concern. For listed companies, audit and remuneration committees are fully independent, whereas the majority of nomination committees are made up of independent directors. The two main roles of non-executive directors, "monitoring" and "advising," require significant firm-specific knowledge and often significant personal investment by outside directors. The skills needed on committees are facilitation, engagement, problem-solving, and decision-making, as well as knowledge and experience in the relevant specialism.

This short chapter provides an overview of the purpose and attributes, contribution, and key challenges for each of the three mandatory committees of audit, nomination, and remuneration. The aim is to enable reflection by practising directors through applying the 20 key questions that must be asked with regards to board committees.

---

2 2019 UK Spencer Stuart Board Index, UK, Spencer Stuart, p. 33.
3 *The Cadbury Report*, 1992. Report of the Committee on the Financial Aspects of Corporate Governance, London, UK, Gee Publishing, pp. 20–36.
4 Grant Thornton, 2019. *Corporate Governance Review 2019*. London, Grant Thornton, pp. 61–62.

Value of committees

Committees set policy and provide both information and decision recommendations to the board. They support the process of governance in helping directors cope with limited time and the complexity of information to review before board meetings. They increase efficiency and accountability, especially to shareholders. It is thought that over half of all board activity takes place at committee level and is then ratified in board meetings. Committees are not only important for the efficiency of the full board but can also contribute to a board culture of cohesion and collegiality. They provide access to resources and act as a potential resource for solving any inherent deficiencies of the full board. Much of the work of the board is prepared by committees, which focus on specific key activities and make recommendations to the board to facilitate decision-making.

The presence of female directors on committees has a positive effect on firm performance, even more so than when female directors are on the main board. This is thought to be due to symbolic integration of women into the governance mechanism. The appointment of women on committees can be a source of competitive advantage and economically more meaningful for firms than if they are on the board.

Committees are often the drivers in emerging markets for increasing the company's attractiveness to international investors. A positive market reaction has been found to firms matching the skills of their directors to committee appointments. When there is a small or largely insider board, then committees positively influence firm performance, whether they are monitoring or advisory in nature. They can also reduce the likelihood of directors "social loafing" or free riding.

Challenges of committees

There is a cost associated with committees, not least non-executive remuneration and expenses, but also time and money spent in engaging, training, and developing them. Their remit to hire outside consultants such as external auditors, recruitment, and compensation consultants also adds to the overall costs of committees. Establishing committees does not exonerate the board from compliance with their legal obligations, and as such, they can face greater scrutiny from shareholders. Larger boards experience higher costs and risk more individual "social loafing" or free riding by directors.

A problem with committees is the segregation of information from the board which is often spread across several committees. This can be overcome to some extent by multi-committee directors (directors who serve on two or more committees). This usually occurs on aligned committees, for example, audit and remuneration committees, or nomination and remuneration committees. These multi-committee directors tend to be outside or non-executive directors with more expertise and experience. Utilising multi-committee directors in this way allow firms to moderate the costs associated with outside directors; however, there is a risk of overloading when directors serve on three or more committees. Directors can also experience conflict with sitting on two or more committees. For example, a director who sits on nomination and remuneration committees may feel torn between how to nominate the best available talent while keeping remuneration levels in line with stakeholder expectations.

There are certain sensitivities with the CEO sitting on committees, especially remuneration and nomination committees. The presence of the CEO can lead to fewer independent directors on the remuneration committee and with potential conflicts of interest in director selection on the nomination committee. The CEO's use of ingratiating or persuasive behaviour towards institutional investors has been shown to prevent the formation of an independent nomination committee. In the absence of monitoring by directors, CEOs tend to get awarded higher pay and bonuses when they sit on the nomination committee.

Fault lines or rifts arising from diversity in the composition of committees and between committee directors can lead to conflict and reduced task satisfaction. This disengagement can hinder committee effectiveness. As committees are typically small, turnover of one director can impact the group dynamics, and this change may signal a loss of skills, which can impact committee effectiveness.

Audit committee

The audit committee is the most established and mature of all committees. They ensure robust accounting and financial processes are followed as well as compliance with disclosure requirements. Audit committees are responsible for the integrity of the financial statements, the performance of internal audit, overseeing financial reporting including disclosure of activities in the annual report, and selecting, overseeing, and improving communication with the independent auditor.

Following the 2008 financial crisis, the *Walker Review* stipulated that all banks, large insurance companies, and other financial institutions should form a separate risk committee. In smaller companies, audit committees may also be responsible for risk management. In the UK, audit committees should comprise at least three independent directors and for small companies outside of the FTSE350, at least two members.

The financial and monitoring expertise of the audit committee chair has a positive influence on financial indicators such as return on assets, return on equity, and the net profit margin. An overlap of the same director on both the audit and remuneration committees can lead to lower executive compensation. The knowledge transfer of tax, risk implications, and accounting practices tends to improve monitoring effectiveness, which is important when managers are less conservative in their accounting choices. The greater the frequency of audit committee meetings, the more corporate risk tends to be disclosed by companies. Committee independence is positively correlated with firm performance; a fully independent audit committee tends to provide more accurate earnings forecasts. For example, independent directors with legal expertise on the audit committee will reduce the likelihood of financial restatements. The greater the expertise on the audit committee, the better the quality and impact of the accounting practices.

Remuneration committee

Remuneration or compensation committees are developing committees, introduced in response to the "fat cat" furore from financial scandals and the 2008 financial crisis. They are responsible for designing and implementing incentives and compensation packages for executive directors and board directors. They should address the six factors of clarity, simplicity, risk, predictability, proportionality, and alignment to culture in remuneration policy and practices.[4]

These committees review and approve the CEO's compensation and senior management compensation one level below the board. Remuneration committees also manage pension rights and are often responsible for policy and approval of employee benefits, bonuses, and salary uplifts. They require the same membership as audit committees in terms of the number of members, and all these directors should be independent. The committee chair should have a minimum of 12 months prior remuneration committee experience.[4]

The presence of a remuneration committee can give greater confidence to investors. The independence of the remuneration committee and the presence of the CEO on this committee don't appear to significantly affect executive compensation. This committee has come under the spotlight with the introduction of shareholder "say on pay," UK legislation which allows shareholders a vote to approve executive long-term incentive plans. This has especially increased public scrutiny of CEO pay according to median pay benchmarks. Maintaining a balance between attractive remuneration for executives and ensuring shareholder and public expectations are met has become a key challenge for this committee.

Nomination committee

As the youngest and least researched committee, nomination or nominating committees are responsible for the selection of both senior executive and non-executive directors with appropriate skills and experience to fulfil their monitoring and advisory roles. They are required to demonstrate formality, rigour, and transparency in the selection objectives and process, including the retention of any independent recruitment consultants or head hunters. This committee increases the likelihood of having effective directors on the board. The nomination committee regularly assesses the performance of the board and the impact the board is having on company and financial performance. It is responsible for board effectiveness via board composition including the process of succession planning.

This committee tends to be chaired by an independent outside director or the main board chair. It should consist of a majority of independent directors. Listed companies have to disclose the activities of nomination committees. The annual report should make explicit any consultants used, the policy on gender and ethnic diversity, objectives for the year, and what progress has been achieved.

The appropriate education and experiential expertise of the nomination committee chair has been found to positively influence financial indicators of the firm and heighten acceptability of the nomination committee and its output. The independence of the nomination committee leads to more robust monitoring of the influence of the CEO. However, the presence of the CEO on the nomination committee has been shown to lead to fewer independent directors being appointed. When a nomination committee is entirely independent, it tends to have a higher sensitivity between forced CEO turnover and firm performance.

Conclusion

There is still much to learn about what makes a great committee and how their contribution to and impact on the board and firm performance can be enhanced. There are likely to be more committees established, including the less traditional committees specialising in activities pertinent to specific sectors and challenges of the business. There will be a demand for greater agility and resilience, not least, post-Covid-19, and therefore more scrutiny, with a focus on the quality of information and decision-making. Moreover, with the coronavirus and the impact of significant disruptive events, risk committees may assume even more importance. The imminent passing of the governance baton from the Financial Reporting Council to the Audit, Reporting and Governance Authority (ARGA) promotes the professionalisation of the audit function, which will have implications for audit committees.

Questions to ask

- Do you follow best practice with the existence of the three main committees?
- How would you rate the performance of each of your committee chairs?
- Do you have written and explicit terms of reference for each committee?
- Are your committees chaired by independent directors?
- What proportion of independent directors sit on each main committee?

- Does the CEO sit on any of the main committees?
- How well do committees operate in terms of group dynamics and decision-making?
- How well matched are director skills to committee appointments?
- Is your audit committee responsible for risk management?
- Does your audit committee optimise communication with external auditors?
- How transparent and robust are processes around director selection?
- How robust and objective are processes around executive compensation?
- How diverse and inclusive are your committees?
- Do you adequately disclose details about suppliers for audit, remuneration, and director recruitment?
- Can you identify any segregation (or duplication) of information which hinders the operation of the board?
- How well are your committees exercising their "monitoring" and "advising" roles?
- Do you need and can you justify additional specialist committees?
- Do you have multi-committee directors on aligned committees?
- Do you have any directors with potential conflicts of interest?
- How often do you evaluate the composition and effectiveness of your committees?

33

MATTERS RESERVED FOR THE BOARD

David Doughty

Key to the board's effectiveness is the relationship between the board and senior management – the foundation of this relationship is a clear understanding of where the board's duties and responsibilities end, and the management's duties and responsibilities begin.

It is vital for this understanding that this delineation is written down in a document which is either referred to as "Matters Reserved for the Board" or "Delegation of Authority." It is a requirement of the UK Corporate Governance Code[1] that "The responsibilities of the chair, chief executive, senior independent director, board and committees should be clear, set out in writing, agreed by the board and made publicly available."

In the unitary board, executive directors wear two hats – they are part of the board team providing direction for the company and they are also the senior managers tasked by the board to deliver its objectives. This

---

1 UK Corporate Governance Code: Frc.org.uk. 2017. UK Corporate Governance Code. [online] Available at: www.frc.org.uk/Our-Work/Codes-Standards/Corporate-governance/UK-Corporate-Governance-Code.aspx.

DOI: 10.4324/9781003201182-39

dichotomy can only be resolved by having the utmost clarity as to what is required of them in each role.

With two-tier boards such as the German management and the supervisory board system, board members are usually not allowed to belong to both boards. In general, the management board has the power to manage and represent the company independently, and the supervisory board has the function to supervise and advise the management board.

The unitary, one-tier board structure is found in Australia, Canada, Hong Kong, India, Ireland, Japan, Macau, Malta, Puerto Rico, Russia, Singapore, South Africa, South Korea, Spain, Switzerland, Trinidad and Tobago, Turkey, the UK, and the USA, whilst the two-tier board structure is common in China, Belgium, Germany, and Indonesia. Both one- and two-tier systems can be found in France, Italy, Luxembourg, Mexico, and the United Arab Emirates

Generally, in the countries above, listed companies are subject to corporate governance codes, similar to the UK Corporate Governance Code or legislation, similar to the US Dodd-Frank[2] and Sarbanes-Oxley[3] Acts. Nonlisted companies, though not required to by law, tend to follow the spirit of the prevailing legislation for listed companies as it is seen to be best practice.

Board checklist

Tick the box, where appropriate, for who has responsibility for the following matters:

Questions to ask

- Does the board clearly delegate authority to management?
- Is there a clear division of responsibilities between the leadership of the board and the executive leadership of the company's business?
- Is there a formal schedule of matters specifically reserved for the board's decision?

---

2 Dodd Frank Act: Wall Street Reform and Consumer Protection Act, Pub. L. No. 111-203, § 929-Z, 124 Stat.
3 Sarbanes Oxley Act: Soxlaw.com. 2015. Sarbanes-Oxley Act Summary and Introduction. [online] Available at: www.soxlaw.com/introduction.htm.

Table 33.1 Board responsibilities for the unitary board

The Unitary (1-Tier) Board	Shareholders	Board of Directors	Executive Board
Strategy and management			
Structure			
Financial reporting and controls			
Internal controls			
Contracts			
Communication			
Conflicts of interest			
Board membership and other appointments			
Remuneration			
Delegation of authority			
Corporate governance matters			
Policies			
Other			

Table 33.2 Board responsibilities for the two-tier board

The 2-Tier Board	Shareholders	Supervisory Board	Management Board
Strategy and management			
Structure			
Financial reporting and controls			
Internal controls			
Contracts			
Communication			
Conflicts of interest			
Board membership and other appointments			
Remuneration			
Delegation of authority			
Corporate governance matters			
Policies			
Other			

- Is it clear that the board is responsible for formally approving interim and final dividends, interim and annual reports, accounts, and communications to shareholders?
- Does the board formally take responsibility for establishing and maintaining the company's purpose, vision, mission and values, and strategy?

- Does the board set a financial threshold above which the chief executive has to obtain board approval for loan capital, capital expenditure, acquisitions, joint ventures, and disposals?
- Is there a clear policy in place with regard to the board's authority to appointment or remove the chief executive, other executive directors, and the company secretary?
- Are board members aware of what is expected of them in terms of their fiduciary duties and legal responsibilities?
- Is there is a clear understanding of where the board's role ends and the senior management team's begins?
- Is there good two-way communication between the board and the senior management team?
- Does the board trust the judgement of the senior management team?
- Has the board discussed and communicated the kinds of information and level of detail it requires from the senior management team?
- Are there clear terms of reference for the board, the directors, and the managers?
- Does the board own the strategic risk register?
- Does the board regularly undertake reviews of its own performance, that of its committees, and individual board members?
- Does the board ensure that the chair conducts a formal annual appraisal of the chief executive?
- Is the board responsible for approval of the overall levels of insurance for the company including directors' and officers' liability insurance?
- Does the board have clear responsibility for major changes to the rules of the company's pension scheme?
- Does the company's annual report contain a high-level statement of which types of decisions are to be taken by the board and which are to be delegated to management?
- Does the board have the authority to obtain outside legal or other independent advice at the expense of the company?
- Is the board clearly responsible for the adoption of significant changes in accounting policies or practices?
- Does the board's "Matters Reserved for the Board" statement include the recommendation to shareholders for approval alterations to the memorandum and articles of association of the company?

- Is it clear that the board is responsible for making any take-over offer for another company or other companies, and considering a response to any such approaches to the company?
- Is the board responsible for reviewing succession plans for the board and senior management of the company?
- Is the chief executive required to obtain board approval of all significant changes to the company's activities including acquisitions or divestments, or entry into a new foreign jurisdiction, or exit from an existing one?
- Is it clearly understood by senior management that the board must be advised of all material litigation either proposed by or commenced against the company, including recommendations for settlement or an alternative dispute mechanism?
- Is the board responsible for recommending to shareholders the appointment or removal of the company's auditors including approval of their fees?
- Is it clear that the board is responsible for considering the balance of interests between shareholders, employees, customers, and the community?

34

SOFT GOVERNANCE

Dr Meena Thuraisingham

The key to board effectiveness and impact

Boards may possess the credentials, qualifications, and skills to govern, but they are only as effective as the quality of interpersonal interactions between the board members.

The process of governing does not occur in a social vacuum. This is the lived experience of non-executive directors (NEDs) who hold multiple directorships and report different experiences in how accountability is practised on different boards, even for similar tasks. Decision-making behaviours are influenced as much by the social factors and context surrounding the decision as by the cognitive demands of the decision. Our research shows that these differences in lived experience are a result of the board group itself representing a *social system* embedded in complex power asymmetries and group identity effects. These social factors shape the use of decision influence and ultimately the exercise of accountability.

Differences in the social reality from board to board create an implicit understanding of the social order of things and can become a self-regulating dynamic. The dynamic exerts subtle pressure for unity, determining what directors choose to do and say in exercising their influence over decisions, and how others' influence attempts are responded to.

Board research and practice associated with board effectiveness have long underestimated the role of human dynamics in and around the boardroom. Hard governance – the more formal instruments of accountability such as regulation, codes, and mandates – while essential because it provides the boundary conditions for good governance to thrive, does not guarantee it. Board dynamics or "soft governance" does.

Soft governance is largely invisible (even to those in the boardroom), poorly understood, and not given the attention it deserves. It is the sum total of the shared history of interactions and ways of working, stated or unstated expectations of directors, and their sense-making of board norms. Several government-sponsored inquiries and commissions have continued to reveal egregious lapses in soft governance both in the UK and in Australia. Recent reviews[1] reveal how the culture of an organisation and its board can undermine its formal governance accountabilities. These findings echo the 2013 findings[2] in which it was observed that "the culture of an organisation can defeat its formal governance."

The dilemmas of soft governance

The work of the director is complex. There are three dilemmas in particular[3] that all directors face, no matter how experienced they are:

- **Informed but heedful**
  Information dilemma (vis-à-vis the very real challenge of information asymmetry): How do I engage with management in a way that ensures I get all the information I need to make decisions, but at the same time retain a healthy scepticism and find other ways to verify and calibrate what I am told? It requires trusting and mistrusting what one is told.

---

1 The 2019 Royal Commission into conduct in the banking and financial services sector led by Justice Hayne.
2 The independent review conducted in the UK by Anthony Salz of Barclays Bank following the LIBOR rigging scandal.
3 Research by R. Roberts, T. McNulty, and S. Stiles 2005.

- **Challenging but supportive**
  Expertise dilemma: How do I use my expertise to provoke the kind of thinking and questioning of assumptions that I think is necessary, but still come across as supportive of management?

- **Detached but involved**
  Role dilemma: As a NED, my relative distance from the day-to-day helps objectivity in what I see, which management, through their closeness to issues, may not be able to see. How do I achieve this without immersing myself in too much detail?

In theory, these dilemmas would be relatively easy to manage because corporate governance is based on the fundamental premise that trust and control are not mutually exclusive, and that a NED can engage in both trust-based and control-based behaviours at the same time. The reality may be harder to achieve as NEDs possess a variety of tendencies or propensities that make them more predisposed one way or another. Skill alone therefore will not help directors navigate the dilemmas of soft governance.

Board capital as the source of a director's influence

A director's background, experience, expertise, and exposure is the source of their identity on the board, characterised here as *board capital*. Far broader than the notion of skill, it is the sum of his or her human and social capital:

- Human capital relates to experience working with diverse and alternative business models; experience working with the diverse strategies needed to make those business models work; experience working with the assumptions underpinning those strategies; and experience working with the variety of consequences of actions taken as a result of those strategies. In essence, human capital relates to a NED's experience working with a diversity of mental models and schema.
- Social capital relates to the social networks and connections acquired through life experience across multiple domains, for example, intergenerational, geographic, educational, socio-economic status, and ideological (one's world view). When engaged in decision-making,

the diversity of NEDs' networks and connections guards against the narrowing of the ideological perspectives and strategic horizons of the board. It provides the NED with better contextualisation skills, especially at a time when the social licence of businesses is being closely scrutinised and the primacy of shareholder value challenged. In essence, social capital relates to the NED's social embeddedness.

Each NED uses an informal and subjective ranking of board capital as an internalised guide to his or her "place" in the group. It is also part of the human condition that we tend to place a higher value on our own career experience, and value the contribution of peers we judge as similar to us. This in turn creates trust-based affiliations and allegiances along board capital lines, generating a power dynamic which predicts how influence attempts in shaping a decision are likely to be mounted and received.

The power hierarchy and its self-regulating character

In the face of a power dynamic, directors are not just passive participants. They don't merely engage in mindless compliance with power structures when required to exercise influence. Instead they engage in conscious and deliberate attempts to gain approval, build rewarding relationships and enhancing self-esteem. Each director at the subconscious level makes an internalised calculation of where he or she sits in this power structure, and the strength of their desire to earn peer respect and acceptance. This internalised calculation shapes how, when, and why they choose to use the voice or remain silent during influencing episodes. Self-censoring divergent views, silencing self-doubt, or undertaking revisions of self-confidence may lead to unjustified support for the views of a powerful director – even when they hold a minority view. It may also lead to higher-power directors subliminally discounting others' contribution, rationalising away doubts or prematurely dismissing counter-positions.

These micro-behaviours create a set of norms and ways of working that advocates and exemplifies "what is acceptable around here," in effect creating the character of the board that becomes self-regulating. It creates pressure for unity and can act as a constraint on "deviant" behaviour because of the desire of a director to fit in as well as earn, retain, consolidate, and grow respect from their peers.

The critical role of director propensities

Faced with the pressure for unity, it requires a fair amount of energy and personal courage to push against powerful individuals and coalitions, and relies on more than the possession of skills or board capital. It relies on propensities to help neutralise the adverse effects of power differentials. In particular, it requires both the *propensity to influence* and the *propensity to be influenced* – and the character strengths these propensities imply. Both these propensities, which imply character strengths such as courage, confidence, fortitude, humility, openness, and candour, must be in balance, especially when facing subtle pressure to conform to the majority opinion. If they are not in balance, independent mindedness is compromised. Added to this is trust propensity: a generalised propensity to rely/depend on others and a faith in humanity shaped early in one's life. It shapes, for example, the degree of healthy scepticism one shows about what one is told.

The skills-based board, which has held sway for decades, is deeply flawed because it ignores the important role that the underlying propensities of directors play. Propensities are deeply wired and take considerable time to change. It requires significant effort to recognise the tendencies that hold us back from being personally effective. Current director selection and board development practices need a rethink.

A typology of culture types and the role of the chair

The chair plays a critical role in ensuring that no one person or subgroup has an oversized influence on deliberations and final decisions. The real challenge facing chairs is how to facilitate agreement and disagreement when faced with a diversity of viewpoints and perspectives. How do they allow robust debate and the proper contest of ideas to thrive, letting a debate run its course while maintaining the psychological safety required for all directors to feel secure enough to disagree with the chair and each other?

A typology of five culture types, shown below (moderated by the effects of power and identity), offers a chair a handy framework which can focus their efforts in improving board culture and managing the associated risks. It is not difficult to see how an overly agreeable board can emerge and how

TYPOLOGY OF BOARD CULTURE AND THE RISKS TO THE BOARD'S COLLECTIVE IMPACT

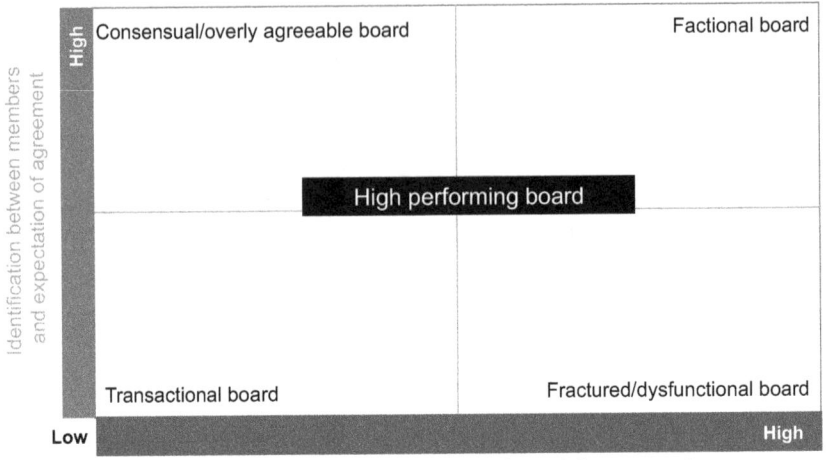

	Low Power differentials and expectations of disagreement	High
High Identification between members and expectation of agreement	Consensual/overly agreeable board	Factional board
	High performing board	
	Transactional board	Fractured/dysfunctional board

Figure 34.1 High-performing board
Source: *Identity, Power and Influence in the Boardroom*, Abingdon, Oxon (Routledge, 2019).

chilling effects on the proper contest of ideas and independent mindedness may materialise.

A board is at its best when there is a healthy equilibrium between the effects of identity and power differentials. When members identify too strongly with each other, the contest of ideas and perspectives becomes less likely, groupthink emerges, and an overly agreeable board develops. The reverse is also true, giving rise to a fractured board. A productive tension between consensus and harmony on the one hand, and dissent and discord on the other, keeps a board dynamic healthy. Directors need to cultivate a taste for both harmony and discord in order to be effective.

Questions to ask

- To what extent is there a shared view on the board that good governance is achieved not only by exercising its duty of care and duty of diligence as prescribed by the law, but also through the quality of interactions and trust-based relationships?

- Does the board have a single shared view of its role in protecting and creating shareholder value, while at the same time aligning with the company's purpose and values? That is to say, are both value and values given equal importance in board deliberations?
- What steps can the board take to ensure there is sufficient cognitive and ideological diversity required to reflect the complexity of the sector it operates in and the broader communities it serves?
- Are individual director contributions drawn from the totality of their commercial experiences, allowing for broader individual contributions beyond a director's specific area of expertise or functional discipline?
- Do the number and scope of the committees reflect the complexity involved in governing the company, and are committee recommendations given diligent consideration by the whole board?
- Do the directors respect and value the distinctive strengths that each brings, actively seeking out and engaging with the views and contributions of each other?
- Are deliberations led in a way that allows all voices to be heard, and do directors feel safe to challenge and disagree?
- How consistently does the chair deal with any single director or sub-group of directors who may have an oversized influence on the direction, content, or pace of board decision-making?
- When faced with a diversity of viewpoints and perspectives, what steps does the chair take to ensure that agreement and disagreement are managed in a way that neutralises the effects of power asymmetries that inevitably exist?
- Are there formal and informal processes created in and around the boardroom to allow members to learn and grow together and reflect on the board's own effectiveness as a group, and is the closed session/in-camera session used for this purpose?
- What steps does the board take to continually refresh and renew its board talent, ensuring it is future-ready in the face of the transformative external forces of change?
- In its board renewal efforts, how much attention is paid to director propensities as compared to skills and experience to allow both consensus and contention to thrive in equal measure?
- To what extent do formal board effectiveness reviews surface and address the undercurrents that impede independent-mindedness, and

what steps does the chair take to systematically address the results of the review?
- How does the board ensure a culture of disclosure exists (over and above simply complying with their legal obligations under continuous reporting regulation)?
- How does the board ensure that management has the same shared view on the underpinning values of openness and transparency?
- How does the board become alert to a "good news culture" that might exist across all management levels?
- What steps has the board taken to ensure informed oversight through the unhindered flow of information between the board and management, characterised by mutual respect?
- How does the board and management ensure the advisers it engages provide advice that engenders trust with its community of stakeholders, rather than simply providing advice on legal protections?
- How does the board ensure that the moral compass used for decision-making is not a relative one, that is, that wrong is wrong even if everyone is doing it, and right is right even if no one else is doing it?
- How does the board ensure that management is viewing all decisions through the prism of public interest and scrutiny? Are *market values* given the same prominence as *market value*?

Part VII

ACCOUNTS

35

ACCOUNTS

Ian Wright

Publication of the annual and interim accounts are a critical component of a board's accountability to shareholders and other stakeholders. The approval and the publishing of the accounts is an activity which cannot be delegated to management or a subcommittee of the board.

Making sure you understand your responsibilities is essential. Generally, directors are individually and collectively responsible for:

- Keeping adequate accounting records
- Preparing financial statements in accordance with laws and regulations
- Selecting suitable accounting policies and applying them consistently
- Making judgements and accounting estimates that are reasonable and prudent
- Preparing accounts on a going concern basis unless it is inappropriate.

Understanding the accounts

It is important to start with a good grounding in the entity's accounts and accounting issues. A board induction programme should include sessions with key persons in the accounts and accounting process such as the chair, audit committee chair, finance director, and financial controller.

Management should provide a written briefing on the topic. The induction process could also include turning the pages on the last published annual report and accounts, discussing significant matters, and reviewing recent audit committee papers.

The board induction programme should include a review of the laws and regulations affecting the entity. In relation to the accounts that may mean specific provisions in company law covering the responsibilities of directors for accounts and any additional requirements in capital market or securities laws and regulations, auditing standards, and governance codes.

Accounting standards

Company law or securities law will likely prescribe the accounting standards that must be complied with. Many countries have adopted International Financial Reporting Standards (IFRS) or IFRS with some limited adjustments, or other similar national standards.

Directors who are not professional accountants are not likely to need a detailed knowledge of the individual standards. However, they should be able to read and understand the parts of the standards that are identified as relevant and ask challenging questions and probe the answers given by management and auditors. Most importantly, directors need to be comfortable with the answers to their questions given by their fellow directors, management, and the auditors.

Documents for review

There should be a number of documents produced leading up to the board's reviewing and approving a set of annual accounts. Some of these documents may be included in audit committee papers as well as board papers, and board members should have access, and the opportunity, to read all of these papers as part of their routine work preparing for a board meeting. The documents should include:

- draft accounts with notes,
- going concern and viability review,

- draft letter of representations required by the auditors from the board,
- accounting papers produced by the executive addressing areas of judgement on selecting and applying accounting policies,
- accounting papers produced by the executive addressing economic assessments such as fair valuations, discounted liabilities, and asset impairment assessments,
- audit plan (including risk assessment), and
- auditor's letter report at the completion of their audit work.

Risk disclosures

Risk disclosures have been a hot topic amongst accounting standard setters and capital market regulators. Whilst specific disclosure requirements may vary by jurisdiction, the annual report should contain the board's assessment of significant financial risks, and the accounts should contain details about the financial market and other financial risks to which the entity is exposed.

Directors will want to review these disclosures and be satisfied that they reflect what worried the board during the year about its finances and its financial reporting.

Whilst some claim that accounting has become overly complicated since IFRS was introduced (so external reporting is different to management accounting), don't be seduced into assuming that's true for your entity. The reality is that for most businesses, what gets reported externally in the accounts should be the same as what gets reported in the monthly management accounts. If you don't recognise the draft profit or loss, ask for a reconciliation comparing the two and for an explanation of the difference.

Eliminating bias

Accounting is designed to portray the results and financial position of the entity concerns in a neutral way, and if there is any bias it should reflect a degree of caution in making estimates and judgements.

Accounting standards are increasingly codifying how transactions and balances should be recorded and measured, but there is often scope to choose from a range of acceptable policies and it's important to know whether in aggregate those choices are neutral, aggressive, or prudent. Ask for a view from the experienced financial professionals. If management feels unable to guide you on whether accounting policies are neutral or not, why not ask for a view from the auditors?

Materiality

The concept of materiality underpins the disclosures required to be made to help shareholders and other stakeholders understand your financial results and financial position. Broadly, something is material if knowledge of it would have an impact on decisions made by shareholders or potential investors.

Generally, materiality is expressed in terms of a small percentage of net profit or net assets. However, accounting standards also explain that something might be material due to its nature rather than just its absolute size. Ask management what is seen as material. The auditors should have explained how they assess materiality in their work in their annual audit planning document.

You may be a director of a simple entity with simple accounting. However, almost all businesses undertake more complex transactions from time to time, and it must be expected that accounting for more complex transactions brings its own challenges. IFRS and other accounting standards require an explanation to be given of significant judgements made when selecting and applying accounting policies. Read the disclosures and make sure you understand the issues described.

Accounting policies

Each significant judgement about the selection and application of accounting policies should be supported by an accounting paper prepared by the executive. Ask for a copy and ask for the chairman of the audit committee to talk you through them. Do any of them seem overly complex and contrived. If so, ask what the alternative accounting policy could be. If the alternative looks simpler, it may be a better one.

Accounting standards and their interpretation do change with time, as does the precise nature of contractual relationships between an entity and its customers, suppliers, and employees. As a result, accounting policy decisions should be revisited regularly. Do not be put off by comments such as "we decided that many years ago," "the papers are in the archive," or "nothing has changed recently."

Some entities appear to have a plethora of accounting policies, many of which are "boiler plate" – text plucked out of the accounting standard. It may be useful to step back and reflect on the policies that are most critical to how profit, and thus the result for the year, is measured.

For many entities, revenue recognition will be the accounting policy that has the most profound effect on reported results, particularly where revenue is generated through a number of service steps. For others, cost recognition can be as important, particularly where costs are incurred well in advance of the provision of services.

Difficult measurement judgements, fair value estimates, and impairment tests

IFRS and other accounting standards have developed with an increased focus on current economics – what things were worth and what you owed, based on the specific conditions in existence at the balance sheet date. That may impact on assets that you must fair value such as stocks and shares and assets that you must test for impairment, such as goodwill and intangible assets. Accounting standards require the assumptions and evidence supporting difficult measurement judgements to be explained in the notes.

Valuing listed stocks and shares should not be difficult as market prices can be obtained quickly. However, models may need to be used to estimate the fair value of assets where active markets do not exist. The measurement objective is to estimate what you could sell them for at the balance sheet date and external inputs should be used for valuation models whenever available. If significant assets are fair valued, you may wish to read the papers on how the valuations have been carried out, taking a special interest in any assumptions.

Impairment tests require future cash flows to be estimated and then the net cash flows to be discounted at the discount rate that would be applied by a potential purchaser of the asset. Note this is not the discount rate that the business might use itself. Directors will have access to cash flow forecasts for at least the next 12 months, which you would expect to be consistent with any impairment test estimates. If the subsequent cash flows show a hockey stick profile, you may wish to ask more questions about how credible those forecasts may be.

Undisclosed commitments and contingencies

Accounting systems struggle to capture commitments and contingencies and as such, future events don't immediately give rise to double-entry booking. It's worth taking a moment to compare what is reported in the notes as commitments and contingencies with your knowledge of the business and to check whether they should be added.

Events after the balance sheet date could give rise to information about assets and liabilities at the balance sheet date where the accounts should be adjusted, or to material matters about the period post the year end but before the date of approval by the board. If the board has been discussing a significant issue in recent weeks, check whether it should be disclosed.

Auditors

Auditors collect the information and explanations that they require in order to form their opinion. Where they find something difficult to verify from independent sources, they may request that the board provide written representations, particularly if the audit evidence has been heavily dependent on representations made by management. The representation letter requested by the auditors should be carefully reviewed and questions may usefully be asked if there is anything unusual.

Governance codes and securities law and regulation vary according to jurisdiction. In most jurisdictions, directors are required to produce accounts that give a true and fair view that presents the results for the year and the financial position of the entity. In some jurisdictions, directors are required to confirm that annual accounts within the context of annual reports are fair, balanced, and understandable.

Once you have read the accounts and explanations as part of the annual report, sit back and consider whether all of the difficult issues discussed by the board in recent months have been properly addressed. If something has not been disclosed, ask why not. If the results don't make sense when compared to what you know about the entity and its transactions, don't stop asking questions until you are content.

Questions to ask

- Do you understand the accounts and accounting policies as well as your responsibilities for the accounts as director of the entity?
- Do you appreciate the accounting standards, laws, and regulations that apply to the entity?
- Do you need to have read and understood all the accounting standards?
- Have you read all of the documents available to you when considering the annual accounts?
- Have you considered and probed the draft financial risk assessments, and do they cover all the accounting matters that the board has spent significant time on in recent months?
- Are the draft annual or interim results similar to the management accounts that you have seen?
- Are the chosen accounting policies neutral or aggressive or cautious?
- Have you thought about what's material to shareholders?
- Have you reviewed and probed the draft disclosures about significant judgements made in selecting and applying accounting policies?
- Have you asked for and read the papers supporting accounting policy choices?
- Have you thought about which accounting policies are the most critical?
- Have you reviewed and probed the draft disclosures about significant measurement matters?
- Are you happy with the assumptions used to estimate fair values?
- Are you happy with the assumptions used in any impairment tests?
- Are you aware of any significant commitments or contingencies not disclosed?
- Have you considered whether all significant subsequent events have been disclosed?
- Have you read what written representations that auditors are asking the board to make – and are you happy to stand behind them?
- Are the draft accounts within the annual report true and fair/presented fairly and is the narrative fair, balanced, and understandable?
- Are there any remaining niggles?

36

EXTERNAL AUDITORS

Helen Gale

The directors of a company are responsible for ensuring that the company's financial statements are prepared in accordance with the applicable financial reporting framework and for overseeing the company's internal control framework. The board of directors may establish an audit committee, as a requirement of law and regulation or as adoption of best practice of good corporate governance. The audit committee is responsible for the appointment of the external auditor, approval of their remuneration and any non-audit service work commissioned. The audit committee is also tasked with challenging the auditor over the quality of their work and ensuring that the auditor's independence is not compromised. It reports on the work done, and the conclusions drawn, in the annual report.

There is certain information that an auditor should routinely provide to those charged with governance in accordance with auditing standards. In addition to these required communications, further detailed questioning will allow the audit committee to more deeply understand and challenge the information presented to them. The audit committee, through its interactions with the auditor and with the other directors and management, has a key role in facilitating a high-quality audit.

DOI: 10.4324/9781003201182-43

Audit timing

Many people have heard of the 5Ps of success Proper Planning Prevents Poor Performance, and this is especially relevant to an audit process. A well-planned audit reaps many benefits, including ensuring that audit efforts are directed at the most significant areas of the audit and improving the efficiency of the audit. A well-planned audit process will also give the directors sufficient time to consider the key areas at the right time in the process.

Directors should liaise with management and the audit firm to ensure that the audit has been properly planned. Questions to assist in this process include:

- What is the audit timetable? How realistic is it and is there flexibility built in to allow time to deal with any unexpected matters arising?
- Is there sufficient time allocated for review of the financial statements by all the parties who need to review the financial statements and other reporting documents?
- Were all deadlines met in the prior year? If not, why and how can the cause of these delays be managed this year?
- When will the work on significant risk areas and critical judgements be performed and reported on, for example at the interim or final stage, or as part of a continuous year-round audit? Will this give the audit committee and management enough time to follow up on any findings?
- What specialists will be involved in the audit and when will the output of their work be reported?

Resourcing the audit

Asking questions about how the audit is resourced provides a lot of valuable information to those charged with governance. It gives directors information to assess the quality of the audit, for example by understanding the extent of use of specialists on complex technical areas or overall partner hours to assess the quality of direction and supervision by the partner. Understanding the audit resourcing also allows directors to understand, and if necessary challenge, the time that is spent on the higher-risk areas and key judgements and how the planned time allocation compared to the actual time spent at the end of the audit. Questions to assist in this understanding include:

- What staff will be allocated to the audit, what areas of work will they be allocated to, and how much time will they spend on each audit area?
- Will there be continuity of staff from the prior year? What knowledge do each of the team members bring?
- What specialists will be used, what areas will they work on, and how much time will they spend on the audit?
- How many hours will the engagement partner spend on the audit and how does this compare to similar audits?
- How can management or the board help with improving the efficiency of the audit?
- How reasonable are the auditor's anticipated hours in relation to the proposed fee based on the work to be performed?

Key judgements

Management makes many judgements and estimates in preparing financial statements, some of which will have a significant effect on the reported results and financial position. Information about the key judgements and estimates made is of value to investors (and stakeholders), as it helps them assess an entity's financial position and performance and understand the sensitivities to changes in assumptions.

- What are the key judgements and areas of estimation uncertainty within the financial statements?
- To what degree is each of the judgements considered conservative or aggressive? How has the auditor assessed this and what information have they used for this assessment?
- How do the judgements and estimates compare to those made by other companies in a similar sector?
- What is the sensitivity or range of possible outcomes, on how changes to estimates could affect the results?
- Could there be improvement to the disclosure in this area, including quantified information such as sensitivities or a range of possible outcomes, on how changes to estimates could affect the following year's results?

Audit scope

The auditor will communicate the significant decisions and judgements they made when setting the audit plan, and further questioning on the audit scope can facilitate a high-quality audit.

- What is the planned scope of the audit and how does it differ from the prior year?
- Will any other audit firms be involved in the audit (for example, auditing subsidiaries of a group). If so, what percentage of assets, revenues, and net income will they be responsible for and how will the audit firm oversee the quality of their work?
- How is materiality determined and why does the audit firm believe that this is an appropriate basis for determining materiality? How does the materiality selected impact the risk assessment and testing to be performed?
- How will the involvement of the internal auditors be coordinated with your audit?
- Do you anticipate any particular problems in this year's audit?

Meeting without management present

The audit committee would normally meet with the auditor without management present at least annually. These meetings allow the audit committee to ask questions on matters that might not have been specifically addressed in the formal part of the audit committee meeting and allow the auditor to provide candid, often confidential, comments to the audit committee.

- What were the key accounting, auditing, or reporting matters that were discussed between you and management?
- Were there any disagreements on these and if so, how were they resolved?
- Did management pressure you on contentious issues by seeking alternative views from other accountancy firms? Could your response on these matters be considered to be a condition of your retention?
- Were any integrity or honesty concerns noted?

Audit conclusions

When the auditor presents their final report towards the end of the audit, the audit committee has an opportunity to ask many probing questions to ensure that they fully understand the findings from the audit and how the audit addressed the significant areas:

- Did the scope of the audit differ from the audit plan?
- Are there any unresolved matters?
- Did you detect any material errors, fraud, illegal acts, or significant deficiencies or material weaknesses in the internal control system?
- Are there any adjustments or disclosure deficiencies that have not been corrected for?
- What factors were considered when assessing the entity's ability to continue as a going concern?
- Was management receptive to any recommendations you made? Were all findings reported by you last year remediated?
- Are there any proposed new accounting, auditing, tax, or reporting rules that will impact the company?

The questions above cover just some of the areas that would be discussed between the auditors and those charged with governance. Whatever particular topic is being discussed, effective communication, active engagement, and probing questioning by those charged with governance will go a long way in facilitating a smooth audit process and a high-quality audit.

37

SOLVENCY AND GOING CONCERN

Heather MacCallum

Assessing solvency and assessing going concern are separate tests that have their own specific criteria. In general the question of solvency is whether an entity will be able to pay its debts as and when they become due and payable. This shouldn't be confused with liquidity, which is the ability to pay current liabilities with current assets. Both liquidity and solvency are important concepts as they both measure the ability of an entity to pay its debts, albeit liquidity has a short-term focus and solvency considers longer-term obligations. An entity is considered to be a going concern unless management either intends to liquidate the entity or to cease trading, or has no realistic alternative to liquidation or cessation of operations. Definitions can vary in law and also by accounting practice applicable to the entity.

Most importantly, it is possible for an entity to be solvent but not a going concern and vice versa. There can be situations which result in insolvent trading not being an offence and indeed the UK government enacted emergency legislation during the coronavirus pandemic which allowed some relaxation in the rules surrounding wrongful trading. Conversely, there may be cases where some entities are insolvent but a going concern. For example, there may be circumstances where a business is fundamentally sound, has forbearance from its lenders, and is able to continue to trade despite being unable to pay suppliers within normal credit terms or meet its debts in the short term. However, as some recent high-profile cases have demonstrated, directors should exercise caution and consider the need to seek appropriate professional legal and financial advice in relation to uncertainties around solvency and going concern.

Solvency

Solvency refers to a business's long-term financial position. A solvent business is one that has positive net worth. That is, its total assets are more than total liabilities. Solvency is most commonly assessed using solvency ratios, which measure the ability of the business to pay off its long-term debts and interest on its debts. Such ratios included interest coverage ratio and debt-to-equity ratio amongst others.

If directors are required to declare solvency in a solvency statement, this generally means 'Does the company have capacity to pay debts which it has incurred as at the time of that declaration?' Directors should also take into account debts which will be incurred in the foreseeable future. Under UK law, directors must have reasonable grounds for believing that the company will be able to pay its debts as and when they fall due. In meeting the reasonable grounds requirement, directors should consider all information relevant to forming their opinion in respect of the solvency statement such as:

- profit and loss forecasts and budgets;
- cash flow budgets including cash balances or overdrafts, the amount and timing of operating cash flows, access to credit lines and undrawn facilities, and the liquidity of non-core investments;
- the timing and amount of payment obligations, supplier credit terms, debt repayment dates, and the end date for any loan repayment or rent holidays, including expected dates for repayment of loans where no repayment dates have been fixed or agreed;
- the ability of customers and borrowers (including related parties) to meet their obligations to the company, including meeting credit and repayment terms;
- the ability to realise current assets such as receivables and inventory;

- known or likely changes in economic and market conditions, consumer behaviours and demand, inventory turnover, supply chains, production processes, and ability to deliver goods and services;
- ability to comply with debt covenants and normal terms of credit, renegotiate debt arrangements, and refinance maturing debt;
- the possibility of withdrawal of financial support by major lenders, debt factoring arrangements, customer supply chain financing, or financial support by a parent company;
- ability of a parent company or shareholders to meet any financial support arrangements;
- the solvency of any entities to which the company has given financial guarantees or offers of financial support;
- the extent and timing of any government support and travel or other restrictions;
- any material contingent or prospective liabilities; and
- any uncertainties affecting the above.

Solvency and going concern key questions

The questions below cover either or both solvency and going concern, and are relevant depending on the type, size, and complexity of the entity.

Financial

1. Is there a net liability or net current liability position?
2. Are fixed-term borrowings approaching maturity without realistic prospects of renewal or repayment?
3. Is there an excessive reliance on short-term borrowings to finance long-term assets?
4. Are there indications of withdrawal of financial support by creditors?
5. Are there any negative operating cash flows indicated by historical or prospective financial statements?
6. Are there any adverse key financial or solvency ratios?
7. Are there any substantial operating losses or significant deterioration in the value of assets used to generate cash flows?
8. How quickly is income converted into cash? Has there been any deterioration? If so, why has that happened?

9. Is there an increasing amount of receivables and what is the age profile? Is there any unallocated cash, and if so, does this indicate an underlying problem within the finance function or payments on account by debtors (or any other reason)?
10. Are there any arrears or discontinuance of dividends?
11. Is there an inability to pay creditors on due dates? Is there an increasing number of creditors and for how long have they been outstanding beyond the expected payment period? Has there been a change in credit terms? Is the age profile of creditors correct?
12. Is there an inability to comply with the terms of loan agreements?
13. If there are cash flow issues, are there any impacts for any other contractual covenants?
14. Is there any change from credit to cash-on-delivery transactions with suppliers?
15. Is there any inability to obtain financing for essential new product development or other essential investments?

Operating

16. Are there any management intentions to liquidate the entity or to cease operations?
17. Has there been any loss of key management personnel without replacement?
18. Has there been any loss of a major market, key customer(s), franchise, license, or principal supplier(s)?
19. What is the risk profile of new clients or contracts and is this a change from previous practice or agreed strategy?
20. Are there any workforce difficulties?
21. Are there any shortages of important supplies?
22. Is there any emergence of a highly successful competitor?

Other

23. If the entity is a financial institution is there any non-compliance with capital or other statutory or regulatory requirements, such as solvency or liquidity requirements?

24. Are there any threatened or pending legal or regulatory claims or proceedings against the entity that may, if successful, result in claims that the entity is unlikely to be able to satisfy?
25. Are there any changes in law or regulation or government policy expected to adversely affect the entity?
26. Are there any uninsured or underinsured catastrophes when they occur?
27. Has there been a substantial decrease in share price?
28. Are there any off-balance sheet commitments or contingencies?

The significance of such events or conditions often can be mitigated by other factors. For example, the effect of an entity being unable to make its normal debt repayments may be counterbalanced by management's plans to maintain adequate cash flows by alternative means, such as by disposing of assets, rescheduling loan repayments, or obtaining additional capital. Similarly, the loss of a principal supplier may be mitigated by the availability of a suitable alternative source of supply. The key question is whether those mitigating factors are realistic, reasonable, timely, and capable of being implemented.

Management's assessment of solvency and/or going concern

In many large organisations, management will draft a detailed assessment of solvency and/or going concern. However, it is important to be aware of limiting behaviours in assessing solvency and going concern such as over-optimism, arrogance, confirmation bias, lack of systemic thinking, or even the challenge of complexity. Key questions which may be applicable include the following:

1. Are the processes to produce supporting information underlying solvency or going concern assessments reliable?
2. Is the information provided consistent with your understanding of the business, the markets in which the company operates, and any other relevant matters?
3. Are the underlying assumptions reasonable? For example, if the business needs further cash or additional funding, have management considered how or where it can be accessed? What assumptions

underlie this and are those assumptions reasonable? Have they been stress-tested? If so, how?

4. Is the range of judgements underlying the assessments too optimistic?
5. How has management considered the impairment of any goodwill and what key judgements underline that assessment? Are those judgements and assumptions consistent with those underlying the assessment of going concern?
6. Is the business model or any part of it flawed. For example, does the entity make a profit or sufficient profit but produce insufficient cash flow? If profit margins are in decline but cash flow improved, does this make sense?
7. Has the business built in any resilience? That is, would it be a going concern under various adverse scenarios? Have those adverse scenarios been stress-tested? If so, how?
8. What is the risk of failure to deliver plans to address any adverse scenarios? Is management able to transform plans into actions if required? What oversight does the board have and is there any follow-through in decision-making which can be undertaken?
9. Is the business prepared for assumptions to be upturned, for example its projected debt refinancing to be unsuccessful? What are the contingency plans and are they realistic? Can they be executed in a timely fashion and what are the obstacles?
10. In terms of challenging the existing assumptions, is there any information that would cause management to change assumptions? If so, what would that information be?
11. Has the business established any early warning indicators for solvency and going concern?
12. Is the business model sustainable? Perhaps only if debts are "taken away"?
13. What's the safety margin and is it mapped and tracked over time?
14. In respect of any tax, legal, or regulatory uncertainties, are there any contingency plans?
15. What is management and/or the board blinded to?
16. Has there been any bad news, and how have the board and management dealt with it?
17. Has management imagined future failure and considered what the warning signs would have been?

On a final note, it's important to note that the risk of insolvency or failing to be a going concern can never be fully controlled or mitigated. Considering an "off-piste" – skiing analogy – one can carry equipment and be prepared for an avalanche, but you can't reduce the risk of an avalanche occurring. However, you can monitor the weather and snow conditions and adapt accordingly. In summary, you can look for the warning signs of an event about to happen and build in resilience to weather the event.

38

INSOLVENCY

Amaechi Nsofor

Solvency for a company is the degree to which its assets exceed its liabilities. Solvency can also be described as the ability of a company to meet its financial obligations and to achieve long-term expansion and growth.

Solvency is generally an important measure of financial health since it is one way of demonstrating a company's ability to manage its operations into the foreseeable future. The quickest way to assess a company's solvency is by checking the equity/value on the balance sheet, which is the sum of a company's assets minus liabilities. An alternative test is the availability of liquidity to meet financial obligations as they fall due.

There are also solvency ratios, which can spotlight certain areas of solvency for deeper analysis.

Many companies experience periods with a negative balance sheet value or an unhealthy quick ratio (liquid assets surplus over current liabilities), which could be signs of insolvency.

A negative balance sheet indicates that a company has impaired shareholders' equity, and this can lead to losses for creditors, business owners, and personal claims against directors. In essence, if a company was

DOI: 10.4324/9781003201182-45

required to immediately close down, it would need to liquidate all of its assets and pay off all of its liabilities, leaving only the shareholders' equity/balance sheet net assets as a remaining value.

Certain events may create an increased risk to solvency, which are key for directors to be aware of and closely updated by the executives. Events like a pandemic, or other unforeseen natural disasters such as flooding or unusually bad weather, can significantly influence the solvency of businesses. The world has been a witness to that during the Covid-19 pandemic, and the impact of climate change is also giving ongoing live examples of the impact it has on the solvency of many businesses.

In addition, changes in laws and regulations can quickly have a negative impact on solvency and rapidly move an organisation towards insolvency. When changes in certain regulations directly impact a company's ability to continue business operations, directors have to act swiftly and keep a very close eye on the solvency situation of the company. Brexit is a good example of a decision that could have widespread impact on many businesses by introducing changes to laws and regulations. It takes businesses a relative long time to change the ways they conduct business, and some are not agile enough to survive widespread changes or sudden shocks and therefore fall into insolvency.

When directors consider whether a company is at risk of insolvency, it is also important to be aware of certain measures used for managing liquidity. Solvency and liquidity are two different things, but it is often wise for directors to look at them together, particularly when a company is potentially insolvent. A company can be insolvent and still generate positive cash flow as well as steady levels of working capital.

While solvency represents a company's ability to meet all of its financial obligations, generally the sum of its liabilities, liquidity represents a company's ability to meet its short-term obligations. This is why it can be especially important to check a company's liquidity levels if it has a negative net balance sheet value/is balance sheet insolvent.

One of the easiest and quickest ways to check on liquidity is by subtracting short-term liabilities from liquid short-term assets (quick ratio). This is also the calculation for working capital, which shows how much money a company has readily available to pay its upcoming invoices/creditors. A company can survive while insolvent for a reasonable time period, but a company cannot survive without liquidity.

Independent business review

If directors find themselves in a situation where a company appears close to entering a distressed or insolvent state, they should consider appointing an external adviser to conduct an independent business review. An external stakeholder, such as the bank or investor, can also call for such a review, which is usually undertaken at the expense of the company. This generally happens when the bank or investors are concerned that the information flow from management is not fit for purpose, or the underlying risks are high so they commission experts in insolvency and finance to establish the solvency and viability of the company.

The adviser should independently assess the business recovery plan the board and executives are proposing to avoid insolvency and determine if the proposed actions are realistic. Sometimes it can be hard for executives and directors to look at the situation at hand from all angles and with the required objectivity.

If directors/stakeholders initiate an independent business review, the directors need to be prepared to provide a range of information. The required information is nothing beyond what should be readily available from any well-run company. It will generally result in a comprehensive report on the company, its business, and its management. The executive management team will be required to take part in the review but may not be part of the final report to the board and/or key stakeholders. This report can also lead to further protective steps, utilising business rescue insolvency tools, to protect creditors.

The below non-exhaustive list shows what an independent business review can include:

- Trading and financial position analysis
- Market place and competition
- Balance sheet and asset values
- Overall risk analysis across the company
- Cash flow projections analysis
- Business strategies/business plan analysis
- Plan for recovery, SWOT analysis
- Management abilities and skills/skill gaps

- Sensitivity analysis on all forecasts
- Corporate structure
- Bank covenants and how they will be met
- External valuation of assets

Red flags to be aware of as directors and stakeholders

It is common for companies to have to cut costs from time to time. However, if a company is tightening its belt excessively in one or more of the below mentioned scenarios, it could be a red flag:

Reduced cash and/or losses – a company that loses money month by month could burn through its available cash quickly.

Debt covenants – at risk of breaching covenants, do the company's revenues generate enough cash to service current debt?

Switching auditors – a sudden change in auditors for no apparent reason will raise a red flag with stakeholders. It can be a sign of a disagreement over the accounts or a conflict with the executives.

Dividend cut – dividend payments to shareholders are usually one of the first items to be looked at in a difficult situation. A board is not likely to cut dividends unless absolutely necessary as it will generally affect the share price/valuation of the company.

Executive team resignations – typically when times are difficult, senior members of the executive management team will leave to take a job at a different company.

Selling assets – a company will generally only sell valuable assets in a situation where they need to raise cash.

Cutting staff benefits – many companies will seek to make cuts to various benefits in difficult times.

The most important thing to do as a director in a difficult situation is NOT to do nothing and NOT to panic. Keep in mind that in an insolvency, directors have a duty to the creditors, not themselves or the shareholders. Therefore, the first thing to do is establish whether the company is insolvent or on the road to becoming so. If directors believe it is, then directors must act to ensure that the creditors' situation is not made worse.

Below are a range of questions that directors should consider asking in a situation where they are concerned with the solvency of the company they serve on the board of:

- What is the definition of insolvency in the jurisdictions the entities are registered and/or operate in?
- What are the fiduciary and other statutory duties of the board?
- What are the individual responsibilities of a director and the collective responsibilities?
- How do the board's duties and duty of care shift from shareholders to creditors as the entity moves through the insolvency curve?
- When is the tipping point after which the board's prime duty of care switches from shareholders to creditors?
- What steps should the board be taking to avoid an insolvency?
- How should the board deal with matters impacting the potential outcome for creditors?
- How should the board deal with shareholders in the run-up to an insolvency event?
- How should the board deal with secured creditors and senior-ranking creditors?
- How should the board deal with other stakeholders, including employees and government?
- Should the board preferentially treat any creditors who rank as a similar class of creditor?
- Are there any further factors for the board to consider in relation to ransom payments and/or critical creditors?
- How often should board meetings be held and should any special processes be adopted at meetings?
- How should the board deal with taking on new credit or extending credit terms?
- How should the board deal with taking cash in advance from customers before supply of services?
- What type of contingency plans should be created by the board facing an insolvency event?
- When should a board consider that the point of no return has been reached and they should throw in the towel?

- What advice should the board be receiving from qualified professionals and when should this be commissioned?
- What investigations into the affairs of the company and conduct of directors are undertaken in insolvency?
- What happens to the role of the board on the appointment of insolvency practitioners?

39

VIABILITY

Steve Maslin

Little has damaged confidence in the capital markets like a sudden and catastrophic loss of shareholder value. The causes may change (tiger economies, accounting fraud, technology innovation, hubris, systemic banking collapse, pandemic), and regulation and oversight have taken off exponentially, but still, we open the financial newspaper pages to see a once famous name disappear almost overnight. How can boards minimise the risk of being the latest casualty?

Financial considerations

Much of the best advice I have received over the years has been the simplest, and nothing has stuck like "there is no long term without a short term." Larger businesses have learned from the 2008 financial crisis and have built up strong cash reserves to withstand further systemic shocks. However, when working with a new board, one of my first areas of focus is to look at the budgetary and forecasting track record. Overuse of exceptional items to meet profit and cash forecasts has been a warning sign in many high-profile collapses for decades, but some management teams do not heed that warning.

When evaluating longer-term financial resilience, boards need to consider over what cycle it is feasible to plan. Research by the Financial Reporting Council (FRC)[1] suggested that when the requirement was first introduced for UK-listed entities to publish a viability statement, boards were typically reporting on a three-year horizon. However, my experience is that internally, boards generally consider a period of five to seven years and sometimes longer.

Providers of capital continually reassess their exposures to certain sectors and individual entities, and it is important that the board continue to examine the likely appetite of investors, lenders, and other capital providers to support their longer-term growth plans and to step in should an unforeseen systemic shock occur. It is a mistake in my view to leave this relationship assessment to the finance team. I have always found that regular engagement with key capital providers gives the board a much more sound evaluation of varying support for the entity's ambitions and where alternative funding relationships need to be nurtured.

Linking viability and risk

Clearly, any viability assessment has to be closely linked to the risk register. I believe it is crucial for the audit committee chair to finds ways of ensuring that the risk assessment process is a dynamic, forward-looking one, and I invariably start a risk dialogue with a "what is on your mind" session with the CEO and key executives. I still hear of too many risk committees where the agenda is primarily a historical assessment of internal audit. The audit committee's private session with internal and external auditors should also be a rigorous discussion as these functions are a valuable external check on management's approach to risk and the source of what risks are concerning comparator entities.

Stress-testing of key risks, now commonplace in financial services, should be a regular feature of any board and risk committee. Stress-testing needs to be more robust than mere sensitivity analysis and embrace how a

---

1 FRC Lab *Risk and Viability Reporting* November 2017.

severe but plausible event could threaten viability. An alternative deployed by some boards is reverse stress-testing, that is, looking at how bad a shock would have to be to threaten the entity's viability and then considering what mitigations can be deployed.

I was lucky enough to witness the media operations room at the London Olympics in 2012. The media provider demonstrated how it was testing its main and back-up systems in real time with mock attacks (national power outage, terrorist incident, fire and so on) to evaluate the resilience of their mitigation plans. As the risk officer put it, asking Usain Bolt to re-run the 100 metres final in a world record time because we lost the feed to 170 countries at the key moment was not an option. It was a great lesson on robust stress-testing.

Purpose and culture

In 2019, Grant Thornton issued research[2] on governance behaviours of the UK FTSE 350 and demonstrated a measurable correlation between good governance and financial performance and resilience. I use this research when evaluating viability as, by logical extension, poor governance behaviour can lead to suboptimal financial performance.

The research highlighted three areas which appeared to underpin this good governance and financial performance:

- Clarity of purpose and a healthy culture that was embedded throughout the entity
- Deployment of robust risk evaluation and mitigation as a value driver, not just a compliance function
- Employment of a rigorous board effectiveness process and acting quickly on the results.

Again, two simple bits of advice I received on clarity of purpose have stayed with me. First was, "if you cannot say that your business is one of the two leaders in its field, you will always be at risk." The CEO who said this continually examined the markets in which his business operated, and investment

---

2 www.grantthornton.co.uk/globalassets/1.-member-firms/united-kingdom/pdf/documents/corporate-governance-and-company-performance.pdf.

was always directed towards services that would be market leading. This did not have to be size-based necessarily, but if another measure of leadership was used, it had to be clearly measurable and demonstrable. Second was a CEO who said, "if your business did not exist, would society invent it?" She was passionate about meeting the Mark Carney test in the wake of the financial crisis. That is, if your business does not show a clear benefit to society, what good is it?

Culture is also a massive part of success and viability. Boards need to be curious about what it really feels like to be a part of the entity, from the reception cleaner to the chair's office and what its people believe is really valued, as this will drive their motivation and behaviour. I have valued the conversations initiated by the more progressive boards in response to recent heightened concerns around race and ethnicity fairness where the experiences of some people are not aligned with those published on the entity's website. These conversations are painful, but necessary, and curiosity about the actual experiences of people is incredibly important in understanding and shaping culture, and thereby building resilience.

Board effectiveness

To build viable entities, the board effectiveness review needs to take a long-term view of skills and experience needs and lead to a plan to fill gaps before they create a problem. I would hazard a guess that most large entities on all key stock exchanges would have IT resilience and cyberthreat high on their risk registers; but how many have built credible experience within the board so that management's response can be challenged effectively?

For listed and unlisted entities, understanding shareholder and potential investor sentiment is an important extension of the board effectiveness review. While I was an audit partner, it always surprised me that gaining an insight into investor sentiment was not hard-wired into auditing standards, and these steps were always a key part of my risk assessment of an entity's viability.

Sustainability

Capital providers are increasingly focused on the entity demonstrating that it has a responsible approach to the environment and use of scarce resources. Following the establishment of the Task Force on Climate Related

Disclosures,[3] entities in sectors such as construction might find that their ability to demonstrate a long-term intention to achieve a responsible environmental approach more of a challenge when trying to access new bank loans than the traditional questions around the business plan.

More recently research published by Bloomberg NEF[4] finds that the Covid-19 pandemic has changed the way investors think of sustainability for the better. The research report states, "Investors are beginning to view companies that prioritize sustainability as more resilient to external shock, making them safer long-term investments."

The power of diverse thinking

I will close by looking at the power of diverse thinking in building resilience and ensuring viability. For me, *Rebel Ideas* by the brilliant *Times* sportswriter and former table tennis Olympian Matthew Syed, is essential board reading when considering viability. This book grabbed my attention when he noted the absence of diverse thinking and challenge as the critical flaw that led to two fatal disasters. First was 9/11, where he put the case that a CIA culture that supposed an elite intelligence service was based singularly on white men with an Ivy League education created a blind spot to the emerging threat of al-Qaeda. Second, was a fatal plane crash, where junior crew members failed to challenge the experienced pilot out of undue respect because, they assumed, he had spotted the emergency signals in the cockpit controls even though it was obvious he was distracted by another problem.

If our primeval sense of tribalism and hierarchy can lead to intelligent and experienced people failing to challenge, even if it places their and colleagues' lives at peril, then we must be open to the danger in the boardroom that even experienced executives and non-executives will fail to challenge sufficiently to avert corporate disaster.

The board cannot maximise the chances of achieving viability unless there is a culture and process of continual, and genuine, challenge.

---

3   www.fsb-tcfd.org/.
4   https://t.co/iYfGp1Zhtc.

Questions to ask

Liquidity

- How reliable are profit and cash forecasts and is there an over-reliance on exceptional items?
- Does management use forward-looking key performance indicators to manage compliance with lending covenants?

Solvency

- How well does the board understand the appetite of key investors and lenders to support future growth and to help to maintain solvency?
- How is the board maintaining a regular dialogue with capital providers to explore mutual business ambitions, outside of the functional finance relationship?

Risk

- What mechanisms are used to ensure that the risk assessment and mitigation is a forward-looking and dynamic one?
- How regularly are risks subject to stress-testing and how rigorous are those stress tests?
- How is the audit committee tapping into relevant experiences of other entities about risks and stress-testing to gain an external perspective?

Purpose

- How does the board ensure clarity of purpose and that purpose is understood by stakeholders inside and outside the entity?
- Can the entity truly claim that each of its business units is one of the two leaders in its market?
- If the entity or individual business units did not exist, would society invent them?

Culture

- How does the board show that it is curious about how well the desired culture is embedded throughout the entity?

- Do our people genuinely exhibit the culture and behaviour that the board desires?

Board effectiveness

- How well are the board, chair, and key committees felt to be working by key stakeholders?
- What will be the key skills and experiences required to achieve plans and challenge business resilience plans over the business plan cycle?

Sustainability

- How well do the entity's plans for a responsible approach to the environment and climate change measure up to other actors in its markets?
- What expectations will key stakeholders (for example, customers, regulators, investors, lenders) place upon the entity over its business cycle?

Diversity

- How does the chair ensure that dissenting views are actively encouraged and the arguments fully explored?
- How regularly are key decisions challenged and debated in the board or relevant committee, or are they routinely nodded through?
- How does the entity explore external views on emerging threats?

Overall

- How has the entity challenged itself that everything feasible has been done to maximise the entity's viability?

The imposition by the FRC for UK-listed companies to publish their viability reports has imposed a helpful discipline – there is nothing like having to commit a plan to writing and subject it to external challenge for driving robust challenge and debate.

40

FINANCE

Jean Pousson

Finance is an essential capability for any executive. Blind reliance on the chief finance officer (CFO)/finance director (FD) and/or other finance professionals will not serve as a defence in any court of law when there are problems. Having said that, most jurisdictions do not expect all directors to be as au fait on finance matters as their financially qualified colleagues, but there are expectations and requirements which have to be met.

The following are a list of questions for boards. The list is not exhaustive, but should nevertheless provide a good, easy, and useful framework. Some are reflective, but many are legitimate questions to ask during the course of a board meeting or outside of the board.

Governance and strategy

Is the board clear as to how the chosen strategy creates value for the shareholders? Is the board at one when the phrase "value creation" is used? What is the relationship with the shareholders? Is the dividend policy aligned with their expectations and the company's strategy?

Although an understanding of the finance impact of strategic decisions is crucial, the board should never forget that corporate strategy drives the finance strategy. Not the other way around.

How influential is the CFO/FD? Is he or she collaborative with colleagues, or does he or she constantly dominate by throwing numbers to make his or her point?

Does the CFO/FD coach other board members on technical matters? Does he or she communicate in clear and easy to understand language? Who appraises the performance of the CFO/FD on technical issues?

How robust are the internal controls? Is the board comfortable about the relationship between the internal auditors and the finance function?

What is the relationship between the CFO/FD and the external auditors? "Combative" or "very friendly" are both worrisome answers. Do the finance people feel relaxed about welcoming external auditors, or is there a feeling of "We need to hide this"?

A clean external audit is not a clean bill of health. External auditors only give you an opinion. They cannot test and verify everything and, in that sense, can provide a certain degree of false comfort. Are external auditors' letters seen by all the board members? Is the entire board comfortable with the materiality test threshold?

Is the audit committee well configured and does it work well within the board? Do the members challenge sufficiently? Is the chair of the audit committee sufficiently influential?

When looking at the risk register, have the risks and impact been monetised? That is, is it clear what the impact on revenues, profits, and cash would be if these items were to materialise?

How quickly are the management accounts produced? In an age of technology, these should not take very long. Are there endless adjustments that need to be made each month/quarter? If so why would that be?

Is the board dashboard fit for purpose? This presupposes that everyone understands the purpose of the organisation! Are the financial and technical items understood by all? Is there a healthy balance of financial and non-financial metrics? Is the reporting on ESG measures in line with good practice? And never forget, what is complicated is rarely useful and what is useful should not be complicated.

Does the CFO/FD communicate in plain and simple language? Does he or she treat simple questions with respect and humility?

Is there a simple corporate structure in place, or is there an intricate pyramid of subsidiaries? Why the apparent complexity? Are the related party transactions (that is, transactions between group companies and/or directors) sufficiently transparent and conducted at commercial arm's length?

Are all board members clear of the avenues to be pursued if they are uncomfortable? Could the audit committee, whistle-blower champion, internal and external auditors be available for counsel if required?

Accounting and financial health

Does the board fully understand all the accounting policies utilised by the company? Could this be easily explained to junior members of staff? Are proposed changes in accounting policies robustly challenged? If the business has not changed, why should the accounting policies change? Numerous accounting scandals have stemmed from this. The board should always treat with healthy suspicion a proposed change in accounting policy which has the immediate impact of improving profits.

The board has collective responsibility when signing off the annual report. Are all the facets fully understood? Does the report comply with the legal true and fair criterion? Are there material or significant post balance sheet items that merit a mention? Is there complete agreement (and understanding) about the adoption of the going concern statement?

Does the tax management regime seem appropriate? Or are the finance folk devoting too much time to reducing or deferring corporate and other taxes? Is the company's effective tax rate in line with peer competitors and previous periods? Where is the tax advice coming from?

Could any director speak comfortably about the financial health of the business? Are professional reviews from debt rating agencies and other similar bodies regularly discussed at board level?

A simple way to summarise a company's financial performance is by addressing the following variables: growth, profitability, efficiency, gearing, and liquidity.

Growth

Have revenues grown? What is driving the growth? Has the mix changed and is it likely to change further? Is that growth sustainable? Is the board comfortable with the forecasts being presented? Are they in line with solid strategic and resource analysis? Are there any dependencies on one customer or industry? Is there a risk mitigant in place, that is, no one customer to make up more than x% of revenues?

Profitability

Is the business profitable? What is driving the levels of profitability? Is profitability per product, per division, or by which other metric appropriate for the business well defined?

Are all the profit margins fairly stable year on year and going forward? Are they acceptable for this type of business? What about the returns on equity and the returns on capital employed? Do they represent a good return on the capital provided? How does that compare with the company's own cost of capital (often called the weighted average cost of capital)?

Are the costs allocated as they should be? Is the board comfortable with the company's costing system? Have all expenses grown in line with increased activity?

Where is the business trading vis-à-vis its break-even point? By how much would revenues have to decline for a profit to turn into a loss? What is the level of operational gearing? A high level of operational gearing (that is, high percentage of fixed costs versus variable costs), makes the business vulnerable to sudden downturns or revenue contraction. However, profitability will be enhanced once the break-even point is exceeded. By contrast, a business with a low level of operational gearing (that is, low percentage of variable costs), is more flexible and can withstand a downturn better but would not achieve the same levels of profitability.

Are the interest charges (finance costs) well covered by the level of profits? Remember, cash matters for repayment and debt servicing. Are the finance costs in line with the borrowings? That is, a simple check is to compare the charge in the income statement against the loans as stated in the balance sheet.

Does the corporate tax charge look adequate? This is a charge and not necessarily the amount actually paid out to the tax authorities. The statement of cash flow is more instructive on that one.

Efficiency

Is the business using all its assets productively? Is the asset level in line with the nature of the business? Are the assets owned or leased? Check on the depreciation policy: Are the valuation criteria justified?

What is the policy on asset replacement? How are decisions made? What are the methods used?

The board should distinguish between discretionary and non-discretionary capital expenditure. Some assets have to be replaced; otherwise, product/service quality drops and the business suffers.

What does the working capital position look like? Is it an unnecessary drain on the cash flow, or is it well managed? Managing inventories, trade payables (debtors), and trade payables (creditors, suppliers) is important as a slight deterioration can cause a significant cash outflow if the business is sizeable.

Gearing

Sometimes referred to as financial leverage, gearing assesses the amount of debt that a business has raised. There are a number of different ways to calculate this, but in essence it is about comparing the debt levels against a number of parameters.

What is the business gearing percentage (that is, interest-bearing debt expressed as a percentage of equity)? Have all liabilities been considered (for example, a pension deficit, a guarantee given, a financial commitment and so on)? Does the board have a gearing policy? The measurements by themselves are just indicators. What is more important is to see the trends over a period of time. Why has the company borrowed? Typical reasons would be to finance a loss, to fund working capital requirements and capital expenditure. Borrowings could also be raised to pay dividends, make an acquisition, fund a capital restructuring, and so on. What about the utilisation? How much more could be drawn down at a moment's notice in line with current borrowing facilities?

What about financial flexibility? Could the business raise additional capital at relatively short notice if pushed? Cash flow is not a reason to borrow. A lack of cash flow is a result of other activities!

Once the rationale for the borrowings has been ascertained, the obvious question is: Can the business afford to service the costs and repayments? Only a full cash flow analysis will reveal this. Have all debt repayments been stress-tested? That is, what if there was an interest rate shock? What if there was a business shock, that is, a drop and/or delayed revenues, loss of a big client, unexpected cost, and so on? Could the debt repayments still be made?

Is the management of banks and other financiers well in hand?

Liquidity

Cash is king. You will only run out of cash once! Sales are vanity, profits are sanity, and cash is reality. These statements have held sway for decades and will continue to do so.

Does the board understand the difference between profits and cash? Does the board understand the cash flow drivers and the cash conversion cycle, that is, how profits eventually turn into cash?

EBITDA ((earnings before interest and tax, add back depreciation and amortisation) is widely used in business and has developed a following. It is a measurement which is a rough proxy for cash flow. It is not free cash flow. Free cash flow is the cash left over (if any) after all cash outlays have been taken into account. Could any board member walk through the statement of cash flow with bankers and other financiers if they were asked to comment on the business liquidity? If ever in doubt, the banking records do not lie. Do they reconcile with internal cash flows provided? Is the business cash positive or cash negative? If cash flow is negative, why? How was the deficit funded? When will this position become positive? A business cannot be cash negative forever.

My final few thoughts are perhaps aimed at individual directors. Do not be fooled by the apparent simplicity of these comments. They are very powerful:

Trust your instincts? No! Obey them! If something doesn't feel right it probably is not right. A good director is tenacious and will never rest until he or she gets a satisfactory answer.

Large profits that you don't understand are far more dangerous than losses that you do. If it looks too good to be true, it probably is. So, question and question again. As a director, you are well within your rights to ask and ask again. And don't ever be satisfied with answers such as "It is for tax reasons," "It is strategic," "We can't afford this," or "It is for legal reasons." A good CFO/FD would never hide behind such vague responses.

Part VIII

COMPLIANCE AND RISK MANAGEMENT

41

COMPLIANCE

Charlotte Valeur

Increased scrutiny from regulators and enforcement agencies has prompted boards to take a more active interest in their organisations' compliance programmes. It should be expected that board members will ask questions about the compliance information presented. A board presentation that doesn't raise questions isn't necessarily an indication of all being well. Instead, it could be a signal that more education of the board members is needed to increase compliance awareness.

To increase the likelihood of a constructive and meaningful dialogue about the compliance programme, directors should know what they are looking for and why they are looking for it. Organisations should have a clear vision on the role and importance of having a comprehensive compliance programme. Understanding the organisation's compliance programme needs to be second nature for boards, in the same way that understanding the finances has become second nature.

Developing a culture of compliance within an organisation is an important part of running any business. Many boards lag behind in taking an active part in building a culture of compliance. It is easy for leaders to become overwhelmed by the risk exposure of their businesses.

DOI: 10.4324/9781003201182-49

Organisational culture is set from the top and cascades down, and directors must make compliance a standard at board level. Training is essential to ensure the development of a culture of compliance from the top to the bottom of the organisation.

The need for boards to build a culture of compliance is increasingly critical. Having unresolved compliance issues, yet to be discovered by a regulator, for example, is an uncomfortable situation for any organisation and its board to find themselves in. However, even more so is a violation uncovered by a regulator that the organisation is then forced to deal with. Compliance issues can also become serious when an organisation is involved in a merger or acquisition. In these circumstances any compliance issues will be red flags that can effectively stop a deal from closing.

Developing a culture that supports compliance is a meaningful way to avoid compliance issues. The ever-increasing volume and complexity of regulation globally will not go away, so developing a culture of compliance and risk management is imperative for any organisation. Due to this increasing complexity, organisations are having to move away from using a box-ticking approach to making the whole organisation embrace compliance and risk as a natural ongoing part of doing business every day.

Developing this compliance culture rests with leadership. The board must both set the standards for a culture of compliance, and then communicate them to the rest of the organisation. Managers develop and influence culture through their own behaviours and expectations of the staff they manage. There have to be consequences when poor behaviour is exhibited, not just with regards to compliance but in general and across the business. At the same time, it is also possible to reinforce a compliance culture through ensuring that remuneration provides the right incentives to support behaviours that reinforce a compliance culture. Other ways to reinforce a compliance culture can be using positive ethical communications that consistently set moral standards and help employees make the right decisions and display the right behaviours.

It is a part of the director's fiduciary duties in most countries to ensure that executive management has a compliance programme in place, exercising oversight of this programme and staying informed as to the programme's content and operation. A compliance failure can lead to serious consequences for the organisation reputationally, operationally, and financially; therefore, monitoring compliance is a critical part of risk oversight and should be treated as such.

The board's role in oversight of an organisation's compliance programme is important to the success of the organisation. This starts with expertise on the board. Does the board have a compliance expert on the board? If not, the board should have access to an independent subject matter expert to support the board in discharging their duties in this area. The role of the compliance officer should include reporting to the board on a regular basis and as appropriate. The compliance officer should have open and unrestricted access to the board without fear of repercussions.

A board should not only ensure a compliance programme is in place but also actively oversee that function. It is a key function that gives the board members the necessary assurances that they need to discharge their duties. Compliance oversight is not something the board can engage outside advisers to support them with. Outside advisers can support the board in monitoring compliance risks, ensuring all relevant areas of compliance is being monitored, and assessing whether existing compliance procedures and processes are appropriate and how they might be improved. Should a serious compliance breach occur, the board should consider engaging an independent organisation or individual to investigate all issues involved with the breach.

An effective compliance programme requires involvement and commitment from senior management, an effective communications system, and an ongoing monitoring system. This is to ensure an organisation-wide adaptation of the compliance programme.

Questions the board should ask about compliance

- Does the board set the tone from the top on the importance of compliance?
- Does the organisation have a clearly stated and formal vision for compliance?
- Has the board approved the strategy for the compliance function to meet its objectives?
- Are there mechanisms in place to measure the performance of the compliance function?

- Does the organisation have a dedicated compliance officer?
- Is the compliance function resourced appropriately?
- How is the compliance programme structured and who created it?
- What is the state of the compliance programme and how is it evolving?
- What do our compliance reporting processes look like?
- Is the board knowledgeable about the content and operation of the compliance programme?
- Do the directors exercise reasonable oversight of implementation and effectiveness of the compliance programme?
- Does the board hold private sessions with the compliance functions on a regular basis?
- Is the compliance programme covering all appropriate areas of compliance?
- Does the organisation's culture support compliant behaviours?
- What does the organisation do to ensure employees are trained in compliance?
- What does the organisation do to ensure the board members are trained in compliance?
- How often should the board receive compliance updates and assurances?
- What process is in place to keep the board informed on compliance issues?
- What process is in place to address potential compliance issues?
- What is the process for employees to be able to raise compliance issues?
- Do we have a whistle-blowing procedure in place for anonymous complaints/reporting of compliance issues?
- Who manages whistle-blowing? (executives/audit committee members/board members?)
- How are compliance risks managed and assessed?
- How often is the compliance programme reviewed and updated to ensure it covers all legal and regulatory changes?

42

CYBERSECURITY

Anjola Adeniyi

No matter where you are located in the world or what type of organisation you serve, cybersecurity is an increasingly complex area, and organisations need either to employ staff who have adequate skills and knowledge or, recognising that there is a global shortage of such skills, ensure that security staff acquire and maintain appropriate skills.

An organisation's board is responsible (and accountable to all its stakeholders) for the framework of standards, processes, and activities that, together, secure the organisation against cyber risk. All boards should be aware of the cyberthreat landscape and should understand what advanced persistent threats are.

Organisations need to develop cyber resilience, via a continuum of tested processes that enable an appropriate response to incidents of all sizes, including those which escalate and threaten the survival of the organisation itself.

The sections below cover the key topics and related questions to ask that are pertinent for directors to be mindful of.

Critical data and assets

Cyberattacks have the potential to be as destructive as major natural disasters. The board needs to have clarity on which of the organisation's data and assets are strategically critical. All assets don't deserve or need the same level of protection. While it would be good to be able to protect everything within security environments, often the truth is that resources needed to do so are out of reach for many companies – and strategic assets absolutely require the most attention.

- Has management defined and located its "crown jewels," that is, critical assets (data and technology systems) which it needs to protect from a cyberattack?
- Where possible can you put a financial value on the data?
- Where do the crown jewels reside, and are they in more than one location? This can be relevant when considering who has access.
- Who has access to the crown jewels, and how are they accessed?
- What controls are in place for protecting the crown jewels, and how do we know they're effective?

Third-party relationships

Cybersecurity vulnerabilities within your third-party suppliers, and vendors, can put your organisation at risk. According to specialist research by the Ponemon Institute,[1] "37% of respondents do not believe their primary third-party vendor would notify them if it experienced a data breach involving sensitive and confidential information. Worse, 73% of respondents do not believe an Nth party vendor would notify them if they had a data breach."

It is still common for organisations to have weak third-party cybersecurity management, with a low budget allocation.

- Does the organisation have appropriate policies, and processes in place for managing cybersecurity risks with partners and third-party suppliers?

---

1 Data Risk in the Third-Party Ecosystem by Ponemon Institute, 2016.

- Does the organisation ensure its partners and suppliers have appropriate policies, and processes across their partners and suppliers?

The board should ensure that third parties have similar arrangements with any downstream organisations being worked with. Data controllers must choose a data processor that provides sufficient guarantees about its security measures. The processor should undertake the same security measures that you would have to take if you were doing the processing yourself. Data controllers may have to audit and inspect the processor, either yourself or an authorised third party.

Awareness and training

The organisation should have a security awareness training programme, and all employees should take the training and test regularly. The training and awareness programme should be relevant to an individual's role such that those with higher-risk roles are given training and awareness at the appropriate level. Some individuals will handle customer data, another may handle sensitive commercial data, and finance functions may be vulnerable to social engineering and fraud, while others may just require general security awareness.

- Does the organisation educate its employees on their role in relation to cybersecurity?

Breach response

The organisation should plan, prepare, and rehearse for a successful cyberattack/data breach. Sample scenarios can be: what do you do if competitors access your IP/trade secrets/critical data? How do you reassure customers if their data is stolen? Everyone, including board members, should understand their roles and responsibilities in a response scenario, expectations from the regulators, law enforcement, customers, and other stakeholders.

It is very common for boards and executives to feel blindsided when a data breach occurs. Keeping abreast of all major cybersecurity incidents and data breach attempts can go a long way and as well as being aware of your top cybersecurity risks. The definition of major will depend on the industry, and the organisation.

- Does the organisation have a robust incident response programme/crisis management programme?
- Does the board keep track of its data breach attempts – successful/unsuccessful?

Budget

- What percentage of the total revenue is the cybersecurity budget, and how does that compare to other companies – by industry, geography, size?
- What percentage of the IT budget is the cybersecurity budget, and how does that compare to other companies – by industry, geography, size?
- What other departments maintain a security budget, and how does that compare to other companies – by industry, geography, size?
- What's the percentage of security budget in those departments, and how does that compare to other companies – by industry, geography, size?

Security strategy

The board should set the parameters for selecting a security framework, and the framework should reflect how those parameters evolve. Below are some of the widely accepted industry frameworks:

- ISO27001 – focuses on legal, physical, and technical controls, and is often requested by customers who already use ISO in other aspects of their business.
- COBIT – a framework emphasising information governance and enterprise risk management.
- NIST – for US government agencies; however, it is used by the private sector and is probably the most mature security framework currently available.
- HIPAA – for the health-care industry
- PCI DSS – for payment data

The organisation may be going through digital transformation, expanding into new markets, or approaching a merger and acquisition. The security strategy should support your business initiatives, and their associated risks should be part of your security strategy.

- Does the organisation use a security framework?
- Does the cybersecurity strategy link with the business objectives?
- Does the organisation's cybersecurity programme account for internal and external threats?
- Does the organisation have a system in place for insider threats?
- Does the board discuss with the chief information security officer (CISO) their key cybersecurity issues, roadmap/strategy, current projects, budget?
- Does the board review the independently produced annual cybersecurity assessment?

Annual financial audits add credibility, promote transparency, and accuracy to the reported financial position and performance of a business. In the same sense, it is considered good practice to have regular independent cybersecurity assessment of an organisation. The annual cybersecurity assessment should cover all cybersecurity domains, identify vulnerabilities in the organisation's cybersecurity programme and, depending on the organisation, it should be from an independent source.

The board must require management to provide an independently produced annual cybersecurity assessment report, in a language accessible to the board. The cybersecurity assessment should evaluate: the security teams, IT and cyber governance, reporting relationships, security controls, security awareness training, and comparisons with the industry and organisations of similar sizes in other industries.

- Does the organisation understand the data privacy laws in all its geographies?

These laws can vary from one geography/jurisdiction to another, with details on the definition of a data breach, and reporting requirements also varying. General Data Protection Regulation requires companies and organisations to report a cyber breach or incident within 72 hours, and notify individuals and data protection authorities.

- How often does the board meet with the CISO?

The board should meet with the CISO, at least annually. Such meetings are an opportunity to understand key issues from the CISO's perspective – security issues, budget, political agendas, as well as discuss the security strategy. The board should set annual improvement expectations on various parameters, including incident response time and levels of compliance with the cybersecurity framework.

- Does the organisation have an established relationship with the appropriate authorities on cybersecurity?

The board should ensure that management has established relationships with the appropriate local and national authorities who are responsible for cybersecurity. Such bodies may include:

- National Cyber Security Centre
- Information Commissioner's Office
- Government Communications Headquarters
- Action Fraud
- National Crime Agency
- Scotland Yard
- Ministry of Defence
- Federal Bureau of Investigation
- Interpol

In some organisations a CISO may report through the chief information officer (CIO), which may create a conflict of interest where the CIO may be interested in operational performance or cost-cutting. Also, having the CISO reporting via the Legal, chief risk officer (CRO), or chief financial officer (CFO) may divorce the CISO from the IT areas. In an ideal scenario, the CISO should have independence with access to the board. It's important the CISO works with the CRO, CIO, chief operating officer (COO), chief privacy officer, chief digital officer, head of businesses and various functional leads. The CISO's reporting line should be considered on the industry and the organisation's dependency on technology. Typically, the higher one is in an organisational hierarchy, the greater influence one has on implementing policies and culture change.

Is the CISO reporting at the appropriate level within the organisation, and how does this compare with the industry and the organisation's dependency on technology – via the CIO, general counsel, COO, CRO, CFO, chief executive officer?

Risk

- Does the board meet with the CRO, at least annually, to discuss how the cyber risks are treated? As part of the day-to-day running of the organisation, management may accept risks which the board may be unaware of.
- Does the board verify the cyber insurance coverage is sufficient to address potential cyber risks?

The board must ensure the cyber insurance policy is sufficient to address the potential cyber risks, by asking management to understand the potential impact of a data breach. The global average cost of a data breach per record is $144, the UK Average is $123, and the UK average cost per data breach incident is $3.10M.[2]

- Is the board aware of the organisation's top five risks in relation to cybersecurity?

The board should require management to provide information on the threats, actors, and their possible methods as well as the major breaches that have happened in the market/industry, and how their defences compare.

- How do you compare with your industry peers?
- Does the board monitor annually whether the enterprise risks relating to cybersecurity are improving or not? The board must monitor enterprise risks related to cybersecurity if they are improving or not from year to year and set expectations for them.

---

2 According to *Cost of a Data Breach* report by Ponemon Institute 2017.

Skills and leadership

Board directors are required to apply the constructive challenge to cybersecurity matters as they do to board discussions on strategy and performance. The board may want to consider additional directors who can bring in cybersecurity skills where needed. The current skills gap in cybersecurity may hinder this, and there are schools of thought against directors with a single functional skillset. Where possible, a board may benefit from a cybersecurity leader who has strong business acumen and can fulfil the role of a non-executive director whilst having a strong cybersecurity skill level. Other options include having access to independent cybersecurity consultants, and director-level training on cybersecurity.

- Does the board have members with a technology or cybersecurity skill?

43

IT GOVERNANCE

Tony Fish

"Finance for the non-finance leader" is the framing for this chapter and I am therefore presenting this as "IT governance questions for non-IT leaders." It will guide those who are willing, keen, and supportive of their peers in the complex decisions that IT demands, through questions and not judgement. IT governance is one of the latest additions to the corporate governance agenda and is not as mature as finance or legal. In short, IT governance enables an organisation to:

- sustain and extend the organisation's strategies and objectives;
- demonstrate that IT is aligned with delivering broader business goals;
- meet all relevant legal and regulatory obligations, including compliance with public listing rules or requirements; and
- assure stakeholders they can have confidence, faith, and trust in an organisation's IT services.

I have left off a link to improving return on investment, financial returns, and efficiency as these measures tend to limit the scope of IT governance to a finance dimension, ignoring the human cost.

The media continually promotes the outcomes from errors in IT oversight as data leakage, outage, and cyberattacks. Each story becomes a new case study, with highly sophisticated attacks being defensible only after the event. IT governance remains itself fixed in a cycle of identifying the problem after the event, learning fast how to adapt, and finding whom to blame for the unimaged event. IT governance lacks the prestige of financial governance and audit, and the budget of legal and regulatory compliance, yet without our IT systems, companies are simply unable to function. As IT has become increasingly sophisticated and specialised, it has often left one person both recommending and making the decisions that a board should agree together. Since the level of detail, technical language, and implications affecting and effecting every aspect of the business is so complex, many leaders find they are unable to operate at the level of detail needed to add value and in such a way that it does not result in frustrating the decision-making processes or a loss of respect. Sometimes it is easier to talk about anything else other than IT. This chapter focuses on how to support those who are accountable for IT governance in their role. IT governance concerns layers of increasing complexity and interdependency. IT governance embraces at one end the integration of discrete hardware, software, and embedded systems and solutions. At the other end, IT governance encompasses how the internal systems depend on third-party solutions and eco-system integration, which has a dependency on the company's own internal resources; those in the eco-system and the interface to and with the customer. Within the simple scope, IT governance demands that:

- a leadership team can verify, test, and trust all third-party suppliers, their systems, their third-party supplier, and all processes, to at least the same level you demand of yourselves continuously;
- other leaders in your eco-system believe you are able to deliver the same verification, test, and trust level to them;
- you can understand the limitations and biases of your internal development and integration and accept, manage, and communicate the risks;
- you understand your peers and staff, their motivations; contexts; and behaviours; and
- the data that you have, and use does not create bias, prejudice, or misleading recommendations.

IT governance possibly demands the widest variety of skills outside of the core disciplines (finance, legal, marketing, operations) and includes: anthropology, sociology, behavioural sciences, economics, moral philosophy, coding, computer science, data science, power planning, physics, building design, and IT. To explore the diverse skills requirements by example, we should ask, "what is your password policy?" It is perfectly possible to make a system 100% secure; however, it will be unusable. There are necessary compromises between usability and security that every board member needs to agree on, understand, and appreciate sincerely. Setting a password management policy too high means that users will write them down; a policy of updating a password too often will lead to bypass, where a user will forward to a personal useable off-system account, or too weak a system, and passwords are easily broken. Taking away your employees' agency with draconian policies means you undermine your core values. Giving employees to much control leads to security breaches. Monitoring staff use of IT creates distrust. IT governance needs a leadership team who can debate these complicated issues without becoming righteous and argumentative. IT always becomes personal and is based on our own preferences. As a second example, "Which design philosophy and policy does the company follow?" Design for security, design for use, design for privacy, or design for the customer first? In reality, probably all four are valid in different areas, but what gaps are created, and where and what are the compromises and risks from different ideals?

IT governance is about

- creating policies that align to, and with, core values;
- balancing risks, understanding the compromises, and being able to explain them;
- aligning design philosophies across the company operating functions;
- delegating what to whom and why;
- continually learning, refining, and updating; and
- responding to a crisis.

IT governance is not about

- agility, which technology, which platform, or whose software;

- security breaches, hacking, permissions, cyberattacks, or root passwords;
- cost allocation, budget controls, and that scale is very hard;
- humans being in the loop, even though this will always remain an IT governance nemesis;
- compliance, procedures, processes, and methodologies;
- development tools, controls, or outsourcing; or
- your personal problems with login, software choices, or phone providers, however important you feel they are.

Questions to support full board engagement for better IT governance

Skills

- What IT skills do we have at this table?
- How do we assess sufficiency in skills?
- Are there any gaps?
- Are we focused on IT governance or IT compliance, and do we know the difference?
- Do we have the skills/resources to cope with every possible IT crisis?
- Will our response to a crisis be good enough?
- Are we able to explain automated decisions made by our IT system?

Alignment

- How are we sure that our IT can deliver our vision and strategy?
- How sure are we that our IT will deliver our vision and strategy?

Policy

- What IT governance/compliance policies do we have?
- Do our IT policies align to and with core values?
- What is our risk profile for IT?
- Is our risk profile for IT aligned to other risk profiles?
- How are we checking that we are genuinely measuring and balancing the risks?

- Who has delegation authority for what IT-related decisions and why?
- How are we understanding and communicating the compromises?
- Is our communication good enough on compromises to stakeholders?
- Do we use our controlled IT environment/platform for everything, or do we depend on something outside of the system (for example, spreadsheets) for control, management, and oversight?
- Is our policy and approach to IT sustainable?

Design

- What design and control philosophies do we have/use?
- What design/control frameworks are we using and why?
- How do we know our philosophies and framework are aligned?
- Do we know what bias is in our philosophies and framework and what the implications or unintended consequences are?
- How do we know we are continually learning, refining, and updating to improve?
- How do we decide on what IT support, tools, and services we use, service, or provide?
- What level of automation do we have, and are we aiming for?
- Who tests the testers, who controls to controls, who questions the alignments?

Data

- What is our data policy and how many do we have?
- What is our data philosophy?
- Do our data philosophy, privacy, and controls align with our values?
- Do we know what bias is in our data, and what the implications are?
- What assurance do we have that information and analysis presented for decisions is true and linked to a source for future reference and checking?

44

FINANCIAL PERFORMANCE MANAGEMENT

Virginia Bombín Moreno

Performance management is about identifying the right short-term key performance indicators (KPIs) to be monitored and measured over time, to evaluate performance and trends, to ensure the organisation is driven towards relevant long-term goals in order to accomplish its mission and maximise value creation.

It is an ongoing process that should be constantly reassessed and improved to ensure the right fit between strategic and business decisions and meeting value creation expectations. Finding the right mix of short-, mid-, and long-term metrics alignment, to boost performance efficiency towards clear financial and business goals, is key.

Economic value

From a financial perspective, the economic goal of an organisation is to maximise its economic value over time. Economic value is based on the future long-term capability of a firm to generate free cash flows from operations, being supported by the appropriate capital structure that minimises the cost of capital with a moderate level of risk, so that the return on invested capital overcomes the cost of capital.

Free Cash Flow from Operations over time is a key metric as it drives the business's intrinsic value. Interestingly enough, free cash flows from operations are determined by the revenue growth rate and the return on invested capital under the following relationship:

Growth rate = ROIC × Reinvestment rate ⇒

Free Cash Flow from Operations = EBIT × (1 − tax rate) × [1 − (growth rate / ROIC)]

Hence, the following parameters will have to be targeted and monitored over time to ensure expected free cash flows from operations will be generated and value created as planned.

- Revenue growth rate
- Gross and Earnings before interest and tax (EBIT) margin
- Return on invested capital (ROIC)
- Operating working capital requirements to grow
- Net capital expenditure requirements to grow
- Effective corporate tax rate

Cost of capital as a risk metric

Projected free cash flows from operations are discounted at the cost of capital to determine the firm's intrinsic value. The cost of capital is made up of the weighted average cost of debt and equity after tax, as shown below:

$$\textbf{Cost of capital} = \text{Cost of debt} \times (1\text{-tax rate}) \times \frac{\text{Debt}}{\text{Debt} + \text{Equity}} + \text{Cost of equity} \times \frac{\text{Equity}}{\text{Debt} + \text{Equity}}$$

44.1

On top of the interest rate policy and the market situation, the cost of debt is affected by the business operating risk. Operating risk is dependent on the recurrence of revenue, the cost structure, and the gross and operating margin volatility. The cost of equity is affected by the debt-to-equity ratio.

Hence, the cost of capital is also one of the relevant metrics to be determined and monitored over time. Increases in the organisation's operating and/or financial risk will raise the cost of capital. Increases in the cost of capital will cause a negative impact on value.

Competitor performance

Competitor performance and strategy become another pertinent set of inputs and data for a board, as relative value drives a firm's market value as much as its own intrinsic value. Hence, benchmarking relevant financial indicators against those of peers is a useful source of high-quality data, when available.

Regarding performance management, the first step is to identify the right short-term KPIs that support the long-term strategic goals and to build a financial dashboard. A **financial dashboard** should provide enough high-level data to the board, for members to draw a general picture as to how the organisation is performing towards value creation in the short, mid, and long term. It should also include enough detailed data in different appendices for the members to drill down into any of the high-level indicators, to reach root-based conclusions.

- Does the dashboard provide a high-level view of how the main short-term financial goals are being achieved in a one-pager? *Short-term goals should ensure long-term goals will be met.*
- Does the dashboard provide data to monitor the different value drivers' performance and trends, at consolidated, regional, and product/service/brand portfolio level?
- Does the dashboard include current versus target for all the indicators on the different periods of time that are being tracked?
- Does the dashboard include an annual one-page peer analysis on the main value drivers' performance to identify areas of improvement and inner strengths?

FINANCIAL PERFORMANCE MANAGEMENT   273

1. **Revenue growth** is one of the key value drivers. In order to increase economic value over time, organisational growth must be accomplished.
   - What is the target size of the company in five years' time, in terms of consolidated revenues?
   - What is the annual growth rate that needs to be achieved on the way to accomplishing the long-term goal?
   - What are the main revenue streams at product/service/brand/regions level?
   - Have they been categorised accordingly to where they are in the life cycle, as high growth, mature growth, stable, and declining?
   - Have specific growth rates been established for each of the main revenue streams that ensure the annual consolidated revenue growth rate is achieved?
   - Is there enough available information to the board to determine if the overall situation is appropriate and fits with the mission and economic goals in the short, mid, and long term?

   Growth drivers: What are the key growth drivers for the organisation to reach its target revenue growth rate?
   - Is it expanding the annual customer ticket as the business competes in a mature market?
   - Is it scaling the number of customers as the segment or region is currently expanding?
   - Is it leveraging current facilities through online channels to improve return on invested capital?

   Customer engagement and satisfaction: Most successful growth companies are those that are very close to their customers. Therefore, an organisation should be capable of identifying its growth value drivers within its strategy.
   - Have the right metrics and channels been identified to keep a close eye on customers' feedback and needs?
   - Have they proved to be efficient on the task of gathering reliable information?

2. **Margins** are at the heart of an organisation's profitability process. Margins are also value drivers. Gross margin speaks of the customers'

perception of value. High gross margin (60–80%) is a cushion that reduces operating risk. Low gross margin (10–25%) increases the break-even point and leaves the company at higher exposure to operating risk when facing declining revenues. Earnings before interest, tax, depreciation and amortisation (EBITDA) and EBIT margins are also of high relevance to the business performance. The relationship between growth and margin is also relevant.

- Where is the organisation strategically positioned in terms of gross margin at consolidated, regional, and product/service/brand portfolio level?
- What are the EBITDA and EBIT margins at consolidated, regional, and product/service/brand portfolio level? How are they performing against budget and in terms of growth? Are overhead costs being efficiently managed to hit margin goals?
- Does the current growth strategy go against margin? If so, for how long? How and when will the situation be reversed?

3. **Return on invested capital**

    ROIC, also known as return on capital employed, is a simple ratio that has a direct relationship with the capacity of a firm to create value, as explained earlier.

    ROIC = EBIT margin × Invested capital turnover × (1 − tax rate)

    Invested capital turnover multiplied by the operating margin after tax determines ROIC. When ROIC exceeds the cost of capital, value is created. Invested capital is made of total net capital expenditures and operating working capital. Hence, invested capital turnover is about the relationship between revenues and the amount of capital invested. When a growth strategy is being pursued, new capital will be required in addition to capital required for assets being replaced or updated (capex).

    - What is the minimum consolidated ROIC to meet the cost of capital? When is it expected to be reached if not yet?
    - Is there information available to the board to determine whether the company should focus on improving ROIC or pushing growth

further to maximise value creation at regional and product/service/brand portfolio level?
- Does the board have a clear target on growth rate and ROIC for the different revenue streams/business units and regions that maximises value?
- What is the actual ROIC at regional and product/service/brand portfolio level, and how has it been evolving over time against budget?
- What is the amount of new capital available on an annual basis? If restricted, what are the rules for capital allocation? What are the products/services and regions that have priority? Value creation should drive these decisions.
- Is there a clear plan for the annual capital expenditures, broken into replacement and new investments, that matches the firm's strategy in the short, mid, and long term?
- How is operating working capital turnover performing at consolidated, regional, and product/service portfolio level against budget and compared to previous periods?
- Are higher operating working capital requirements, at different regions, offset by higher margins?
- What are the plans to keep on optimising operating working capital, without increasing risk?

ROIC, together with the revenue growth rate, are the free cash flow from operations drivers:

- What's the current and expected cash flow from operations?
- If positive and stable, what portion of it will be deployed to capex to self-finance growth and replace obsolete assets? What portion of it will be used to distribute dividends or buy-back shares?
- If negative, when is it expected to turn positive? How is it going to be financed?

4. **Cost of capital as a risk metric:** Intrinsic business risk can be broken into operating and financing risk.

   Operating risk is about EBIT's volatility when revenues change over time.

- What's the break-even point in terms of revenue?
- What is the composition of the cost structure in terms of variable versus fixed expenses?
- Does the company have sufficient recurrent revenue to break even?
- What is the worst-case scenario in terms of potential drops in revenue? Would that lead to a crisis situation?
- How could fixed expenses be converted into variable? How long would it take?

Financing risk: net debt-to-equity ratio, solvency assessment, and the relationship between net debt and EBITDA are prevalent indicators.

- Has the board determined the target debt-to-equity ratio and the net debt/EBITDA ratio that minimises the cost of capital with a moderate level of risk?
- How are these ratios related to those of peers? Falling far from peers' results will cause a negative effect on the cost of capital, and hence on value.

The capital structure together with the operating risk of a firm will determine the cost of capital. The cost of capital will be the rate at which expected free cash flows from operations will be discounted to estimate intrinsic value. Hence, it has a direct impact on value. Companies that do not use debt capital are not maximising shareholder value. On the other hand, when there's too much debt in the capital structure, it will cause a negative effect on value as risk increases.

Many private companies do not estimate the cost of equity, especially those owned by few shareholders. In order to drive a company towards value creation, it is vital to determine the required rate of return and discuss the meaning and implications of this with the shareholders (based on market data), so that the cost of capital can be identified. Otherwise, how do directors know what the hurdle rate is for the company's invested capital and for new opportunities?

- Does the board have a clear strategy on the appropriate capital structure that suits shareholders' appetite and culture for risk that can ensure the firm's viability in the long term?

- Are there specific guidelines to determine the cost of capital at project and regional level to ensure sound economic decisions that drive long-term value creation are in place?
- Are plans to raise new capital to cover investment needs being rolled out as scheduled?

5. **Dividend policy** establishes a commitment with shareholders that should be met.
    - Is there a dividend policy in place?
    - If so, will the company be capable to meeting it? If not, what are the reasons? How long will it take to reverse the situation?
    - If there has been a strategic decision not to distribute dividends, has it been explained to shareholders?

6. Regarding **share price performance**, when applicable.
    - What is the total shareholder return (TSR) on an annual basis?
    - What is the accumulated TSR for the past five to ten years? Compared to peers and appropriate indexes?
    - Is it in line with the board plans? If not, what's the reason behind this?

45

RISK OVERSIGHT, MANAGEMENT, AND CONTROLS

Rajiv Jaitly

Risk management as a board subject has emerged from the shadows of theory to become a practical way of setting and managing corporate objectives for those charged with the oversight and governance of organisations. Risk management means different things to different people, and many categories of risk have been defined and encompass different types of corporate concern, whether extending to enterprise, investment, liquidity, operational, or other forms of risk management.

"Doing the right thing," defined as conduct risk, has become a prescribed form of risk categorisation, particularly for financial services' firms. The conduct or behaviour of firms and its employees has been pushed to the forefront. Providing the right outcome for customers and meeting their needs is now an important focus for boards. A spotlight is being shone on how effective boards are in assessing information and statistics to determine whether firms are meeting and delivering value to their customers. If firms are falling short, the board needs to take decisive action and track this until they are back on track.

Risk management is of course not always the avoidance of risk. Enterprises do need to balance risks with rewards, but may take the view that some types of risks are accepted and managed whilst other risks are avoided altogether. The removal of all risk would also eliminate all opportunity and in any event would never be a practical or sustainable strategy for a business. Indeed, managed risk may be good for a business.

Risk and risk management, boards, and corporate governance, are all topics of ongoing research but the principles articulated by the UK regulator, the Financial Reporting Council, remain applicable to all organisations. The major reports written in 2011 and 2012[1] are summarised as follows:

> the board must determine its willingness to take on risk, and the desired culture within the company
>
> risk management and internal control should be incorporated within the company's normal management and governance processes, not treated as a separate compliance exercise
>
> the board must make a robust assessment of the principal risks to the company's business model and ability to deliver its strategy, including solvency and liquidity risks. In making that assessment the board should consider the likelihood and impact of these risks materialising in the short and longer term
>
> once those risks have been identified, the board should agree how they will be managed and mitigated and keep the company's risk profile under review. It should satisfy itself that management's systems include appropriate controls, and that it has adequate sources of assurance
>
> the assessment and management of the principal risks, and monitoring and review of the associated systems, should be carried out as an on-going process, not seen as an annual one-off exercise, and
>
> this process should inform a number of different disclosures in the annual report: the description of the principal risks and uncertainties facing the company; the disclosures on the going concern basis of accounting and material uncertainties thereto; and the report on the review of the risk management and internal control systems.[2]

The questions we have set out below have emerged from our discussions through the lenses of both executive and non-executive roles on boards whether as chief risk officers, chief operating officers, non-executive chairs

---

1 Boards and Risk 2011 Financial Reporting Council and The Sharman Inquiry 2012.
2 www.frc.org.uk/getattachment/d672c107-b1fb-4051-84b0-f5b83a1b93f6/Guidance-on-Risk-Management-Internal-Control-and-Related-Reporting.pdf.

of audit finance and risk committees of boards or as members of boards setting strategy for a business and managing issues as they arise or through the scanning of risk horizons. Risk as viewed by a board encompasses three very broad areas:

1. Strategic – to ensure that risk management is embedded in the corporate objectives of the board
2. Cultural – to ensure that the people in the organisation led by its board have embraced risk management as part of the culture of the organisation
3. Operational – to ensure that the strategic and cultural embedding of risk management is operationalised so that it becomes a practical rather than theoretical tool in managing the risk of the business

The questions on risk management matters that we feel all board members should ask about an organisation they are charged with governing include the following:

- How does the organisation define risk?
- Has the organisation defined what its appetite for risk is?
- Does the organisation have a risk management policy?
- How is risk managed and reported?
- How does the organisation operationalise its risk management policy, and is there a clear risk management framework in place?
- Who is responsible for the executive function of risk management and to whom does it report?
- Is the risk management function independent from the business and able to demonstrate robust challenge on all risk matters?
- How often does risk management appear as an agenda item on matters considered by the board and its committees?
- To whom are the functions of risk management delegated by the board and what authority do they have to manage risk?
- Has the organisation defined what its key risk indicators are?
- How has the organisation defined the key risk indicators?
- Do you understand how these risk indicators are compiled (data quality) and reported (monitoring)?

- Who gets to see, review, and comment on these indicators and how often is this done?
- Are risks categorised and assigned to "risk owners" with the appropriate seniority to demonstrate they are effectively managed and or mitigated?
- How are risk issues escalated within the business?
- How are risks to the business recorded?
- Is there a corporate risk framework and risk register?
- How often is the risk register updated and reviewed?
- How often do the risks on the register change ratings?
- Who owns the risk management process?
- Is the risk management process one for "meting out justice," or is it a process for a learning organisation?
- Is the risk management framework an insurance-based structure, or is it a framework that is embedded in all organisational processes?
- Who tracks risk events and how are risk issues closed off?
- Is risk management treated as a part of internal audit, or is it treated as a separate function?
- Can people within the organisation articulate what its critical risks are?
- Does the organisation operate a three-lines-of-defence policy?[3]
- Are the organisations' corporate objectives and view of risk aligned?
- How are divergences in opinion on matters of risk managed?
- How process driven is risk management?
- Is there a healthy tension between management and the risk and compliance functions?
- Is there a scorecard process for risk management, or is some other process used to rate and manage risks?
- Have the controls that provide for safe ratings on risks been tested? How often are these key controls tested for reliability?[4]

---

[3] These are: First line of defence: Management controls and internal control systems; Second line of defence: Organisational compliance functions such as compliance departments and internal audit; Third line of defence: External assurance such as through independent audit.

[4] Also referred to as avoiding the "green-washing syndrome."

- Are board papers manageable, or are board members expected to read the equivalent of a medium-length novel in preparation for meetings?
- How often are risks stress-tested?
- Does the organisation self-assess and review long-term viability?
- Are there any pressures that would prevent disclosure and dialogue between executives and board members?
- What does the organisation do with its risk management information? How serious are the discussions around risk management at board level?
- What level of transparency does the business demonstrate with its external advisers such as its auditors?
- How transparent is the organisation within its own hierarchy?
- Does the organisation encourage the recording of breaches, errors, and near misses in the pursuit of learning as a way of risk management?
- Are the financial, taxation, and business regulatory requirements understood and complied with?
- How seriously does the organisation guard its reputation in its interactions with stakeholders?
- Does the organisation understand who its key stakeholders are and what that means for the organisation and its viability?
- What risks has the organisation dealt with in the past and how likely are those risks to materialise again?
- Does the organisation have the appropriate skills to identify and manage risk to it?
- How are emerging risks captured and considered by the board, particularly if it impacts the firm's risk profile?

In writing such a chapter as this it feels incumbent on us to try and describe what a good risk management environment set by a board might look like and of course, whilst each organisation will have differences in what it does and the culture it creates, some basics remain constant, and so we have tried to frame what good looks like in a brief paragraph with general application.

A good risk framework would exist where an organisation's board has set a clear corporate strategy understood by the entire organisation and reflected in its mapping and management of risks to deliver that strategy. The board will be clear about how the organisation will deal with those risks, whether by instituting controls, conducting periodic reviews, carrying insurance, or avoiding or, indeed, accepting risks. Risk management would be embedded in the culture of the organisation as something used as a learning tool to improve outcomes, operational safety, and the sustainability of the organisation in delivering its strategic objectives, and would be reflected in the risk outputs of the organisation, which would be practical and used by management to learn and improve its operations beyond being theoretical outputs or something used to mete out punishment. Finally, these risk outputs would be translated into practical operational controls, risk indicators, risk maps, risk registers, and assurance frameworks that were reliable, accurate, complete, operationally useful, and which delivered the strategic objectives of the organisation.

Part IX

COMMUNICATIONS

46

REPUTATION

Alice Hunt

Reputation has shot up the boardroom agenda and remains firmly in the minds of non-executive directors (NEDs) as scandal after scandal has besieged UK plc and beyond.

Reputation is inextricably linked with trust. It is also notoriously complex to define, something which many more progressive organisations seek to do in the development of their organisational purpose.

Measuring reputation is also fiendishly difficult, though by no means impossible. Finding a way to assess the health of an organisations' reputation will enable the board of directors and the executive team to establish a reputational bellwether that will inform strategic choices and help weigh the risk of a particular decision.

Reputation also falls into a frustrating category for board members and their executive teams of having somewhat intangible benefits when the going is good. As a result, the investment required to build and maintain reputation can sometimes slip down the agenda. This can be extremely short-sighted, particularly given events that have an adverse impact on reputation such as product recalls, executive scandal and misconduct, cyberattacks, and data breaches are all on the up.

DOI: 10.4324/9781003201182-55

At the same time, the value of reputation has increased considerably. Investors increasingly place a premium on the shares of companies that are recognised for maintaining a strong reputation.

Organisations which appropriately assess their appetite to invest in reputation and then adhere consistently to it, will be far more likely to survive adverse reputational impact and emerge from a crisis more resilient and with deeper stakeholder relationships (see chapter on stakeholder management and engagement).

Reputation management is an organisational discipline which sits at the very heart of the modern boardroom. Equipping yourself with the right curiosity, the right mechanisms to interrogate and understand reputation and the reputational implications of key decisions in executive and non-executive muscle which will only need to grow stronger.

"Reputation arrives on foot and departs on horseback." It is, in other words, hard fought, and without appropriate safeguards it can be lost with breathtaking speed.

So what role do NEDs have in ensuring they are asking the right questions at the right time? Just as a board has an integral role in defining the strategy and purpose of an organisation, so too do they have a role to play in helping the organisation define their reputation:

- What does the organisation want to be famous for?
- What does the board want people to say about the organisation when you "aren't in the room"?
- What does the board want the reputation of the organisation to be today and also over time? Will this change? How?
- How do the organisation's purpose and reputation come together? If there are gaps, how does the executive team plan to bridge these?

Understanding reputational trends

- How might the organisation's reputation change over time and why?
- What are some of the external factors and trends that might impact the organisation's reputation?
- Do you as a board member have a real understanding of them? If not, what are you doing to ensure you have that knowledge?

- What processes does the organisation have to ensure they are constantly refreshing this knowledge and understanding?
- Are the insights, as in reputational insights that are brought to the board for information and discussion, genuinely helping the organisation and its board of directors see around corners?
- Who else is feeding into reputation insights and how?

Striking the right balance

- What's the right reputational stance for your organisation to take?
- What's the board and the executive team's appetite for investing in reputation, and are they able to sustain that investment?
- How does reputation relate to the organisation's risk appetite and risk management?
- How does reputation relate to value creation in the organisation?
- How does reputation relate to growth and return on capital levers for the organisation such as:
  a. Growing your customer base?
  b. Expanding your sustainable product offering?
  c. Price increases?
  d. Supply chain and operational efficiencies?
  e. Talent attraction and retention?

Accountability and support

- What are the expectations of shareholders, rating agencies, customers, and employees with regard to reputation? Does the board have a clear understanding of these, and has the executive team got a plan to meet or indeed exceed these expectations?
- Who is the custodian of reputation and who is accountable for reputation in the organisation? Is this clear and do they know?
- How is this responsibility shared across the board, the executive team, and beyond?
- What has the organisation done to ensure its employees understand the reputation of the business and what their role is in maintaining it?
- Are you as a NED clear where the areas of strength and weaknesses are in your current reputation?

- What is the executive team doing to mitigate these weaknesses?
- Has the board created an expectation amongst the executive team members that creating a culture of positive assertiveness to ensure challenge on diversity and inclusion and environmental, social, and governance (ESG) criteria?
- What is the diversity and inclusion strategy for the organisation that will attune it to reputational issues that may arise from diversity or a lack of it?
- Is the executive team spending time on the things they can control or cannot control?

Measurement

- How is reputation measured? Is the executive team measuring what really matters?
- Does the board and the executive team fully understand the difference between purchase consideration drivers and more fundamental drivers of trust?
- What is the process for surfacing this measurement in the right places in the organisation – for example, in product design?
- What are other companies doing in your competitive set and what are the benefits they are driving from improvements in reputation?

Reputation escalation and management

- How are issues that are reputationally sensitive surfaced in the organisation? Is there a formal process?
- How does reputation sit with the whistle-blower policy?
- Are there crisis management exercises that are regularly held to test these processes and the individuals who are responsible and accountable for them?
- Are there clear roles and responsibilities for the board and executive team in the event of a crisis?

Reputation and brand

- Is there equilibrium between your brand and your corporate entity?

- How is the executive team ensuring that marketing activity is aligned to and sensitive to corporate reputation?
- Is the board clear about what the executive team has done to reflect reputation in the employer brand to ensure strong talent attraction?
- Is the employer brand aligned to reputation and is it something colleagues would recognise and that is written into every job description and recruiting touchpoint?

Repetition

Like so many areas of scrutiny, ensuring that these are questions you ask again and again will be key to ensuring the reputational health of an organisation is consistently and successfully managed.

47

CORPORATE BRAND

Elliot S. Schreiber

Many executives and directors are surprised that the value of intangible assets to the organisation's market value are five times greater than that of tangible assets.[1] Intangible assets are a major driver of long-term business value, and affect capital allocation, organisational governance, and financial reporting.[2] However, because most executives and directors are more familiar with and attuned to conventional accounting and financial analysis, there often is less understanding of intangible value economics and business impact analysis. Many international accounting and financial standards organisations and accounting and regulatory bodies are seeking to address the long-standing need to better understand and measure the financial value of brand.[3]

The corporate brand provides a "window" for stakeholders to see the company and make assumptions about what it stands for, it values, its

---

1 pcloseup.com/2019/06/04/21-trillion-in-u-s-intangible-asset-value-is-84-of-sp-500-value-ip-rights-and-reputation-included/.
2 https://sfmagazine.com/post-entry/october-2019-the-financial-value-of-brand/.
3 https://sfmagazine.com/post-entry/october-2019-the-financial-value-of-brand/.

DOI: 10.4324/9781003201182-56

strategy, whether to join the company, the quality of its management, and its value as an investment. One issue facing executives and boards is that finance and marketing speak a different language and often are in conflict. While marketing might discuss "net promoter scores," finance is more concerned with return-on-investment, margins, and asset turns. Marketing, public relations, and finance need to work together to focus on how the brand can create value for both stakeholders and the company.

How the corporate brand is managed impacts reputation, investment decisions, alignment of people, and pricing decision, among others. There is also brand or reputation risk with which executives and directors should be concerned. Directors should recognise that they fulfil their duty of care when they assure themselves that the organisation is managing this important intangible asset fully to maximise and protect value.

What is a brand?

Anything can be branded. Companies, non-profits, universities, countries, cities, and people use branding to differentiate and create value, whether it be sales, contributions, applications, tourism, or publicity. In this chapter, however, we will focus on the corporate or organisational brand.

The corporate brand has three components: symbols (logo, corporate signature, corporate identity, and so on), attributes, and associations, which are those characteristics and values that attract and retain stakeholders. While more time and most money are focused on the development of the logo and the maintenance of the corporate identity guidelines, the greatest financial value to the corporation comes from the brand attributes and associations. That is, the symbols of the brand are owned by the company and provide trademark and patent value, but the attributes and associations create value with and for stakeholders that can be enhanced and sustained over time. Employees also are an important part of the corporate brand, since the attributes and associations of the brand should be consistent with the corporate values and culture. The greater the employee ability to "live the brand," the better the corporate reputation.

Not every organisation needs to have a publicly recognised brand. However, every successful organisation's brand needs to resonate with its stakeholders. There are many organisations that are not well known outside of their industries that are successful because they manage their corporate brand well with their customers, investors, employees, and others.

Every organisation has a brand, whether they invest in it or not. Employees, customers, and investors join, buy, and invest in a competitive environment. If a company is not well known or has attributes and associations that do not align with stakeholder expectations and needs, it is difficult for them to compete against better known competitors who invest in and better manage their brand.

- How well has the organisation done to identify the attributes that it wants to be known by, as well as with what it wants and does not want to be associated?
- Are the key assumptions of executives about the corporate brand in line with market opportunities, customer expectations, and the competitive marketplace?
- How involved and committed are the CEO and the executive team with the development and communication of the brand's attributes and associations?
- Are the brand attributes aligned with our organisation's values?
- Are the attributes of our brand sufficiently differentiated from the brands of competitors?
- Has our corporate brand had an impact on the sales of our various products and services?
- Is the board clear about what the CEO and his/her team have done about branding the organisation for current and future employees to ensure top talent attraction and retention?
- How does the executive team know that the attributes and associations of the brand are meaningful and of benefit to key stakeholders?

How brands create value

When the brand attributes and associations are communicated, they create a promise to stakeholders. The promise creates expectations. If experience is equal to or greater than expectations, value is created. However, if expectations are greater than experience, value is lost. Brand value, then, is akin to reputational value in that both are the result of whether stakeholders believe that their expectations have been met. Measures of brand equity determine how well the organisation is doing in meeting or exceeding those expectations. It is important for executives and boards to recognise that measures of brand equity typically look at the value of the brand to the consumer. Questions need to be asked to determine the value of the brand to the company.

- What valuation methods are we using to assess the value of our corporate brand versus others in our industry? How are we doing?
- Is there alignment between the corporate brand and the various product brands in the company? How are they being aligned?
- What are we doing if there is a lack of alignment between our corporate brand attributes and those of the product/service brands?

Brand risk

"A happy customer tells a friend, an unhappy customer tells the world," is an old business adage. Since the advent of social media in 2004 and smartphones in 2007, telling the "world" has become more possible, not just with words but also with photos and videos. Some 3.5 billion people, or 45% of the world's population, use social media to get their news, connect with family and friends, and share information about brands.[4] More than 50% of customers use social media to research products and rely on so-called social media influencers for brand recommendations.[5]

Marketers know that social media is important to create value for their brands, but they also know how fragile that value can be when the brand is attacked. Many companies have had crises result from information – some of it wrong or distorted – shared on social media. There also are groups on social media that look for issues they do not like and share this with others in an attempt at what is now called "cancel culture" or "public shaming." Actions that at one time might have gone unnoticed or could have been easily contained and managed, can now flare into full-blown crises.

- What is the company doing to monitor what is being said about the company in social media and does it have crisis plans in place for potential vulnerabilities?

4 www.oberlo.com/blog/social-media-marketing-statistics.
5 www.lyfemarketing.com/blog/social-media-marketing-statistics/.

- How well is the company using social media, not just to promote the brand but also to monitor and listen to what is being said about the company and to adjust if expectations change?
- How are executives ensuring that marketing activity is aligned with and sensitive to corporate reputation?

The role of public relations in branding

Marketing has traditionally been the "owner" of branding. While that is particularly true in consumer products companies and with product or service brands, public relations play an important role in corporate branding.

The corporate brand is enhanced in large part by employee engagement, corporate advertising, and earned media, all areas of public relations strength. In addition, as noted above, social media has increased in importance both for creating as well as defending the brand value. These are other areas where public relations should play a major, if not leading role. Public relations should have in place crisis plans for potential threats against the brand.

- Before we communicate our brand externally, what have we done to engage employees so that they can "live the brand"?
- Are we linking brand to our reputation risk management activities? Is the board committee responsible for risk management considering brand and reputation risk?
- What are we doing to maximise the value of our brand activity beyond corporate advertising?
- Do we know who our key influencers for or against our organisation are and are we engaging with or monitoring them?
- How is the executive team making certain that employees adhere to the brand attributes so that they are consistently communicated to customers and other external stakeholders?
- How is the organisation doing versus competitors in gaining positive media coverage of our corporate brand reflecting the attributes we desire to be known by?

48

SOCIAL MEDIA

Marshall Manson and Craig Mullaney

An early twentieth century, a political and communications axiom exhorts leaders and businesses to resist the temptation to "pick a fight with people who buy ink by the barrel." A useful truism, to be sure, for a world where newspapers and professional media organisations were key forces in defining reputation. These days, as countless examples have brought to life, no one needs to own a printing press in order to have a major impact. Social media platforms and mobile phones equip everyone with the tools to capture and distribute content and, therefore, enable anyone to have influence, sometimes only for a moment.

This wholesale realignment and democratisation of communications hold profound consequences for business. Every business leader, and the boards to which they are accountable, needs to appreciate the powerful role that social media can play in shaping your business's reputation and how it engages key audiences. The landscape offers real opportunities, but there are also critical risks to manage and mitigate.

In this chapter, we explore social media at a strategic level, and offer a series of questions that directors should be considering as part of a broader business strategy. We will also offer some specific thoughts on practical steps that any business or institution might consider.

Before we consider implications, we must first define our terms: social media is any internet-dependent platform that enables two or more people to establish a durable connection and share information. The most common examples are household names: Facebook, Twitter, LinkedIn, Instagram, Snapchat, and Tik Tok are all platforms that fit the definition. Each fuels content sharing and public or partially public interaction between people. Platforms like WhatsApp, Telegram, and WeChat also enable content sharing and conversation. While interactions on these platforms are private and, in some cases, highly encrypted, that doesn't make them any less social. Indeed, in some ways, the internet's oldest form of social media is email.

The role of social media in society is, of course, increasingly a cause for debate. Many believe that major platforms like Facebook and Twitter are under-regulated and a source of harm. Some are concerned that the platforms are amplifying extreme voices or contributing to the polarisation of politics. But no one should underestimate their significance. Indeed, their centrality to public policy debates underscores how much these platforms matter to serious enterprises, including business.

From a business perspective, the most commonly understood role for social media is within marketing. Nearly all of the platforms offer opportunities, in one form or another, for businesses to distribute content to customers (or consumers for businesses that sell through retailers). However, the opportunity for businesses goes well beyond marketing. The same tools that enable engagement with a customer or consumer audience also allow connections with other audiences, for example, investors and other key reputational stakeholders.

If opportunities are abundant, so too are the risks. During an incident or crisis, social media helps information spread in seconds instead of minutes or hours. This provides benefit to an organisation seeking to quickly set the record straight or reassure investors, customers, and employees. However, it also routinely provides a venue for critics to find an audience for a negative story. Social media can enable rapid organisation by critics or supporters at great scale. It can provide a vehicle for employees to voice concerns. And in an age where state actors are using social media to destabilise politics and attack businesses, social media can be an enabler for their activities, too.

Most importantly, social media has driven a change in expectations for businesses. Consumers, investors, B2B buyers, policymakers, and employees expect greater transparency and access than ever before. In particular, these key audiences expect leaders to use social media as a tool to communicate more effectively and more directly than in the past. Recent events have accelerated this trend by forcing us all to be more reliant than ever before on digital platforms to keep us connected.

With all of that in mind, we identify some key questions that directors should consider when it comes to social media.

Reputation

- How is social media activity being used to protect and enhance your company's reputation?
- To what extent are you using social media to understand perceptions of your company among key audiences, from customers to investors?
- Is your company using social media as effectively as your competition?
- How does your company look in Google? Does your reputation, as reflected in Google, match the reality as you see it? Social media activity can influence Google's reflection of your reputation.
- Do you have a framework in place to mitigate reputational risks?
- What role will social media play in the event of a crisis or incident? What systems will alert you of a problem online and what response scenarios have you rehearsed?

Risk and compliance

- Is the executive team as fluent in digital media as your customers, employees, or investors?
- What policies do you have in place regarding board or executive team communications via non-corporate digital channels, for example, WhatsApp, SMS, a private group on social media?
- Have social media profiles for the executive team and board members been reviewed to identify and mitigate any potential security or reputational vulnerabilities?
- Does the company have a social media policy for its employees?

Crisis

- How are you using social media to assess risk and inform decision-making during a crisis, incident, or issues management situation?
- Have you established a chain of command and protocol for crisis scenarios, both related to your company and for broader public tragedies?
- How vulnerable would you be to a social media campaign driven by a well-known NGO?
- How would your company respond to a coordinated social media campaign by an activist group?
- If your company website became inoperative, what is your plan for communicating with customers, investors, and other stakeholders?
- How would you respond to a coordinated disinformation campaign by a state or non-state actor targeting your organisation?
- A prominent politician has attacked your company in a social media post. Under what circumstances would you respond and how?
- An activist investor has bought all the search terms on Google related to your company and they are directing clicks to a memo advocating for a new board slate. Do you know how to respond?

Customers

- Is your social media activity delivering value for business development and/or marketing? Done well, social media can help build brand value and drive sales.
- Is the company using social media effectively to improve customer experiences? Successful activity could result in reduced call centre volume or freeing up sales resources.
- If a crisis forced the closure of your retail or customer support locations, what role would social media play in continuity of operations?

Investors

- How are you using social media platforms to engage investors? According to Brunswick's annual survey of institutional investors,[1]

---

[1] 2020 *Digital Investor Survey*, a report from Brunswick. www.linkedin.com/pulse/surprise-increase-investor-trust-digital-sources-marshall-manson/.

75% have made a final investment decision based on something they read or saw online, and social media platforms LinkedIn and Twitter are vital information sources.
- Is the investor relations team effectively sharing the investor narrative to key audiences online during key moments such as earnings announcements?

Executives

- How is your executive team using social media? Do their efforts compare favourably with your competition?
- Do you have a social media playbook for announcing a planned key leader transition? What about an unexpected transition due to a workplace conduct or health-related issue?
- Do the board and CEO have a platform to communicate with the entire company in the event of an office closing or crisis outside normal business hours?
- Do your executives' social media communications add to or detract from the company's reputation?
- Would a prospective customer or employee see your company's purpose, values, and culture reflected through the executive team's online communications?

Seventy-three per cent of FTSE 350 employees in the UK believe it is "important for CEOs to actively communicate about their company on social media," and 80% believe that CEOs should use social media to communicate during a crisis situation.[2] During the recent pandemic, CEOs and other business leaders used social media more than ever before to connect with employees, customers, investors, and other stakeholders.

Human capital

- How is your company using social media to perpetuate conversations with employees and provide opportunities for them to interact with leadership?

2 *Connected Leadership*, a report from Brunswick. www.brunswickgroup.com/perspectives/connected-leadership/.

- How is social media helping you find, attract, and retain great talent?
- Do you have a clear policy and guidance in place for employees on how their social media activity relates to their role in the company?
- Have you explored new or unexpected social media platforms to best communicate with employees on the channels they use most?
- Are you equipping employees with content and platforms to advocate on behalf of the company?

49

SHAREHOLDER RELATIONS AND COMMUNICATION

Claire Fargeot

"Managing expectations" has historically been the mantra for the careful balancing of board-level shareholder relations and communication. Investors have always demanded "openness and transparency" in communications from their targeted or invested companies. Boards of directors, however, have generally tended to err on the side of caution, particularly when things have not developed as planned. This tension has led to growing pressure for greater board transparency and more open communication from activist investment funds, hedge funds, governance professionals, NGOs, and other stakeholders.

Shareholder activism has been on the rise since the global financial crisis for both large and small enterprises, and there appears little sign of that abating. Shareholders are looking for assurances that the enterprise has a solid strategic direction and a viable business model. Within the listed company space, shareholders are looking for access to management and reporting that includes trackable metrics that measure performance and long-term sustainable growth with a sensible approach to executive compensation that is directly linked to strategy delivery, operational and financial results, and meaningful non-financial measures.

DOI: 10.4324/9781003201182-58

Today's regulatory environment is changing for the investment community as well as for companies, and institutional investors are required to intensify oversight of their portfolio companies, disclosing their governance policies, voting practices, and engagement activities. The financial crisis made plain the failures that resulted from too heavy a reliance on purely quantitative analysis to evaluate an organisation's performance, and investors are taking intangible assets and non-financial performance metrics into account in their company evaluations. This enlarged reporting and analytical framework has important implications for companies, and specifically for directors, as responsibility for environmental, social, and governance (ESG) issues and sustainability falls to the board. It is the directors, rather than management, that are answerable for ESG and sustainability issues by shareholders.

Managing expectations

In many international markets the board's role is broadly defined, requiring directors to balance a multitude of competing demands (managing conflicts of interest, including those resulting from significant shareholdings, dealing with workforce representation, and ensuring that the influence of third parties does not compromise or override independent judgement), in addition to their oversight duties. In these markets the need for transparency is even more compelling than in the more highly regulated markets, such as the UK, the EU, and the USA, where comprehensive legal, disclosure, and accounting standards are well established. The provisions contained in the UK Code[1] act as a reminder of what is expected of UK premium-listed company directors in terms of shareholder relations and engagement:

- In addition to formal general meetings, the chair should seek regular engagement with major shareholders in order to understand their views on governance and performance against the strategy. Committee chairs should seek engagement with shareholders on significant matters related to their areas of responsibility. The chair should ensure that the board as a whole has a clear understanding of the views of shareholders.

1 UK Corporate Governance Code 2018

- When 20 per cent or more of votes have been cast against the board recommendation for a resolution, the company should explain, when announcing voting results, what actions it intends to take to consult shareholders in order to understand the reasons behind the result. An update on the views received from shareholders and actions taken should be published no later than six months after the shareholder meeting. The board should then provide a final summary in the annual report and, if applicable, in the explanatory notes to resolutions at the next shareholder meeting, on what impact the feedback has had on the decisions the board has taken and any actions or resolutions now proposed.

Outside the listed company space, certain boardrooms are particularly opaque, with complex shareholding structures such as state-owned enterprises or large private organisations dominated by controlling groups or founding families. Directors that are large shareholders too, such as in many private equity-backed organisations, have to respond to their outside investors' interests as well as look after their own. All in all, managing expectations is not as easy as it sounds, and the experience of increasing levels of transparency has not always been a comfortable one for many directors.

Dealing with activists

Listed-company approaches for dealing with activists have tended to rely on direct targeted engagement methods such as formal letters, orchestrated meetings, and selective outreach campaigns. When the situation becomes more critical, approaches rely much more heavily on external expertise, such as crisis PR agency support or proxy solicitation. However, such an approach is reactive and does not tend to support a long-term basis for positive relations and a prevention of shareholder activism. The prime concern for any board should of course be to act in such a way that it leaves no space for activism – being proactive rather than reactive. As soon as shareholders express concern, it should be dealt with efficiently with a view to removing that particular concern completely. Past experience tends to dictate that if a board does not respond, then shareholders will become more vocal and active. Boards looking to reduce shareholder dissent should follow strategies that are likely to provide an effective prevention approach, such as providing access to key senior team members and pertinent information when requested and so on.

Becoming a transparent board

Board transparency is the recognised accountability mechanism for organisations subject to principles-based, comply-or-explain governance systems. However, this system is not perfect as explanations are only required where companies are non-compliant. As a result, this exceptions-based reporting approach tends to encourage related communication that has gaps, being fragmented and oftentimes, unrelated to other disclosures. Both companies and shareholders would benefit from an annual board narrative and a structured programme for directors to communicate and engage with shareholders.

The board of directors is essentially responsible for its statutory duties, (including ESG and sustainability issues), whilst management is responsible for everything else, including the day-to-day business operations, financial performance, and the execution of strategy. Being clear about this differentiation provides the basis for what can be discussed with shareholders, and meetings planned for the board to meet directly with shareholders should be done so in reflection of this and with care.

Generally speaking, board effectiveness communication requires improvement, with only 51% of companies providing good or detailed explanations in this area and only 46% providing sufficient detail on outcomes.[2] Shareholders view regular board evaluation as an important accountability mechanism for corporate boards. Ideally, the board should commission independent board evaluation experts to conduct an effectiveness review in order to gauge shareholder satisfaction with the board, executive leadership, and overall strategic direction. This review should examine the governance practices, interviewing directors and senior management, observing the board in action, carrying out a shareholder perception survey, and studying the board packs. The findings should be communicated in a non-attributable way to the entire board and a work plan for improvement should be communicated to stakeholders via the annual report.

2 Grant Thornton 2020 (UK) *Corporate Governance Review*

Questions to ask

- Does the board recognise the importance of listening to, and understanding the views of its shareholders so that this information can be used to inform decision-making?
- Does the board understand how and via what means the shareholders want to be communicated with?
- Is the board approach and narrative on shareholder relations and communications clear?
- Is there an effective mechanism of tracking shareholder relations and communication?
- Has the board clearly defined and communicated its own remit?
- Does the board tell a compelling story about its own board effectiveness?
- Does board effectiveness have a commitment to the business goals, ESG, and sustainability?
- Are the shareholders and stakeholders convinced of this?
- What are the views of the current shareholders and stakeholders on the board's effectiveness?
- Does the board regularly conduct an evaluation of its own governance practices and standing? If not, why not?
- Does the board have access to the relevant information for appropriate shareholder relations?
- What are the aspects that shareholders and stakeholders take issue with (or have taken issue with, in the past)?
- Does the board engage with activist investors (now and has it done so in the past)?
- Does the board have clarity on the objective of its engagement campaign?
- Is the board informed as to what topics are on the agenda?
- Is the board clear on who should speak for the board?
- Is it clear with whom the board should engage?
- Does the board understand when and how engagement should occur?
- Is it clear who from management should participate in the engagement process?
- Is it clear what is missing from the current communication to shareholders and stakeholders?

50

STAKEHOLDER ENGAGEMENT AND MANAGEMENT

Alice Hunt

Effective stakeholder engagement and management is an essential part of any non-executive director's (NED's) toolkit. This may be driven by the strategic, legal, or statutory requirements you have to engage with certain stakeholder groups or, just as importantly, driven by reputational considerations.

Taking the time to listen and understand the perspectives of others and using the insight drawn from these stakeholders to inform strategic decisions and scrutinise the actions of an organisation is key. Doing so can both improve the quality of decision-making and insulate you and your organisation from previously unknown or little understood risks.

Stakeholder engagement and management is the process by which you identify, monitor, and build relationships with stakeholders, with the aim ultimately of improving those relationships and of building common understanding of what can be quite diverse perspectives. It typically involves systematically identifying or mapping stakeholders, understanding and analysing their needs and expectations, and where appropriate, building a plan to engage with them.

Let's take a moment to examine the benefits of stakeholder engagement and management on a personal and organisational level.

DOI: 10.4324/9781003201182-59

On a personal level a NED who is able to effectively engage with myriad stakeholders will be able to see the advantages and pitfalls of a number of different perspectives. He or she will then be able to offer these on behalf of those stakeholders in a boardroom context. In doing so, they become more effective scrutinisers of the decisions and actions of the organisation they are entrusted to advise.

Organisationally, the systematic management of stakeholders is becoming ever more important in a world where reputational risk can come from a wide variety of sources.

Stakeholders come in many shapes and sizes, from individuals who hold great influence or expertise over a particular area, to large organisations often with their own reputations and stakeholders to manage. This means engagement can be complex and can often be frustrating, as even when the individuals you are engaging with understand your view of the world, there may be organisational agendas which prevent them from being able to actively support your position.

Big or small, the starting point for all stakeholder engagement should be an understanding of their stance towards your organisation.

Clear mapping of stakeholders to understand their level of influence over your reputational and commercial success and to understand their current view – positive to negative – will enable the organisation to plan and prioritise engagement levels.

Too often, organisations start dialogue with stakeholders from their own perspective, attempting to persuade and recruit support through sheer force of personality. Taking the time to truly understand your stakeholders' starting point in a conversation, their view of the world, their view of your organisation and, critically, the areas where they themselves are under pressure is the key to successful stakeholder management and engagement. Listening will take you a long way.

Like any relationship, it is rare that a one-off meeting will be enough to build mutual trust and understanding, and so consideration should also be given to the regularity of engagement and at what entry points of the organisation this happens.

Alongside this clarity on who owns the relationship within the organisation it is essential to ensure a consistency of engagement and visibility of the interactions with the stakeholder. Many organisations do this through the use of customer relation management tools. These come with a health warning that they can be expensive and maintaining them can become an industry in itself. A robust stakeholder management process that is well coordinated and built on levels of trust in an organisation can often be just as effective if not more so.

Regular communication amongst those charged with owning stakeholder relationships will help coordinate interactions and assess the status and quality of relationships.

The following questions are designed to help NEDs scrutinise the stakeholder engagement and help challenge executive teams to be more effecting in their stakeholder engagement and management.

So, what should organisations be asking about the way their stakeholder management and engagement is run?

Legal or statutory requirements

- What are your legal and/or strategic objectives to undertaking stakeholder engagement/consultation/management? For example, a government or regulatory consultation on certain issues.

Mapping stakeholders

- Have the organisation's stakeholders been segmented by audience?
- Are the board members clear about the stance of stakeholders towards your organisation today?
- Are they positive or negative towards you and what is their level of influence over your organisation's goals?
- Has this been systematically mapped by the organisation?
- Is this map been regularly revisited and updated by the executive team and the board?
- Who is responsible for mapping stakeholders in your organisation?
- How regularly do the executive or board interact with this stakeholder mapping?
- Are you clear on where you want to get all stakeholders to in terms of their view of your organisation?

Understanding our stakeholders and what influences them

- What has been done to understand what is driving the stakeholders' view of your organisation?
- Is this insight up to date?
- Who and what are the key internal and external influences on your stakeholders?
- Can they be leveraged in any way to move your stakeholders to a more positive perception of you?
- Can you identify any mutual goals or territory where you have common views?

Maintaining the relationship

- How often do the board or executive team need to engage with certain stakeholders?
- Who is responsible for managing that engagement plan?
- Is your organisation appropriately mirroring the seniority of the stakeholders they are engaging with, and are there multiple points of entry into the stakeholder organisation that are being managed?
- What are you doing to check in and see whether your stakeholders feel like they are being listened to?
- Can you point to tangible actions the organisation has done to address the concerns of important stakeholders?
- What is the board's role versus that of the executive in interacting with stakeholders?
- Are the NED's connections being effectively leveraged?
- Are you comfortable with the level of resources that has been allocated to managing stakeholder relationships?
- Are there some stakeholders that have been deprioritised and are you comfortable with the implications of that deprioritisation?

Part X

EXTERNAL PRESSURE AND DISRUPTION

51

CRISIS MANAGEMENT

Charlotte Valeur

In light of the growing frequency of extreme weather phenomena and global pandemics, we must ask ourselves if this level of crisis management is the new normal. Crisis management throws boards understandably into short-term fire-fighting; however, it is extremely important for directors to keep their eyes and minds firmly on the longer-term purpose and values of the organisation.

Boards need to maintain a sense of perspective which will enable them to rise above the need to ensure immediate survival. This chapter offers some thoughts for board members to guide them in their deliberations during these kinds of crises.

What are boards of directors there to do as a top priority? They ultimately exist to take legal responsibility for the organisation. The board hires a senior management team to run the organisation on a day-to-day basis on their behalf. At a time of existential crisis, the board should remember that it is ultimately responsible. Without getting in the way of management, it may therefore feel that it needs to take a more involved role than under normal circumstances.

Specific issues for boards

During a crisis like a pandemic or natural disaster, the board needs to closely monitor management's actions, assessing whether management is taking appropriate steps and providing additional guidance, challenge, and direction where necessary. It also needs to demonstrate accountability to all stakeholders.

In particular, non-executive board members (NEDs) can potentially offer a more independent and objective perspective on board decision-making than may be possible for management. The latter will be immersed in solving the daily emerging operational problems. In contrast, NEDs can keep in mind a more holistic view of the business, the organisation's ultimate purpose, its values, and the likely impact of decisions on a broad range of stakeholders. These are key qualities in the midst of a crisis.

In order to do this, the board needs to remain well informed of developments within the organisation – as well as be attuned to the potentially rapidly changing external situation.

Some of the key questions which boards will need to ask, include the following:

Health and safety

- Safety first. Have we ensured our employees, customers, suppliers and so on are safe?
- Do we have appropriate communication plans in place?
- Do we have appropriate policies to protect employees, the company, and society at large?
- Do we closely monitor the guidance and requirements of government and the authorities, and ensure that they are fully complied with at all levels of the organisation?

Financial impact and cash flows

- What are the near-term and long-term impacts of the crisis?
- Do we fully understand and challenge the assumptions underlying revenue/cash projections?

- What are possible alternative financing arrangements?
- What are the options for possibly restructuring current debt obligations?

Risk oversight

The board will oversee management's efforts to identify, prioritise, and manage the principal risks to business operations during a crisis. In a crisis situation, the board will almost certainly need more regular updates from management between regularly scheduled board meetings. Depending on the nature of the risk impact, there may be key new roles for one or more board subcommittees. These may be newly formed crisis committees, which are specifically targeted on the crisis at hand. The board's consideration of, and decisions regarding, the crisis-related matters should be recorded and justified in meeting minutes.

- How is the board noting their deliberations and actions during the crisis?
- Should we constitute a crisis committee?
- What are the terms of reference (TOR) and objectives of the crisis committee?
- How often do the board and the crisis committee meet during the crisis?

Business continuity

The board should determine if business continuity plans are in place, and if they are still appropriate. Questions to consider are:

- Will our employees be affected? (pandemic/illness, adverse weather such as tornadoes, storms, flooding and so on)
- If so, what is the minimum staffing levels?
- Is remote work access possible across key functions?
- Is our supply chain affected?
- Have we assessed the risks associated with disruption to our supply chain?
- Do we have alternative sources of supply?

- Will our production/services be disrupted?
- What are the risks that the organisation cannot fulfil its contractual obligations?
- What are the relevant provisions in customer and other contracts we have? (force majeure, events of default and so on)
- Is any legal compensation available or owed?
- Do we have insurances covering crisis related losses?

Key person risks and succession plans

- Do we have succession planning for key persons in place?
- Is the planning deep enough? (In case of a pandemic, many managers could become ill.)

The board's functioning

- Is the board able to fully discharge its duties during the crisis? (different ways of holding board meetings, availability of board members, manage adverse weather conditions, manage pandemic lockdown and so on)
- Is the board appropriately organised to provide guidance and oversight as the crisis deepens?

Communications

A clear crisis communications plan will support the organisation to communicate internally and externally in a calm and thoughtful manner. This in turn will help build confidence with stakeholders.

- Do we have a crisis communications plan in place?
- Who are the key stakeholders to communicate with in a crisis?
- How do we communicate with them?

Reporting and disclosure

The boards of publicly traded companies in particular, but also other kinds of organisations, must consider whether they are making sufficient public disclosures about the actual and expected impacts of the crisis on their business and financial situation.

- What public disclosures are we/should we be making?
- How often should we make public disclosures about the impact of the crisis?

Stakeholders

- How does this crisis affect our shareholders?
- How does this crisis affect broader stakeholders?
- Are we directing the organisation in a way that works for all key stakeholders?
- How does this affect the organisation's reputation and long-term prospects?

Remuneration

- Do we need to revise or suspend incentive or bonus plans in light of the crisis?
- Are the existing pay schemes encouraging the appropriate behaviours of pulling together in a highly cooperative manner?

Annual shareholder meeting

In a crisis such as a pandemic or natural disaster, the board will need to consider if the annual general meeting can go ahead. Should it be postponed or – if allowed by the articles of association – can it be conducted as a virtual-only shareholders meeting or a hybrid meeting (that permits both in-person and online attendance)?

When the crisis makes a substantial negative impact on the organisation, the board needs to consider the following

- What are our going concern and solvency (balance sheet and cash flow tests) positions?

- What are the interests of our creditors?
- When do we need the input and advice of an external insolvency expert?
- Should we accept any new sources of credit or customer orders? If we do, what personal legal and financial problems will that create for individual directors in the longer term?

52

DIGITALISATION

Claudia Heimer

All board members are now digital directors. This chapter provides guidance for those wishing to fully contribute to board work – irrespective of their technological proficiency. The key questions that I recommend here originate from a 2015 panel on digitalisation for boards for which I convened Charlotte Valeur, Mohima Ahmed (Apps for Good), Charles Bennett (SAP SE), and Ingo Rammer (thinktecture). We noticed that boards were asking the wrong questions, leading to glacial speeds of digital transformation. The imperative for the entire board to be digitally literate was clear.[1]

Back in 2015, approaches to accelerating a board's digital savvy were still bolt-on. They were mainly short familiarisation sessions with tech-savvy people, reverse mentoring of board directors by those of the younger generation. A year later, we saw board members join executives on field trips to Silicon Valley, the first digital natives joining boards, and the World Economic Forum challenging boards to create a digital mind.

---

1 Contributions to this chapter also came from Anne Lesueur, former head of digital at L'Occitane en Provence, and Rainer Nagel of Atreus, who specialises in digital talent.

DOI: 10.4324/9781003201182-62

Fast-forward a few years, again, and the father of self-driving cars, Sebastian Thrun, challenged every company around the world to think of itself as a technology company if it did not want to be left behind (FAZ, 6 February 2018[2]). It has been extremely challenging to integrate younger and tech-savvy people on boards over the last five years, and we now understand that immersing oneself in the digital world cannot be delegated away to an individual. Even after fast-tracking digital journeys following 2020 events, companies now run the very real risk of losing out to competition if they do not complete their digital transitions. Declaring victory after adapting elements of their supply chain and customer experience will no longer be enough. The following checklist is designed as an iterative cycle that can be explored in more depth at any point.

What type of digital transformation do we want to see?

Knowing our market and empathising with our customers' real needs, what would we imagine our company doing next? What would further short cut or change the current way of satisfying that need? Once we have assessed this potential, how would technology help us with that?

What type of digital transformation will we want to help shape our industry? Based on our ongoing competitive analysis, where do we see the potential for change? Given our company's purpose and value system, what digital future is desirable?

What is technologically possible for us in ten years' time?

As a result of what we think possible, what should people in the company already be talking about today? Of course, we want to be interested in what is possible today. Yet are we overly focused on what we can do right now to immediately drive revenue? As the board, we must keep up the future perspective. Of course, this also means that as board members we need to be interested in what the company is already doing with available technology.

---

2 Christian Fueller (2018) "Wartet nicht auf die Zukunft, macht sie selbst!" FAZ.

How does data influence our strategy?

The time for gathering all the data that we can has passed. The computational power available to us remains impressive, but keeping data for data's sake is no longer the smart thing to do. It is now about being clearer on what questions to ask of the data and ensuring that we protect our consumer's data. Do we know where we are as a company in that process? Who contributes to framing the questions, training our machine learning systems, and how are they connected into the customer journey? Are we vulnerable to unconscious bias in the way that we go about this? How do we currently mitigate this risk? How vulnerable are we to data leaks and cyberattacks?

Do we fully understand the ethical dilemmas we will have to face by using data and technology in new ways?

Operating in an unregulated environment driven by the latest innovation can be exciting. Yet the price tag eventually comes, even if decades later. The era of gentlemen's agreements is over. We are all sitting in a glass house. Social media and its power of mobilising large sections of society expose the company to greater reputational risk than ever before. Board members are ultimately liable in grey areas that not even technical experts, on their own, completely understand. What is the social and environmental impact of our strategic decisions, now and in the future? How do these factors relate to our company purpose and values?

How do we articulate our strategic ambition today?

Digital cannot be an end in itself. What do we want to achieve? How do we evolve our business model and our technology accordingly? Which parts of our business model will we keep? Which ones must change? Even if business prospects based on our established business model continue looking good, how long is this likely to continue? What new possibilities are out there? There are some old rules of the game that still apply in the digital age, and growth is one of them. Just focusing on efficiency improvement has never been enough. Speed is ever more critical, particularly as global competitors keep changing the rules – and increasingly cutting out whole chunks of the supply chain and taking years out of the go-to-market cycle. How will technology help us grow, and grow fast? Who is part of the discussion? Are we taking advantage of crowdsourcing (part of) our strategy process to the people in the company? What place does the customer have in our strategic process?

Does our CEO believe 100% in the importance of digital?

Innovation cannot be delegated to a single individual such as a chief digital officer, and certainly not when the CEO is not living and breathing it. Is the topic at the top of the agenda in every business meeting? Does the CEO ask informed questions about it? Is he or she making sure that everyone else on the executive board is also behind the digitalisation process of the enterprise?

The CEO needs to champion a change in management model: it cannot be about fear and control anymore. In the digital world, the CEO must stop pretending that he or she was ever in control. An over-reliance on face-to-face business meetings is part of old-school management rituals that we might now be more ready to re-examine. The future-proof management model needs to genuinely combine good governance with good stakeholder engagement inside and outside the company. This model is likely to be closer to a network organisation where everyone takes responsibility and decisions are taken as closely to the market as possible. Management, in this context, is less about centralising decision-making, and more about giving strategic orientation, setting guidelines, defining and modelling what is culturally acceptable, and moderating conflict. It earns its position of power every day, rather than live off its achieved rank.

Where are we on the journey from command and control to a fully accountable and networked workforce?

How are we contributing to a mindset where not knowing is part of our strategic advantage?

The unknown unknowns are taking over. Do we admit this to ourselves at the board? Anyone who expresses high degrees of certainty about the future might be fooling themselves, yet no longer the people around them. Even the digitally illiterate understand that. Incremental scenarios based on the status quo can no longer be the answer to our strategic challenges. We must make not knowing part of our standard way of operating – deep and wide across the company. How are we doing this at present? And how well? What is the role that our company value system plays when we must take decisions without having all the answers?

How do we keep challenging ourselves and learning?

The board must take charge of its own development in this time of exponential complexity and uncertainty. Anything can come out of left field. Instead of waiting for the next crisis to renew itself and stretch, boards must ask themselves: How can we challenge ourselves? How can we do even better? How do we keep ourselves curious, alive, sharp, and prepared to do things that we don't know how to do?

How do we learn? How do we individually, and as a board prefer to learn? Depending on our learning style, we might want to push ourselves completely out of our area of expertise and of our industry by looking at topics and visiting industry events that are completely outside of our known frame of reference. How can we then reflect together and join the pieces of the puzzle of our (new) individual perspectives?

How do we guard against inconsiderate and wasteful ways of encouraging a "learning culture"?

There is a dark side of tech and venture capitalism that encourages cultures in which it is assumed that 95% of innovation will fail and that it should fail fast. This attitude drives dysfunctional behaviour, cynicism, and wastes a lot of money. This can be corrosive inside companies, even if more and more large companies experiment with new ideas by funding start-ups before fully integrating them when they have been successful.

How can we help innovators inside our company, or in our partner ecosystem demonstrate that their business model works before investing further?

How do we continuously experiment to stay ahead?

An open culture must permeate the entire organisation, and it must be alive at board level. Every board director is at the table for a reason. Every board director is expected to contribute, with grounded experience in industry or a particular area of expertise. This does not make for a dynamic that invites us to put aside what we already know. On the other hand, we do not have to face the unknown in a constant state of anxiety because we are out of our individual and collective comfort zones. There is a method to the madness. Is the board familiar with any of the approaches derived from creative design and rapid prototyping work? Does it have a common language based on this type of iterative thinking? How "digital" are we at the board? Have we delegated this to one of us, or are we truly ready to embrace a digital mindset for the entire board?

How can we guard against the alpha of tech?

Tech attracts people who can be withdrawn and nerdy, yet it also attracts a particular type of alpha who can be ultimately corrosive. They can become easily defensive, and shut down newcomers, juniors, women, and basically anyone who thinks differently. Using combative rhetoric and what appears to be chains of perfectly rational argument, they shut down every idea that is not their own. And they can get away with it, cloaked in the glow of being digital experts. This is ultimately destructive to the organisation because it shuts down people in key accounts, sales, and marketing.

How can we stimulate the power of working cross-functionally to create, support, evaluate, and learn together?

What are the questions that we have not yet asked ourselves?

What other questions are there? Is there another way to ask them? Who can help us ask those? Even if there is evidence suggesting that the business case for diversity might not be as strong as many would suggest, the value of different perspectives around a table is uncontested. And since 2020, we see a resurgence of viewing diversity as a question of equity. Despite our best intentions, we will still fall prey to our biases, which are a lot more conscious than we would like to believe. Diversity and, crucially, diversity of thought must be on every director's "digital" checklist and repeat the questions: What else is out there? What else could we do? What other questions could we be asking? Digital is not about technology. It is about thinking. It is also about culture.

53

DISRUPTION

Simon Devonshire

Context is a powerful thing

Business is not for the faint-hearted. Companies do not operate in a vacuum. At any given moment there are any number of forces that can cause disruption. Whether that is the consequence of:

- competitor activity,
- innovation, or
- environmental/circumstantial events.

Disruption often originates from sources that are totally beyond the control of those that it impacts. New technology and innovation are transforming how people live, work, learn, travel, shop, and entertain. That is why this is arguably the most fertile time to be entrepreneurial, and equally so, the threat of disruption has never been greater.

Understanding the opportunity landscape

In order to understand and manage the effects of disruption, it is important to also understand innovation and how it causes disruption.

Innovation causes disruption when customers choose a new product or service in preference to the established player.

The cost of innovating has never been lower, and so the barriers to innovation have also never been lower too. Consequently, innovation is coming from every angle. Businesses are no longer being disrupted by the usual suspects and the usual players.

Although boards may want to talk innovation, the most dominant conversation in boardrooms is "**disruption**." There is a big difference:

- Innovation is a positive state. Innovation represents "offence." Innovation is about the future of an organisation.
- Disruption is negative state. Disruption represents "defence." Disruption is about the preservation of the organisation's past.

It seems the relationship between innovation and disruption is inversely proportional. The more positively impacting innovation is, the more negatively severe its disruptive consequence can be.

Contemporary businesses build communities

The repeat behaviour common to successful entrepreneurs is their consistent ability to leverage innovation as a tool with which to build communities, ecosystems, and rapport.

Innovation is a topic that stakeholders want to hear organisations talk about. Innovation is a key with which to unlock the permission to engage, the permission to build rapport. Innovation is key to demonstrating a company's vision, mission, and values. The delivery of innovation is a powerful proof-point, and when innovation is effectively leveraged, its impact and influence can be more effective and more compelling than traditional advertising.

- Innovative organisations are inventive, progressive, agile.
- Disrupted organisations are stale, anxious, defensive.

And so, the question that boards should be asking themselves is:

- Is our organisation a **disruptor**, or is it **being disrupted?**

And irrespective of the answer:

- What is the evidence?

Problem statements

The repeat behaviour common to successful entrepreneurs is that they are especially good at defining what problem they are solving. In the language of investors, this is referred to as a "problem statement" – investors look for entrepreneurs who can powerfully articulate the problem that their business solves. Innovation demonstrates that your organisation knows what problem it is solving and that it is passionate about solving it. The boardroom question is:

- What problem does our organisation solve?

Rules and regulation

The biggest difference between incumbent businesses and up-start newcomers is their relative conformity to "the rules." Infuriatingly, new entrants don't play by the old rules. With regard to corporate reverence to regulators, there is a real risk of "doing what was said, not what was wanted." Some corporates disingenuously hide behind regulatory constraint in order to avoid "innovation-hard-yards." And so key questions are:

- What are the biggest regulatory constraints that hold back the transformation of our customer experience?
- When was the last time the CEO met the regulator?

The risk of conformity

There is so much that directors can learn from early-stage ventures and the investors who back them. Investors share a common belief that conformity only ever yields average results.

Sticking to convention is often the root cause that allows disruptors to disrupt. For example, supermarkets like Sainsbury's and Tesco are indelibly attached to stocking as many brands and varieties of products as possible. That is their convention. They are being disrupted by Aldi and Lidl, which not only fail to subscribe to that convention, but worse, do the exact opposite. And so, the question that directors should be asking themselves is:

- What are the established conventions of this business?
- What are the beliefs, attitudes, and behaviours common in our industry or sector, and what specifically would represent the most notable paradigm shift if incumbent conventions were deliberately ignored?

The unusual suspects

The competitive landscape is constantly shifting – more rapidly now than ever. The threat of new competition may not necessarily come from the usual suspects. It may in fact come from completely outside your industry sector. Not only must organisations watch their peers, but they must also actively watch and track the funding and progress of start-ups in their sector too. More challenging still, is the need to monitor start-ups from outside the sector because disruption may come from entirely new sources previously disassociated with the core business.

- Which start-ups are attracting the most publicity, investment, and attention in the sector?
- If Amazon were to launch in this market, what might their service look like?

Old school, new school

It is not just competitors that look different, but the way business is being done is fundamentally changing as well. The classic professional disciplines are changing face too. Key functions such as marketing have changed beyond recognition. No function is immune to the degree of change that is happening (even if some inaccurately believe that societal changes are somehow less applicable/relevant to them). The problem with the old-school approach is that it:

- fails to understand and leverage the power of communities and eco-systems;
- does not get digital and data;
- still wants to compel by telling rather than demonstrating; and
- doesn't understand the science and process of validation.

The key questions directors should be asking in order to better understand which areas are stuck in the old school, or have migrated to the new school, are:

- To what extent does the workforce/senior leadership team work flexibly?
- What new technology does your department intend to implement in the next 12 months and what benefit will it deliver to your key stakeholders?

Non-incumbent thinking

Disruptors are fresh thinking. They are not encumbered. New talent is the antidote to a lack of thought diversity. Diverse thinking is difficult to quantify. Helpfully, diversity of recruitment is much easier to measure. The most anxious businesses most fearful of disruption, are also those that have a tendency to hire from their established competitors. And so, the key question is:

- What percentage of new hires are from outside the organisation's sector?

Differentiation

Disruptors disrupt not by being the best – they win business by being **better**. The key questions about differentiation are:

- What makes customers compelled to choose this organisation's products versus the alternatives available?
- What makes the organisation's product better than the competition?
- What's the next new product feature that will be launched, and when will it land?

Protecting legacy revenues

New entrants have the liberty of not having to protect legacy revenues. It is easier for new entrants to demolish established industry margins. The protection of legacy revenue can distract attention and resources from the creation of new revenue from the delivery of new products and services. The questions that this provokes are:

- What products and/or customers currently deliver 80% of the company's revenue?
- How would the company replace that revenue if it had to?

The innovator's dilemma

Rarely will new products deliver substantive incremental revenue in comparison to legacy revenue. Corporate expectations and demands for new products are invariably unrealistic – corporates want new ventures to yield too much revenue too quickly. Often that means new products are at best a disappointment, and worse, not even worth pursuing in the first place. This is known as the "innovators dilemma." Unrealistic revenue expectations are a common insurmountable barrier to corporate innovation.

For new innovation to succeed, its success must be calibrated in more than simply the revenue generated. The introduction of a new product is unlikely to yield transformative revenues – but perhaps it might help drive substantial awareness and interest in existing products. The question this provokes is:

- How do we as the board evaluate new innovation opportunities?
- What are the right metrics to measure innovation performance and success?

Innovation is predictable

Some forms of disruption are unpredictable; however, most competitor disruption is signposted way in advance of it hitting the market. Three examples that bring this to life are the following:

- Scientists are compelled to publish.
- Corporates are compelled to patent.
- Start-ups are compelled to raise funds.

These examples effectively broadcast the direction of travel and the innovation that is coming. Universities are home to scientists; they are fertile breeding grounds for innovative start-ups; universities prize their collaborations with corporates. So the questions directors should be asking are:

- Which universities are consistently yielding thought leadership and scientific breakthroughs in our core industries?
- How should our organisation partner/collaborate with the best universities that work in this field?

The megatrend megatrend

There have always been megatrends, an ageing society and the rise in obesity being just two examples. What makes this era so remarkable is that there now seems to be the following:

- There are more megatrends than ever before.
- The megatrends feel more significant than ever before.
- The megatrends are more measurable than ever before.

The advantage that megatrends create for innovators is: inevitability. And so the question that boards should be debating is:

- What are the megatrends that will affect this industry most?

The elimination of doubt

One of the most negative consequences of disruption is **uncertainty**. Uncertainty causes **doubt**. The impact of doubt in organisations is that it causes people to throttle-back. Throttling-back can have a devasting impact on productivity. Productivity is vital to business success.

The best antidote for doubt is visible leadership and the constant reiteration/reaffirmation of business strategy. Nothing beats a whites-of-the-eyes delivery from the CEO combined with fluent/coherent unscripted answers to challenging questions. The key questions therefore that directors need to ask are:

- How frequently does the CEO present to key stakeholders, especially staff?
- What are the headline messages over the course of the next six months?

Adaptability

In periods of change and disruption, people need to learn how to adapt quickly. The repeat characteristic of successful entrepreneurs is that they are especially adaptable.

- What programmes are in place to teach staff the practical advantages of an entrepreneurial mindset and acquire resilience and adaptability?

The MPA

The repeat behaviour common to successful entrepreneurs is their ability to **focus**. Once an organisation is clear about what problem it solves, the key question directors need to ask is:

- What is singularly the Most Powerful Action that will move the success of this organisation furthest forward?

In summary

The key questions directors should be asking are:

Defensive: Is this organisation going to be disrupted?
Offensive: What are its opportunities to disrupt?
Capability: Is your team capable of seeing the opportunity?
Initiative: Does the organisation have the competencies to do something about it?
Purpose: What problem does the organisation solve?
Differentiation: What makes this organisation's product better than the alternatives?

54

ARTIFICIAL INTELLIGENCE

Lord Clement-Jones

Corporate governance and AI: time for a rethink?

Worldwide, artificial intelligence (AI) presents opportunities in a whole variety of sectors: healthcare, education, financial services, marketing, retail, agriculture, energy conservation, government, smart or connected cities, and indeed regulatory technology itself. Allied with biotechnology and data analytics, it can be used to tackle a huge number of worldwide problems, where the predictive, analytical, and problem-solving nature of AI can make a huge difference in improving performance, research outcomes, productivity, and customer experience. AI is already having a major impact on our lives, and many countries are setting comprehensive strategies to take advantage of it.

The House of Lords Select Committee on AI that I chaired took an optimistic view of the UK's potential, but[1] we also said that for successful development, we need to mitigate the risks such as the loss of public or stakeholder trust if AI is not seen to operate on ethical principles such

---

1 https://publications.parliament.uk/pa/ld201719/ldselect/ldai/100/100.pdf.

as intelligibility, openness, fairness, and lack of bias, especially as there is a strongly polarised narrative around AI: "the worst or best thing for humanity," according to the late Professor Stephen Hawking.[2]

Concerns in the USA over bias displayed in predictive policing and criminal justice algorithms such as COMPAS,[3] and the more recent debate over the grade standardisation algorithm deployed in the UK's secondary education system are classic examples of how to lose public trust in AI.[4]

We have an abundance of international ethical codes such as those promulgated by the Organization for Economic Cooperation and Development (OECD), the Council of Europe, the European Union (EU), the G20, and others[5] which provide the basis for a common set of international standards, and business is increasingly expected to comply. But as Brent Mittelstadt's paper published in the journal *Nature* puts it, "Principles alone cannot guarantee ethical AI."[6]

The question is not now about how we adopt an international ethical AI framework, but how we bridge the gap between the "what" of responsible AI and the "how" in terms of corporate behaviour, AI design, and regulatory intervention. It is clear that AI even in its narrow form will and should have a profound impact on implications for corporate governance generally. Global organisations such as the Partnership on AI recognise that corporate responsibility and governance on AI is increasingly important,[7] likewise, the World Economic Forum, which has developed a number of corporate governance tools.[8]

---

2 www.theguardian.com/science/2016/oct/19/stephen-hawking-ai-best-or-worst-thing-for-humanity-cambridge#:~:text=Professor%20Stephen%20Hawking%20has%20warned,future%20of%20our%20civilisation%20and.
3 www.propublica.org/article/how-we-analyzed-the-compas-recidivism-algorithm.
4 www.telegraph.co.uk/news/2020/08/15/pupils-can-now-use-predicted-grades-appeal-a-level-gcse-results/.
5 www.oecd.org/going-digital/ai/principles/#:~:text=The%20OECD%20Principles%20on%20Artificial,Council%20Recommendation%20on%20Artificial%20Intelligence.
   https://ec.europa.eu/digital-single-market/en/news/ethics-guidelines-trustworthy-ai.
   https://ec.europa.eu/digital-single-market/en/news/ethics-guidelines-trustworthy-ai.
   www.g20-insights.org/wp-content/uploads/2019/07/G20-Japan-AI-Principles.pdf.
6 www.nature.com/articles/s42256-019-0114-4.
7 www.partnershiponai.org/new-partners-to-strengthen-global-community-of-practice/.
8 www.weforum.org/projects/ai-board-leadership-toolkit.

Detailed guidance is available too on a country-by-country basis. Singapore has issued its Model AI Governance Framework.[9] In the UK, well-respected organisations such as the Institute for Business Ethics, whose report *Corporate Ethics in a Digital Age* have issued a masterly briefing for boards.[10] Investors in the USA and UK such as Analytics Ventures, Fidelity, and Hermes are now imposing their own governance expectations too.

Poor data governance is often at the heart of public mistrust, but there are a wide range of actions boards need to take beyond complying with data protection legislation such as the EU's General Data Protection Regulation (GDPR)[11] and data protection and privacy legislation applicable in other jurisdictions.

Boards must have the right skill sets to understand what technology is being used in their company and how it is being used and managed, in order to fulfil their oversight role. Do board members understand whether and how AI is being used and managed, for instance, by their human resources department in recruitment and assessment or in keeping track of employee movements?

Understanding the different aspects of business context in which AI can impact is crucial. How many boards appreciate the full range of applications of AI which are potentially available?

Boards need to ensure they are informed about the implications of the automation of many tasks before deployment of AI solutions takes place. Will the introduction of an AI solution augment a role or substitute for it?

Companies need to be transparent about the impact of AI solutions on their workforces and on decision-making. They need to accept that they are fully accountable where the introduction of new technology makes a significant impact on employees and customers.

Whatever the scale of introduction of AI, there will be major disruption in the workplace, and concerted retraining to meet demand for new skills will become a major and continual necessity.

Conformity with ethical principles and standards of course has to be central to the introduction of new technology. If boards are going to retain

---

9 www.pdpc.gov.sg/-/media/files/pdpc/pdf-files/resource-for-organisation/ai/sgmodelaigovframework2.pdf.
10 www.ibe.org.uk/resource/corporate-ethics-in-a-digital-age.html.
11 https://gdpr.eu/.

stakeholder trust, they need to adopt an overarching ethics framework which ensures that certain principles on the deployment of AI solutions are followed; such as beneficial purpose, personal privacy, transparency of use, that algorithmic decision-making is explainable and that data being used for training, testing, or operational inputting does not exhibit bias.

So, in sum, boards need to be aware of the questions they should ask and the advice they need, and from whom, when considering the adoption of AI solutions.

- Does the board have the right skills and knowledge to consider the risks and issues?
- Does it understand how data, algorithms, and other technologies are being used in the business, especially to make key decisions or prediction?
- How is ethics around technology included in board governance? How often is ethics and technology discussed by the board?
- Does the business mainstream oversight of compliance with ethics into its audit and risk committee or set up a separate ethics advisory board?
- How is the board communicating the importance of an ethical approach to AI adoption? How are new staff taught about the ethical values of the business?
- Has it received assurance that any ethical risks around the adoption of new technology are being managed? Is ethics considered when reviewing or signing off new AI projects or use cases?
- Furthermore, if AI solutions are externally sourced, are these ethical requirements engrained in procurement processes?
- Are appropriate accountabilities in place? How does accountability between the business leadership and technology specialists fit together? Who is accountable at board level for these issues?
- What tools does the business have available in exercising oversight in terms of AI risk assessment and ethical audit mechanisms? Has the board, in seeking assurance on the standards for training testing and operation of AI solutions, considered other relevant tools such as: algorithmic impact assessment, AI risk assessment, ethical audit mechanisms, consumer assurance through Kitemarking, standards for ethically aligned design.

- Risk management is central to the introduction of new technology such as AI. What is the risk appetite of the business for the adoption of new technologies? How is risk assessed?
- To what extent are "unexplainable" models relied on in decision-making? Developers and those applying AI solutions cannot and must not shelter behind "black box" excuses.
- Where there is automated decision-making, to what extent have controls been reviewed to ensure that there is a "human in the loop"?
- To what extent should individual AI system designers and engineers within the business be explicitly required to declare their adherence to a set of ethical standards? This is particularly relevant to AI developers.
- Importantly, is the board satisfied that they have the necessary diversity and inclusion in the AI workforce with different perspectives when developing technology which enables them to spot problems of bias in training data and decision-making?
- Are there mechanisms for employees to raise concerns about ethical questions, such as whistle-blowing processes?
- Is the business open and engaged with key stakeholders around ethics and technology? To what extent has the business published its ethical approach and engaged customers and others in discussions and feedback?
- Where the business is regulated, to what extent is it engaged in discussions with regulators about any changing requirements? Is there recognition of the potential for role for regulatory sandboxing as a number of regulators such as the UK's Financial Conduct Authority and the Information Commissioner's Office in particular have recognised and promoted?[12] This permits the testing of a new technology without the threat of regulatory enforcement but with strict overview and guidance, and can speed up innovation and scaling up of adoption of AI projects.

At the end of the day there are even broader issues to be addressed. The rise of AI marks a real opportunity for radical changes in corporate governance on a global basis.

---

12 https://ico.org.uk/about-the-ico/news-and-events/news-and-blogs/2020/03/combining-privacy-and-innovation-ico-sandbox-six-months-on/.
www.fca.org.uk/firms/innovation/regulatory-sandbox-prepare-application.

Many of the above questions raise the issue of what the core ethical values of the business are. How do these values fit with a current business model and strategy?

In my view AI can and should contribute positively to a purposeful form of capitalism which is not simply the pursuit of profit but where companies deploy AI in an ethical way for a purpose to achieve greater sustainability.

With all the potential opportunities and disruption involved with AI, boards across a variety of jurisdictions and business contexts need to adopt a strong underlying set of corporate values so that the impact and distribution of benefit to employees and society at large are fully considered for a purpose not exclusively driven by returns to shareholders.

In this context, Sir Ronald Cohen, chairman of the Global Steering Group for Impact Investment, at CogX2020 in London spoke about the need for a "universal impact accounting system."[13]

The World Economic Forum has recently published "Integrated Corporate Governance: A Practical Guide to Stakeholder Capitalism for Boards of Directors,"[14] which emphasises that

> the COVID-19 pandemic and resulting humanitarian and economic crisis have reminded us that firms are themselves stakeholders in the sense that they have an intrinsic interest in and shared responsibility for the resilience and vitality of the economic, social and environmental systems in which they operate.

The Big Innovation Centre – now an international think tank – has played a leading role in the debate with their "Purposeful Company Project,"[15] which was launched back in 2015 with an ethos that

> the role of business is to fulfil human wants and needs and to pursue a purpose that has a clear benefit to society. It is through the fulfilment of their chosen purpose that value is created.

Since then, several important reports have been produced on the need for an integrated regulatory approach to stewardship and intrinsic purpose

---

13 www.youtube.com/watch?v=0HHgZDeMVEs.
14 www3.weforum.org/docs/WEF_Integrated_Corporate_Governance_2020.pdf.
15 www.biginnovationcentre-purposeful-company.com/.

definition, and on the changes that should be made to the Finance Reporting Council's UK Stewardship Code.[16]

In the USA, the B Corp movement[17] has been a leader in this strongly growing community of interest, determined to raise standards of corporate governance.

To finally insert a cautionary note, however, corporate governance, however sound, is not always going to be sufficient. Brad Smith, president of Microsoft, in his recent book *Tools and Weapons*,[18] warns us:

> Many business leaders are absolutely aware of the need for good corporate behaviour but the end of the day ethical principles and good corporate responsibility guidelines however may not be enough.

That takes us on to when and where, in terms of AI applications and business sectors, we assess the associated risks as requiring that we should go further and adopting legislation and regulation, but that discussion is for another occasion.

---

16 www.biginnovationcentre-purposeful-company.com/intrinsic-purpose/.
www.biginnovationcentre-purposeful-company.com/the-need-for-an-integrated-regulatory-approach-to-stewardship/.
www.biginnovationcentre-purposeful-company.com/review-of-the-uk-stewardship-code-thoughts-for-change/.
17 https://bcorporation.net/
18 Brad Smith *Tools and Weapons: The Promise and the Peril of the Digital Age* Hodder & Stoughton (2019).